✓ **W9-CFC-705**

OFF THE BEATEN PATH® SERIES

EIGHTH EDITION

OFF THE BEATEN PATH®
DAKOTAS ➡

A GUIDE TO UNIQUE PLACES

LISA MEYERS McCLINTICK

gpp®
travel

Guilford, Connecticut

All the information in this guidebook is subject to change. We recommend that you call ahead to obtain current information before traveling.

To buy books in quantity for corporate use or incentives, call **(800) 962-0973** or e-mail **premiums@GlobePequot.com.**

Editor: Amy Lyons
Project Editor: Heather M. Santiago
Layout: Mary Ballachino
Text Design: Linda R. Loiewski
Maps: Equator Graphics © Morris Book Publishing, LLC

ISSN 1540-4382
ISBN 978-0-7627-5668-1

Printed in the United States of America
10 9 8 7 6 5 4 3 2 1

About the Author

Lisa Meyers McClintick is an award-winning travel writer and photographer based in St. Cloud, Minnesota. She focuses on Midwest, family, and adventure travel, frequently writing for *Midwest Living, AAA Living,* the *Minneapolis Star Tribune* and *Log Home Living* among other publications. Her favorite Minnesota and Midwest destinations can be found on her blog at www.10000likes .blogspot.com. Her Dakota traveling team includes her husband, Bob, who grew up in Worthington, Minn., near Sioux Falls, and their children: Jonathan, 10, Katie and Kylie, 6, and their sidekick, Gracie, a border collie who lives for long rides.

Acknowledgments

Special thanks to South Dakota Tourism, North Dakota Tourism, regional chambers of commerce, Diana Lambdin Meyer and Stephanie Dickerell, and everyone who chimed in with expertise and affection for the beautiful Dakotas.

Contents

Introduction

I've always joked that I needed to live within a 10-minute drive of cornfields. It could be an innate need for openness and the desire to escape the bustle and visual clutter of often homogenous cities and suburbs. The Dakotas feel refreshingly real. Here, in the wide open landscapes and along rivers and rolling bluffs, you can almost hear the voices of generations past. There's a sense of timeless Americana in many of the small towns—a warmth and a welcome, an echo of ethnic roots, a strong work ethic, and sense of pride. You can slow down, hear yourself think and soak in simple pleasures such as watching a storm dramatically build and thunder across rippling grasslands, seeing a V of geese arc into a prairie pothole gilded by sunset, and feeling like famed explorers Lewis and Clark standing on a quiet bluff above the Missouri River where Native Americans farmed in vast villages. Along buttes and through Badlands wild horses still roam free and buffalo rumble and nuzzle cinnamon-colored calves.

The mysteries of this land—as well as the strong character of the people—beckon time and time again, casting spells in roundabout ways: the sweet, singsong accent of the Dakota people; the cozy main street cafes; the small-town parades and rodeos that liberally fill summer calendars; the stunning sense of history chiseled into Mount Rushmore—and nailed into the very foundation of the Maltese Cross Cabin in North Dakota's Theodore Roosevelt National Park. The Dakotas offer a smidgen of everything that defines America: natural beauty, arts, culture, outdoor recreation and shopping.

ruraldistinctions

North Dakota has 641,481 people, while South Dakota boasts a population of 804,194. To put that in perspective, consider the city of Los Angeles, which has a population of 3.8 million—and that's metro only. New York City has more than 8 million residents.

North Dakota covers 69,299 square miles, while South Dakota weighs in as the bigger twin with 75,956 square miles, ranking them 19th and 16th, respectively, in the nation in terms of size. Look at the population, though, and they're 48th and 46th with an average of 10 residents per square mile.

Geographically, both North Dakota and South Dakota are generously endowed with pristine lakes, clay-streaked buttes, thick forests, blue-tinged prairies, and, of course, the mighty Missouri River. The Mighty Mo splits both states into East River and West River, with the flatlands of East River coveted for their agriculture, and the hills and forests of the West River praised for their beauty and frontier inspiration.

Dakota weather can be unforgivingly cold in the winter, especially in North Dakota, with windchill factors that magnify the effects of the plummeting thermometer. The wise traveler, always mindful that long stretches of road in these states can be quite desolate, will pack lots of warm clothes and have the car serviced and stocked with provisions. Agriculture is a mainstay of the economies in North Dakota and South Dakota, but there are other avenues of economic strength as the states build on tourism, gaming, and other resources.

In North Dakota, the discovery of oil in 1957 heightened natural resource development. The oil crisis of the 1970s spurred increased exploring and development, as well as the mining of the state's immense lignite reserves. Northwestern North Dakota's oil industry is on the upswing again, spurring jobs and offering stability in a down economy. South Dakota's Black Hills, meanwhile, can still claim the Northern Hemisphere's largest underground gold mine.

History binds North Dakota and South Dakota tightly. Both were part of the Dakota Territory, organized on March 2, 1861. Both became states on November 2, 1889. The lands that explorers Lewis and Clark so dauntlessly traveled are today part of not only the Great Plains but also the Midwest and the West. The settlers' stories are assuredly familiar, but Native American voices also are clearly heard. Indeed, Dakota means *"friend"* or *"ally"* in Sioux.

As you might expect, Dakotans are fiercely independent, hardworking people with an enduring pioneer spirit. The work ethic is as real and sturdy as the sunflowers that stretch toward the summer sky. Immigrant groups of Germans, Scandinavians, and Czechs flocked to South Dakota, where these folks traveled to find a piece of land to call their own. In North Dakota, the mostly Nordic settlers, were likewise lured by the promise of fertile land.

Native American people have endured displacement, turmoil, and change. Yet today the tribal culture here still resonates in such events as the spectacular powwows, and in the exquisite beadwork, quillwork, and star quilts of Native American artists.

Essentially, the Dakotas are a seamless terrain, and maybe that is why visitors sometimes have a hard time telling them apart. But the Dakotas are hardly carbon copies of one another.

North Dakota, for instance, borders two Canadian provinces: Saskatchewan and Manitoba. The International Peace Garden on the North Dakota–Canadian border recognizes the friendship of the United States and Canada through stunning flowers and touching memorials.

Long before the Four Faces were carved in South Dakota, the lure of gold in the Black Hills enticed fortune seekers, and lively frontier towns were established with equally colorful inhabitants. Visitors today can walk in the footsteps of characters such as Calamity Jane and Wild Bill Hickok for an instant trip back into the Old West.

Some travelers still snub the Dakotas (like the rest of the Midwest) as fly-over land. But those of us in the Heartland, as well as Europeans seeking a true American experience, know better. Sure the drives to get from here to there can be long—even a little mind-numbing—but the rewards are immense. It's here, off the beaten path from most of the country, where you can also walk in footsteps of Laura Ingalls Wilder and Sitting Bull. You can excavate mammoth bones, spelunk in some of the world's longest caves, mountain bike a world-class track in the North Dakota Badlands, and enjoy some of the nation's best bird-watching, hunting, and fishing. You can dance to Norwegian fiddles, polka with German–Russians, tell stories over a cowboy campfire, or lose yourself in the brilliant splendor of a powwow where rhythmic drumming echoes like a dozen heartbeats.

This is a land rich with the history of explorers—yet there are countless treasures yet to be discovered and adventures yet to be lived. Enjoy finding yours.

Restaurant and Accommodation Pricing

The restaurant cost categories refer to the price of entrees without beverages, desserts, taxes, or tips. Those listed as inexpensive are $10 or less; moderate, between $10 and $15; and expensive, $20 or more. Places to stay listed as inexpensive are $100 or less per double per night; moderate, $101 to $200 per night; and expensive, $201 or more per night. Rest assured, however, that spending a vacation in the Dakotas is almost always pleasantly affordable and magical.

NORTHEASTERN SOUTH DAKOTA ➡

By a fortunate accident of nature, the northeastern area of South Dakota, also known as the Glacial Lakes Region, features prime boating and recreational areas, with sixteen state parks and two national wildlife refuges. Serendipity appeared in the form of glaciers some 20,000 years ago, and more than 120 lakes and miles of prairies were left when the glaciers retreated. This area is referred to as the Young Drift Plains by geologists, but residents simply call it the Lakes Region. For the most part the area is swampy plain, dotted with lakes and marshes. The notable exception is the wide, flat valley of the James River. I-29, which runs north-south, and US 12, which runs east-west, help keep travel and commerce flowing from Sioux Falls, in the southeastern corner of the state, to Rapid City, in the west.

Fertile Valley

We'll begin on US 12 in the northwest corner of the Fertile Valley region. *Aberdeen* lies in the rich valley of the James River. The area was first settled by the Arikara Indians, who introduced farming to the region. Others were to follow by

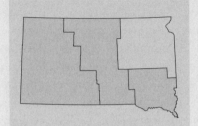

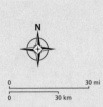

N

0 _____ 30 mi

0 _____ 30 km

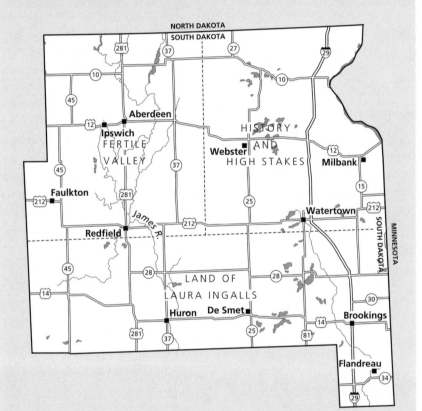

NORTH DAKOTA
SOUTH DAKOTA

281 37 27 29

10 10

45

12 Aberdeen

Ipswich HISTORY

FERTILE AND

VALLEY 37 Webster HIGH STAKES Milbank

45 12

15

Faulkton 25

212 281 Watertown 212

Redfield James R. 212

45 28 28

14 LAND OF

LAURA INGALLS 30

Huron De Smet Brookings

281 37 25 81 14

Flandreau 34

29

SOUTH DAKOTA

MINNESOTA

train and wagon and on foot. Settlers came to forge new lives from eastern states, the Scandinavian countries, Germany, Russia, and the British Isles.

Established in 1881 near the Milwaukee Railroad, the town was named for Aberdeen, Scotland, the hometown of Alexander Mitchell, president of the railroad. Aberdeen soon became known as the Hub City in recognition of the network of rail lines that converged there. Culture flourishes today in this community of more than 24,071 people. Northern State University, established in 1901, and Presentation College, the state's newest four-year college, bring history, higher learning, and the arts to the region.

The *Highlands Historical District* is located on Main Street between Twelfth and Fifteenth Avenues North. Seventeen homes were built here between 1907 and 1969. The district earned the lofty title of Highlands because it rose 3 feet higher than the commercial sector, which was located in a slough. When the first houses were built, only prairie grass covered the area, so young trees were brought up from along the James River and transplanted here to line the sedate streets. Many architectural styles have melded in the district over the years, and the result is a fascinating study in both modern and classical structures. Compare the stately 1909 Georgian revival home at 1206 North Main St. with the sturdy yet elegant lines of the 1929 neocolonial brick residence at 1404 North Main St. Although these are still private homes, some are open for tours. Call the Chamber of Commerce at (605) 225-2860, the Convention and Visitors Bureau at (800) 645-3851, or visit www.visitaberdeensd.com for more information.

For a refreshing change of pace, stop by the *Red Rooster Coffee House* at 202 South Main St. In addition to the java fare, the coffeehouse offers croissant sandwiches, soup, bagels, hummus sandwiches, nachos, and baked goods. In true coffeehouse fashion, Red Rooster also features live performances from

NORTHEASTERN SOUTH DAKOTA'S TOP HITS

Bramble Park Zoo	Mellette House
Dacotah Prairie Museum	Moody County Museum and Complex
Easton's Castle	Redlin Art Center
Gladys Pyle Historic Home	South Dakota State Fair
The Highlands Historical District	Storybook Land
Laura Ingalls Wilder Pageant	Wauneta's Gardens

many local artists, anything from old time jam, to bluegrass, to cover bands. The performances are usually at night. Visit http://redrooster.ning.com for information or call (605) 225-6603.

When you reach the dead end of Second Avenue Northwest, you have arrived at an isolated, strangely ominous home called **Easton's Castle.** Drive by and inspect the Jacobean revival style of architecture that was popular in England in the 1830s. Multiple windows, peaked roofs, and gables distinguish this style. Samples of the home's French-made wallpaper, which remains intact, have been documented in the Cooper Hewitt Museum of Design of the Smithsonian Institution.

In March 1973, Easton's Castle was added to the National Register of Historic Places. The current owners, Sam and Jacintha Holman, adapted the home and barn as a veterinary clinic in 1967. Their loving care is evident throughout the castle. Jacintha recalls the home's restoration:

> "Much has been written about the joys and tribulations of owning an old house. Nothing can compare with the gradual intrusion of a thriving, twenty-four-hour service business into a twenty-room house with the comings and goings of five hippie children and friends during the 1970s. From the road to the top of the chimneys and barn cupola, the rehabilitation turned into constant maintenance and repair. Eventually, the aura and wonder of the place took over."

The longest residents of the home were the C. F. Easton family, who bought the property in 1889. Matilda Gage, a secretary in Mr. Easton's banking business, was a frequent visitor, and she recorded her memories of the castle. Matilda was the inspiration behind the character of Dorothy in the *Wizard of Oz* stories, which were penned by her uncle, L. Frank Baum (there were fourteen *Oz* books). When Matilda died in 1986 at the age of 99, she left her Baum memorabilia to the local **Alexander Mitchell Library** in Aberdeen. If you're interested in visiting the Baum collection, contact the library in advance.

The library was founded by Andrew Carnegie, a boyhood friend of railroad president Alexander Mitchell. It's located at 519 South Kline St. and is open from 9 a.m. to 8:45 p.m. Mon through Thurs, 9 a.m. to 5:45 p.m. Fri, and 9 a.m. to 4:45 p.m. on Sat. Call (605) 626-7097 for more information.

The Land of Oz extends beyond the recollections of Matilda in Aberdeen. L. Frank Baum was enamored with the Wild West and moved here from New York in 1888. He opened a variety store called Baum's Bazaar that fall, but he was dismally lacking in business acumen. After closing the store, he purchased the town newspaper, renamed it the *Aberdeen Saturday Pioneer,* and proved to be a top-notch journalist. Baum's stories were witty, satirical, and sometimes controversial, but the town's happenings were always reported with great passion. Scholars suggest that the populist prairie might have inspired the Land of Oz, a fairyland where the common man and woman become hero and heroine.

Those too young to care about literary analysis can join in the Oz fun at **Storybook Land,** located one mile north of Aberdeen on US 281. The park features characters from *The Wizard of Oz*. Other larger-than-life stories re-created here are "Jack and Jill Went Up the Hill," "Cinderella," "Jack and the Beanstalk," and "Humpty Dumpty."

The entrance to the park features Dorothy's farmstead, including her house, a petting zoo with farm animals, a barn and silo, a windmill, an antique farm tractor, and a pony ride concession. There's even Munchkin Land (a small cornfield that is planted and harvested annually), the Yellow Brick Road, and other beloved sites from the *Oz* books and from the movie. Admission to Storybook Land is free, although rides and food are extra; it is open daily Apr 15 through Oct 15, during the daylight hours, dependant on weather. Call the park at (605) 626-7015 if in doubt.

Aberdeen's newest theme park is the **Land of Oz,** a ten-acre park north-west of Storybook Land in Wylie Park. It expands on the Wizard of Oz themes already so lovingly and gaily presented in Storybook Land. Open during the daylight hours Apr 15 through Oct 15. Admission is free. For more information log on to www.aberdeencvb.com/sbl.htm.

Just outside the gates of Storybook Land you'll find **Wylie Park.** With more than 200 acres of grassland, the park features a spectacular variety of wildlife. You can camp, swim, picnic, and golf. The park is open year-round, weather permitting, and admission is free. Events are held throughout the year, including Haunted Forest the third weekend in Oct. Visitors are guided

AUTHOR'S FAVORITES IN NORTHEASTERN SOUTH DAKOTA

Dakota Sioux Casino
Watertown
(605) 882-2051

Gladys Pyle Historic Home
Huron
(605) 352-2528

Ingalls Homestead
De Smet
(800) 776-3594

Pickler Mansion
Faulkton
(605) 598-4285

through thirteen different spooky scenes led by ghoulish guides. A matinee walkthrough is available for younger children, who are invited to wear costumes and collect candy at every scene.

The park's man-made lake, with more than 1,000 feet of shoreline, features an unsupervised swimming area. The lake is stocked with fish each year for those under age 16 to fish, and paddleboats and canoe rentals are available. On a few Saturdays in the summer, ski shows are performed on the lake. Check the Parks and Recreation guide at www.aberdeen.sd.us for specific times.

The park's pavilion—built in 1912—was once the stage for Lawrence Welk. The pavilion was added to the National Register of Historic Places in 1978.

Wylie Park Campground offers paved roads and camp pads, ninety-two sites, seven cabins, and modern restrooms and shower facilities. New to the campground is a three-bedroom lodge that sleeps eight and has kitchen and bathroom facilities. For reservations, call (605) 626-3512 or toll-free (888) 326-9693.

Regional cuisine is at **Minerva's** (yes, it's affiliated with the much-storied original Minerva's in downtown Sioux Falls) in the **Best Western Ramkota Hotel** (605-226-2988). Just like its sister restaurants, Minerva's whets the discerning appetite with the finest aged beef, fresh seafood, pastas, fancifully dressed salads, and more. In fact, *USA Today* named the bison rib-eye steak as one of the 50 Great Plates of America. The restaurant is open for breakfast from 6:30 to 10:45 a.m. Mon through Sat and 7 to 10 a.m. Sun; lunch is served from 10:45 a.m. to 2 p.m. Mon through Sat, 10 a.m. to 2 p.m. Sun; dinner is served 4:30 to 10 p.m. Mon through Sat, 4:30 to 9 p.m. Sun. Happy hour is 4:30 to 6 p.m. and 9 to 11 p.m., Mon through Fri. Located at 1400 Eighth

TOP ANNUAL EVENTS

Arts in the Park
Aberdeen, June
Contact the Aberdeen Arts Council,
(605) 226-1557

Storybook Land Festival
Aberdeen, July
Contact the Aberdeen Arts Council,
(605) 226-1557

Laura Ingalls Wilder Pageant
De Smet, last weekend in June and first
two weekends in July
(800) 776-3594

South Dakota State Fair
one week starting Labor Day weekend
(800) 529-0900
www.sdstatefair.com

Ave. Northwest. Check out www.minervas.net for complete lunch and dinner menus. Reservations are suggested; call (605) 229-4040.

Before leaving Aberdeen, check out the **Centennial Village,** located at the Brown County Fairgrounds, near the intersection of Twenty-fourth Avenue Northwest and Brown County 10. The village features 19th-century structures, including a post office, a pioneer press, a harness shop, a bank, a saloon, and a general store. Centennial Village is open for two weeks during the Brown County Fair in Aug and by appointment. Call (605) 225-2414. Admission is free.

Just west of Aberdeen on US 12 is the cozy burg of **Ipswich,** which was settled in 1885. One of the more splendid relics of Ipswich's past is the First Baptist Church, which boasts some of the finest fieldstone architecture in the state. The community library, a charming Hansel-and-Gretel-like stone structure, also stands as a testament to the benefits of tender loving care. Outside the library is the mysterious Prayer Rock, a giant boulder with handprints supposedly carved by a Native American medicine man.

The home of **J. W. Parmley** (319 Fourth St.), one of the early movers and shakers in Ipswich, is open to the public. It features family and town memorabilia, as well as pioneer and military displays. The two stone fireplaces in the home were constructed from an eccentric array of rocks, shells, and minerals collected during Parmley family travels. An iron fence post, allegedly from a fence around Sitting Bull's grave when his remains were buried at Fort Yates, forms part of one fireplace. Through the efforts of area native Phyllis Herrick, the home became a museum. Herrick's exhaustive research filled in the town's history with tidbits about the benevolent Parmley. Subsequently, J. W. Parmley's descendants took interest in the project and have supported her efforts to this day. "The Parmleys have been such good offspring," Phyllis said. Great-great-grandson Richard Parmley donated land for Parmley Memorial Park, and the historical society also has acquired the Parmley Western Land Office in downtown Ipswich.

"I was born and raised here and so was Mr. Parmley, and I remembered him when I was in high school," Phyllis said. At the time US 12 was called the Yellowstone Trail. Parmley was known as the father of the Yellowstone Trail. Phyllis and her family lived in Minnesota for twenty-five years, and when she returned, she sadly found the home to be empty. "I just thought it should be preserved. So four other people and I purchased it, and we got the consensus of the town," she said. Subsequently the town's one-room museum, which had been located in the basement of the library, was moved to the Parmley home.

"Parmley was a great rock collector, and he collected anything of interest to put in the two fireplaces. He traveled quite a bit, so he was always bringing things home," Phyllis said, and hence the fireplace is laden with quirky pieces such as seashells and screws. Parmley also had a practical mind, and his home was made of concrete—even the floors and the bathtubs. His previous residence had been destroyed in a fire, and most likely Parmley was determined not to be burned twice, so to speak.

For more information call (605) 426-6580 or visit www.sdmuseums.org. The home is open Memorial Day through Labor Day, Wed, Fri, and Sun from 2 to 5 p.m.

After US 12 was finished, enthusiastic Ipswich folks created a memorial stone arch over their portion of the Yellowstone Trail. When the highway was widened in 1973, the state insisted that the arch be moved. Moving the arch was no small feat since each pillar weighs more than 100 tons, so the state legislature appropriated money to make sure it wasn't homeless for too long. It now stands in the city park.

Northeast of Aberdeen, the **Sand Lake National Wildlife Refuge** boasts 21,451 acres of wildlife and waterfowl in grasslands, forest, lake, and marsh. The area surrounding the refuge was once vast, rolling grassland interrupted only by the slow-moving James River. Settlers arrived in 1887 and brought sweeping changes to the landscape. Farming and grazing depleted essential wildlife habitat, causing waterfowl to dwindle to alarmingly low numbers by the 1930s.

Congress established Sand Lake in 1935 to preserve critical habitat for nesting and migrating waterfowl. Today, millions of ducks, geese, and other wildlife make Sand Lake their home. In fact, 266 species of birds have been recorded at the refuge since 1935, including white pelicans, snow geese, and Western grebes.

Most people choose to drive through the refuge. A nicely illustrated, self-guided auto-tour guide is available. Along the 15-mile route there are twelve numbered stations, which correspond to symbols and text in the brochure. Station Two, for instance, affords an overlook where two important duck-nesting habitats can be seen. Station Eight is perfect for bird-watchers. Great horned owls occasionally roost here, and mallards, pintails, and the smaller blue-winged and green-winged teal also can be seen.

The refuge was designated a Wetland of International Importance under the guidelines developed by the Ramsar Convention on Wetlands in 1971. This makes Sand Lake the only such wetland in the Upper Great Plains, and one of only sixteen in the United States.

To reach the refuge from Aberdeen, take US 12 east to CR 16 (Bath Corner, 7 miles east of Aberdeen). Drive 20 miles north, through Columbia, to the refuge entrance. You can visit the refuge seven days a week, from daylight to dark, between early Apr and mid-Oct. The Visitor Center and Main office are open Mon through Fri, 8 a.m. to 4:30 p.m. and some additional weekends depending on the availability of volunteers. For more information, call (605) 885-6320 or visit www.fws.gov/sandlake.

Only an hour's drive from Aberdeen (take SD 45 south from Ipswich, then go west on US 212) is the **Pickler Mansion** in **Faulkton,** a friendly town of 785 people. John A. Pickler served four terms as South Dakota's first U.S. representative-at-large, and his wife, Alice W. Alt Pickler, campaigned for the suffrage cause. Fellow suffragette Susan B. Anthony was one of the more famous guests in the home, and some of her original letters found here are on display.

The home, a twenty-room Victorian house on the prairie, is complete with a secret room and a 2,550-book library that features Civil War and congressional sections. Called the Pink Castle (its distinct pink color was chosen by pioneer artist Charles T. Greener in 1894), the mansion is open daily from Memorial Day through Labor Day from 1 to 5 p.m. and at other times by appointment. Call (605) 598-4285 for a guide. Admission is $5.25 for adults and $2.60 for children 10 and under.

While you're at the Pickler Mansion, also visit the **Maloney Schoolhouse Museum** (605-598-4285), 6 blocks south of US 212 and Ninth South Avenue, then turn right into the driveway. This completely restored schoolhouse shows how "the three Rs" were taught to all grades within one room, certainly unique by today's educational standards but quite common in early plains life. Open by appointment. Admission is free.

Two blocks north of US 212 at 1202 Elm St. is **Wauneta's Gardens,** where master gardener Wauneta Holdren has lovingly tended her plants on the hillside banks of Nixon Creek for the past three decades. Although this is a private two-and-one-half-acre terraced flower garden, Wauneta kindly shares her botanical wonders and her wealth of knowledge with more than 2,000 visitors each year during the summer months. While she's slowing down a bit, visitors are welcome to admire more than 250 varieties of iris and 70 to 80 varieties of daylily and peony, as well as poppies, petunias, and other flowers. "I've done all the work by myself. The Lord willing, I will keep it open as long as I can," Wauneta said.

let'splayball

If you continue east on US 12, you'll find the birthplace of American Legion baseball in **Milbank,** home to 3,640 people on the South Dakota–Minnesota border. American Legion baseball began at a 1925 convention of that organization in Milbank. A historical marker commemorating the birth of American Legion baseball is located near the community baseball field. Former American Legion players include Yogi Berra, Johnny Bench, Jim Palmer, Frank Robinson, Greg Gagne, and Jack Morris.

"I just enjoy having people come in." She introduced more butterflies into the gardens by growing special plants—including milkweed—that attract the winged beauties. "I'm trying to educate people on the simplicity and the joy of having a garden," Wauneta said. "I have never considered it work." Visitors are asked to contribute a donation. Reservations are suggested for groups. Call (605) 598-6208.

Faulkton is called the Carousel City because it is home to the state's only electrically operated permanent 1925 Parker carousel. The carousel features nineteen original aluminum-cast horses. Located on Ninth Avenue South, the **Happy Times Carousel** can be enjoyed for free Wed evenings and Sat and Sun afternoons and evenings during the summer season. Call (605) 598-4285 for hours of operation.

History and High Stakes

The town of **Webster,** 53 miles east of Aberdeen on US 12, is home to an outlet store that carries home fashions guaranteed to fluff up any interior. Dakotah pillows, comforters, duvets, throws, and table linens are carried in fine department stores nationwide, and their quality and design make **Dakotah Creative Home Furnishings** (605-345-4646) equal to a Ralph Lauren Polo store on the prairie. The outlet store is open from 9 a.m. to 4 p.m. Mon through Fri.

For an interesting and educational way to spend your time, visit the **Day County Museum** (214 Eighth Ave. W; 605-345-3765), located in the basement of the Day County Courthouse. Hundreds of articles are on display, affording visitors an enjoyable glimpse into the past. There are many items of Indian

The Legend of Sam Brown

The Dakotas are rich with legends great and small. One such hero is *Sam Brown,* probably not a household name but a tremendous equalizer in the annals of prairie history nonetheless. In 1866 Sam was chief scout for Fort Wadsworth, now known as Fort Sisseton. He was told of an approaching Sioux Indian war party, and Sam sent a warning message to a fort farther north. Sam mounted his horse and set off to scout a camp 60 miles west. When he arrived, he discovered that the war party was simply several Indians delivering word of a new peace treaty. Sam knew that in order to prevent bloodshed, he must intercept his warning. Struggling through the freezing rain and snow of a ruthless spring blizzard, he managed to reach the fort by morning. But as he slipped from his horse, exhausted and half frozen, he was unable to stand. Sam Brown's heroic 150-mile ride cost him the use of his legs. He never walked again.

significance, including a bow and arrow, spears, arrowheads, beautiful beaded items, stone tools, a drummer's stick, and three beaded war clubs. Among the farm equipment used by early-day settlers is a horse net made about sixty years ago, cow and sheep bells, single and double oxen yokes, an iron hoe, and a hand corn planter. One of the more unusual items is a hair wreath made in 1865 from human hair, which was either crocheted, knitted, or wound around cardboard to make flower petals. The museum is open Mar 1 through Nov 1, from 1 to 4 p.m., only on Wed and Fri. Admission is free.

From Webster take US 12 east to I-29 and go south until you reach the crossroads of I-29 and US 212. It is here that you will find **Watertown.** Known as the Lake City, Watertown quite naturally lives up to its name; the town is situated along the Big Sioux River and

countytrivia

Watertown is located in Codington County, which was named for a Congregational minister and legislator, G. S. D. Codington. The county was formed in 1877, and Watertown was chosen as the county seat in 1878. Interestingly, Watertown is fed by Mineral Spring, which supplies highly mineralized water. It's no surprise that the water's bitter taste quickly repels any geese or ducks lighting on it.

is bordered by Lake Kampeska and Lake Pelican. Originally called Kampeska, the settlement owed its boom to the railroads. The primary industry here is agriculture, which is diversified in small grains, row crops, and livestock. Its enviable location near the crossroads of US 212 and I-29 makes it an important trade center not only for northeast South Dakota but also for west-central Minnesota. Watertown (population 20,237) is located 180 miles west of Minneapolis, 100 miles north of Sioux Falls, and 350 miles from Rapid City.

Pioneer and local history through World War II and Native American artifacts are the focal points at the **Codington County Heritage Museum** (formerly the Kampeska Heritage Museum). Located at 27 First Ave. SE, the museum is open 8 a.m. to 5 p.m. Mon through Fri, and 1 to 5 p.m. Sat Memorial Day through Labor Day and from 1 to 5 p.m. the rest of the year. The exhibits change periodically and focus on the homestead era in Codington County. War memorabilia, exhibits on local culture, and Indian beadwork from the early reservation period are among the displays. Admission is free; donations are accepted. Call (605) 886-7335 or visit www.cchsmuseum.org for more information.

If you meander into the residential area on the north side of town, you'll find more history at the **Mellette House** (421 Fifth Ave. NW). South Dakota's first governor, Arthur C. Mellette, was the model of honesty and conscience—qualities one almost always dreams of, yet rarely expects to find in today's politicians. Mellette was appointed governor of the Dakota Territory by President Benjamin Harrison and later was elected governor of the new state of South Dakota. A drought that lasted well into the 1890s plagued his term, but Mellette used his own personal resources to alleviate the dire circumstances in his state.

The Mellette House, an 1883 Italianate villa, was built on the so-called Mellette Hill. The home was the venue for many extravagant receptions and social gatherings for which guest lists glittered with names of dignitaries, close friends of Mellette, and political associates. When Mellette's close friend W. W. Taylor defaulted on a large amount as state treasurer, Mellette suffered a reversal of fortune as well. As one of the bondsmen, Mellette turned over all of his real estate and other assets, including his own home, to the state as reimbursement. In the process, Mellette went bankrupt. After leaving office, Mellette successfully practiced law until 1895, when he and his family moved to Pittsburg, Kansas. He died one year later. Although the state returned the Watertown home to Mellette's widow, the family never occupied the home again. Over the years the site of once-glamorous galas slowly decayed into a nondescript redbrick house. Fortunately, the Mellette Association intervened and restored the home to the luxurious state it had known with the Mellette family. The home is open May 1 through Oct 1, Tues through Sun from 1 to 5 p.m. Call (605) 886-4730 or visit www.mellettehouse.org. Free guided tours are available, but donations are welcome.

Powwow Etiquette

Powwows are a wonderful chance for non-Native Americans to learn about the culture, and most powwows are open to the public. They can last anywhere from a few hours to several days and frequently include craft displays, rodeos, ethnic foods, and cultural exhibits.

To be a courteous guest at a powwow, here are a few tips:

- It's generally acceptable to take photos or videos, but check beforehand.
- Ask permission before taking someone's photo outside of the dance circle.
- Stand at the "Grand Entry" to pay respect to the dancers. Remain standing for the Great Sioux Nation's national anthem.
- The dance area is considered sacred; don't enter it unless invited.
- Many powwows lack seating, so bring along a lawn chair or blanket and make yourself comfortable.

Twenty-four massive granite columns, visible for miles, lure the visitor to the **Redlin Art Center** at 1200 Thirty-third St. SE. Built by Watertown artist and native Terry Redlin, the center houses more than 150 of Redlin's original paintings. His works capture the charm of rural life that flourishes just outside the center's door. A high-tech planetarium offers educational entertainment for the entire family. The Center is also home to a collection of artifacts from Langenfeld's Ice Cream and Dairy, owned and operated by the family of Terry's wife Helene. The art center is open 8 a.m. to 5 p.m. Mon through Fri, 10 a.m. to 4 p.m. Sat, and noon to 4 p.m. Sun. Special holiday hours are available at www.redlinart.com. Admission is free. Call (877) 873-3546 for more information.

On SD 20 in northwest Watertown, the **Bramble Park Zoo** brings you face-to-face with more than 500 mammals, reptiles, and birds representing more than 100 varieties from around the world as well as those native to the Great Plains. See an exotic jaguar or watch the beauty of a pheasant as it struts its stuff in one of the largest waterfowl and pheasant collections in the United States. The zoo provides for and breeds threatened and endangered species. See deer, arctic foxes, and badgers roam outside. On weekends in the summer, zoo keepers offer special talks. The zoo is open year-round, weather permitting, from 9 a.m. to 8 p.m. in the summer, and from 10 a.m. to 4 p.m. in the winter. Admission ranges from free to $5.50, based on age. Call (605) 882-6269 or visit www.brambleparkzoo.com for general information and special events.

Fifty-seven miles north of Watertown, **Fort Sisseton State Historical Park,** about 25 miles west of **Sisseton,** is the home of the annual Fort Sisseton Festival the first weekend in June and the Frontier Christmas in Dec. The park also offers camping, cabins, boating, canoeing, hiking, and fishing. See www.sdgfp.info/parks or call (605) 448-5474 for details on hours and other information. Call (800) 710-2267 or visit www.campSD.com for reservations.

Another attraction (only 6 miles north of Watertown on Sioux Conifer Road) is **Dakota Sioux Casino** (800-658-4717), featuring blackjack with the highest bets in the state ($100 maximum, $3 minimum). Or take a chance on one of more than 220 reel-slot machines. The casino, with restaurant, lounge, and live entertainment, is owned and operated by the Sisseton–Wahpeton Sioux tribe. The community of Sisseton is located just off I-29 on SD 10.

The **Joseph N. Nicollet Tower and Interpretive Center** is located 3.5 miles west of Sisseton. It is dedicated to the French mapmaker who could very well be a sort of real-life Lieutenant Dunbar from the Academy Award-winning movie *Dances with Wolves.* (The Kevin Costner movie, by the way, was filmed in South Dakota). Nicollet spent 1838 and 1839 creating the first accurate map of the vast area between the Mississippi and the Missouri Rivers. He was trained as an astronomer in Paris, and he took highly accurate notes

Winter Driving Tips in the Dakotas

- Listen to the forecast before departing and postpone travel if inclement weather is expected.

- Avoid traveling alone. Inform others of your timetable and primary and alternate routes.

- Keep your gas tank near full to avoid ice in the tank and the fuel lines.

- Adjust your speed to the conditions and increase following distances.

- Remember that bridges and overpasses are usually more slippery than other parts of the road.

- Always carry a survival kit in your vehicle. Your kit should be equipped with a can of sand or kitty litter; tire chains; flashlight with extra batteries; candles and matches; an empty coffee can (to be used to burn the candles for heat and to melt snow for water); caps, mittens, boots, and sleeping bag or blanket for everyone; nonperishable foods, such as granola bars or dried fruit; booster cables; battery-operated radio with extra batteries; first-aid kit; and cellular phone with fully charged batteries.

in his journals that recorded more than his precise mathematical calculations. Like those of the fictional Dunbar, Nicollet's journals also illuminated a love for the prairies and respect and understanding of Native people. He wrote in 1839 of the Coteau des Prairies (Hill of the Prairies):

"May I not be permitted to introduce a few reflections of the prairies? . . . Their sight never wearies . . . to ascend one of its undulations, moving from wave to wave over alternate swells and depressions; and finally to reach the vast interminable low prairie, that extends itself in front, be it for hours, days or weeks, one never tires; pleasurable and exhilarating sensations are all the time felt. . . . I pity the man whose soul could remain unmoved under such a scene of excitement."

Today, the 75-foot observation tower with three floors affords a breathtaking view of the great valley carved by glaciers some 40,000 years ago.

The "mother map" of the Midwest is displayed at the foot of the tower. Nicollet presented the map to the United States Senate in 1841. The central feature is the Coteau des Prairies, which, at an elevation of more than 2,000 feet, is the highest point between Winnipeg, Manitoba, Canada, and the Gulf of Mexico and the Appalachians and the Black Hills. Original artwork by nationally recognized wildlife artist John S. Wilson is displayed in the Inter-pretive Center, as are paintings depicting the Dakota Indian people Nicollet described in his journals. The tower is open from May to Oct, 10 a.m. to 5 p.m. Mon through Fri and 1 to 4 p.m. Sun. Call (605) 698-7621 or visit www.sisseton museums.org/nicollet_tower.asp for more information. Free admission.

While you're in the area, also stop by the *Stavig House Museum* on First Avenue in Sisseton. The museum follows the lives of Norwegians in the area, through many walks of life, from entrepreneur to humble fisherman. During the summer, the home is open from 10 a.m. to 4 p.m. Mon and Thurs through Sat, 1 to 4 p.m. Sun. Open by appointment and for special events in the winter. A guided tour costs $5. Visit www.sissetonmuseums.org/historic_buildings.asp or call (605) 698-4561 for more information.

Land of Laura Ingalls

If you take I-29 south from Watertown for 44 miles, you'll reach the state's largest university, South Dakota State University, in Brookings, home to 18,504 people. Its varied components contribute much to the town's economy and culture. Open year-round, the *McCrory Gardens and State Arboretum,* at Sixth Street and Twentieth Avenue, features twenty acres of formal display gardens and forty-five acres of arboretum. Called the prettiest quarter section in the state, the gardens include fourteen formal theme gardens and a rose garden with more than thirty varieties, an herb garden, a children's maze, a historic gas station renovated as a garden cottage, and a memorial to the late Governor George S. Mickelson.

The gardens were named in honor of South Dakota State University pro-fessor S. A. McCrory, who headed the horticulture department from 1947 until his death in 1964. McCrory had envisioned a research garden displaying trees, shrubs, grasses, and flowers that were—or could be—a part of South Dakota's landscape. That vision is still the prime directive for all the work done at the gardens. You can view the lovely gardens during a self-guided tour, available from dawn to dusk daily. Admission is free; call (605) 688-5921 or visit www .sdstate.edu for more information on the gardens.

The university's *Prairie Repertory Theatre* has a slate full of comedies, musicals, and dramas each summer. The group is celebrating its 40th season. Call (605) 688-6045 or visit www.prairierep.org for more information. The *South Dakota Art Museum* (Medary Avenue and Harvey Dunn Street, named for a well-known artist in the state) has a stylish look and has graciously served the state for more than thirty years. It features permanent galleries, changing exhibitions, lectures, workshops, and guided tours—all with the artist, the teacher, the student, and the public in mind. Harvey Dunn once told his students, "If you ever amount to anything at all, it will be because you are true to that deep desire or ideal, which made you seek artistic expression in pictures."

Dunn's artistic desire earned him national recognition and exhibition space in the South Dakota Art Museum and the Smithsonian Institution in Washington, D.C. The United States Postal Service also paid tribute to Dunn by putting his painting *Something for Supper* on one of twenty stamps that honored America's greatest illustrators. The pane of stamps, unveiled in 2001, featured artwork by Robert Fawcett, Arthur Burdett Frost, Rockwell Kent, Frederic Remington, and Norman Rockwell, as well. The original *Something for Supper,* completed in 1940, can be seen at the South Dakota Art Museum. Other artists represented at the gallery include Paul Goble and Oscar Howe. The museum is open from 10 a.m. to 5 p.m. Mon through Fri, from 10 a.m. to 4 p.m. Sat, and from noon to 4 p.m. Sun. The museum is closed Sun, Jan through Mar. Admission is free, although there may be a charge for special programs. For more information, call (605) 688-5423 or visit www.southdakotaartmuseum.com.

fishingformore

Walleye dominate the fishing scene in northeastern South Dakota, and most are caught trolling over hard gravel or sand bottoms. Other fish found in the area are smallmouth and largemouth bass, white bass, bullheads, yellow perch, and northern pike. More than 120 glacial lakes dot the northeastern landscape of the state. Anglers who travel to this rolling farm and ranch country will find that the lakes range in size from several acres to more than 16,000 acres. There are fourteen state parks and recreation areas and several municipal and private campgrounds in the region. Resorts can be found at most of the larger lakes, but a few of the glacial lakes remain undeveloped and may be surrounded by private land.

While you're on campus, stop by the university dairy bar in the **Dairy Micro** building, where you can choose from more than ninety-five ice-cream and sherbet flavors, get an ice-cream cookie, or sample the twenty-four cheese varieties, butter, and milk. All products are made from milk produced at the SDSU Dairy Research and Training Facility north of campus, and students do the processing. It's open weekdays from 8 a.m. to 5 p.m., and tours are available (605-688-5420).

South of Brookings and 30 miles north of Sioux Falls is the **Royal River Casino** (800-833-8666; www.royalrivercasino.com), located in **Flandreau** off I-29. The casino, owned by the Santee Sioux tribe, has rejuvenated the community of 2,311 residents. The town, situated along the Big Sioux River, was first settled in 1869 by twenty-five Christian Santee Sioux families who bravely gave up their tribal rights—and their surnames—so that they could homestead.

Religious themes recur in Flandreau through several historic churches built in the 1800s. Most notable is the ***First Presbyterian Church*** on North SD 13, the oldest continuously operating church in South Dakota.

For a historical perspective on the area, the ***Moody County Museum and Complex*** (706 East Pipestone Ave.) shows antiques and collectibles from the area's pioneer past. You can visit an authentic one-room schoolhouse, a Milwaukee railroad depot built in 1881, and the Riverbend Meeting House, Flandreau's first framed building, built in 1871. The complex is open from 10 a.m. to 3 p.m., Mon through Fri and by appointment. Call (605) 997-3191 or visit www.cityofflandreau.com for more information.

Local events include the ***Good Old Summertime Festival*** during the 4th of July and the ***Santee Sioux Powwow*** during the third week of July when residents don authentic costumes to perform traditional ceremonies.

For an overnight stay in Flandreau, try the ***Talk of the Town Bed & Breakfast Inn,*** located at 201 West Pipestone Ave. in a 1904 arts and crafts home. A gourmet breakfast is served every morning, featuring homemade breads and muffins. Call (605) 997-5170 or visit www.bbonline.com/sd/talk for more information.

Generations of children and grown-ups have found their way to the real Little House on the Prairie, located in the heart of Kingsbury County in ***De Smet,*** 30 miles west of Oakwood State Park at the intersection of US 14 and SD 25. Fresh-faced little girls in crisp gingham bonnets evoke the stories of the town's most famous writer each summer during the ***Laura Ingalls Wilder Pageant,*** and the saplings that Pa Ingalls planted so long ago are now mature cottonwoods. Laura moved here as a child in 1879, and the prairie town figured prominently in six of her pioneer adventure books. You can see eighteen sites mentioned in the books, including the house Pa built for his family in 1887 and the railroad surveyor's shanty where the family first lived in De Smet. Scenes from *These Happy Golden Years* are re-created during the outdoor pageant, held the last weekend in June and the first two weekends in July. Tours start at the headquarters and gift shop, located 3 blocks east of the city library. Tour hours are from 9 a.m. to 6 p.m. daily Memorial Day through Labor Day, 9 a.m. to 5 p.m. in the fall and spring. Tickets are $8 for everyone 5 years and older, and free for those under 5. Call (800) 776-3594 for more information about the homestead or visit www.ingallshomestead.com. To learn about the pageant visit www.desmetpageant.org, or call (800) 880-3383 for advance tickets.

Head west on US 14 and enter another county for more intimations of what life on the prairie is really like today. ***Huron*** is the county seat of Beadle County, and it wears its distinction well. The town is the administrative center for a handful of federal and state agencies, and town promoters claim Huron

An Angel in South Dakota

South Dakota considers **Cheryl Ladd** its Hollywood Girl, even though more than thirty years have passed since the Huron-born blond beauty portrayed Kris Munroe in *Charlie's Angels*. The popularity of the series never seems to wane, especially with big-screen remakes of the series starring Lucy Liu, Drew Barrymore, and Cameron Diaz.

Ladd was born Cheryl Stoppelmoor in Huron, South Dakota. Her singing—Ladd joined a local band in high school—proved to be her ticket to stardom. After years of acting classes, appearances in commercials, and guest-starring roles on TV, Ladd joined *Charlie's Angels*. She also has recorded two albums, *Cheryl Ladd* and *Dance Fever*, which were big successes in Japan.

Ladd has continued to act in movies and TV. She also writes children's books with her husband, Brian. Their daughter, Jordan Ladd, also caught the acting bug. She was in the hit film *Never Been Kissed*.

is the trade and farm-products processing center for a 10,500-square-mile area. Not surprisingly, Huron is the second-largest area in the state for livestock sales and among the top in manufactured products.

Huron also has claim to the first elected female U.S. senator, Gladys Pyle, who served in the Senate during the 1930s. This pioneering feminist's home, the **Gladys Pyle Historic Home** (376 Idaho Ave. SW), is open to the public. The 1894 Queen Anne–style building features stained glass, ornately carved golden oak woodwork, and Gladys's original furnishings. The home is open from 1 to 3:30 p.m. Mon through Fri, 1 to 4 p.m. and 6:30 to 8:30 p.m. Sat, 1 to 4 p.m. Sun, and closed on holidays. Admission is $1.50. Call (605) 352-2528 or visit www.southdakotabeautiful.com for more information.

Also in the annals of political and state history is Hubert H. Humphrey, the former senator and vice president of the United States. A mid-1930s atmosphere is quaintly preserved in the **Hubert H. Humphrey Drugstore** on Dakota Avenue, which was owned by Humphrey until his death and still is owned by the Humphrey family. The vice president worked in the drugstore, which his father owned, during the Great Depression. You don't have to pay a cent to enjoy the nostalgia—and both the era and the man—in the drugstore. It's a refreshing detour from today's ubiquitous big chain stores. The store is open from 8:30 a.m. to 6 p.m. daily. Call (605) 352-4064 for more information.

Memoirs of Humphrey and his wife, Muriel, are found at the **Centennial Center** (48 Fourth St. SE). Listed on the National Register of Historic Places, this Gothic-style structure is more commonly known as the Old Stone Church. It was built in 1887 of huge granite boulders from a farm northeast of Huron. The museum also has railroad items, Indian artifacts, and other memorabilia. Call (605) 352-1442 for more information and appointments. Donations are accepted.

Need another reason to visit Huron? Consider the ***South Dakota State Fair,*** one of the biggest agricultural fairs in the nation. It celebrated its 125th year in 2010. You haven't experienced true, dyed-in-the-wool Americana without attending a state fair, especially in South Dakota. It is simply a heartwarming occasion, sticky with cotton candy, delirious from roller-coaster rides and rodeos, and full of down-home events. Rodeos, grandstand shows featuring the current stars on the country music charts, 4-H club projects, and a promenade of the newest and fanciest farm equipment and machinery embody all that is sweet to the rural lifestyle. Don't forget the spine-tingling carnival rides (or the carousel for younger or sensitive tummies). The fair runs for a few days in Sept. Daily admission is $5 for adults and $3 for kids age 6 to 15. Visit www.sdstatefair.com or call (800) 529-0900 for more information.

The ***Dakotaland Museum*** is also located on the fairgrounds with more than 5,000 artifacts celebrating the heritage and history of Huron and Beadle County. Admission is $1 for folks 12 years of age and older. The museum is open from 9:30 to 11:30 a.m., 1 to 4 p.m. and 6:30 to 8:30 p.m. Mon through Fri; and 1 to 4 p.m. and 6:30 to 8:30 p.m. weekends and holidays. For more information, call (605) 352-4626.

Located 15 miles northeast of Huron, ***Lake Byron*** has consistently been one of the top producers of trophy walleye. Expect to catch perch, crappie, pike, and bullheads as well on this 1,750-acre lake. If you're not into dropping a line, try water-skiing, ski-boarding, camping, or picnicking.

Where to Stay in Northeastern South Dakota

ABERDEEN

Best Western Ramkota Inn
1400 Eighth Ave. NW
(605) 229-4040
http://aberdeen.ramkota
.com
Moderate

Lighthouse Inn Express and Banquet Center
12800 South Shore Dr.
(605) 225-5007
www.thelighthouseinn
expressandbanquetcenter
.com
Moderate

Ramada Inn
2727 Sixth Ave. SE
(605) 225-3600
(800) 272-6232
www.ramada-aberdeen
.com
Moderate

Super 8 Motel
2405 Sixth Ave.
(605) 229-5005
(800) 800-8000
www.super8.com
Moderate

BROOKINGS

Comfort Inn
514 Sunrise Ridge Rd.
(605) 692-9566
www.comfortinn.com
Moderate

Fairfield Inn and Suites
3000 Lefevre Dr.
(605) 692-3500
(800) 228-2800
www.marriott.com
Moderate

**Holiday Inn Express
Hotel and Suites**
3020 Lefevre Dr.
(605) 692 9060
www.hiexpress.com
Moderate

DE SMET

**The Prairie House Manor
Bed and Breakfast**
209 Hwy. 25 S
(605) 854-9131
(800) 297-2416
www.prairiehousemanor
.com
Moderate

FLANDREAU

**Talk of the Town Bed &
Breakfast Inn**
201 West Pipestone Ave.
(605) 997-5170
www.bbonline.com/sd/talk
Moderate

HURON

**The Crossroads Hotel
and Event Center**
100 Fourth St. SW
(605) 352-3204
(800) 876-5858
www.huroneventcenter
.com
Moderate

WATERTOWN

Best Western Ramkota
1901 Ninth Ave. SW
(605) 886-8011
(800) 528-1234
http://watertown.ramkota
.com
Moderate

SELECTED CHAMBERS OF COMMERCE

**Aberdeen Convention & Visitors
Bureau**
10 Railroad Ave. SW
P.O. Box 78
Aberdeen, 57402
(800) 645-3851
www.visitaberdeensd.com

Aberdeen Chamber of Commerce
516 South Main St.
Aberdeen, 57402
(605) 225-2860
www.aberdeen-chamber.com

**Brookings Area Chamber of
Commerce and Convention Bureau**
414 Main Ave.
P.O. Box 431
Brookings, 57006
(605) 692-6125
www.brookingssd.com
www.brookingschamber.org

Huron Chamber & Visitors Bureau
1725 Dakota Ave.
Huron, 57350
(605) 352-0000
(800) 487-6673
www.huronsd.com

Sisseton Chamber of Commerce
1608 Highway 10, Suite 10
Sisseton, 57262-0221
(605) 698-726
www.sisseton.com

**Watertown Area Chamber of
Commerce and Convention & Visitors
Bureau**
1200 Mickelson Dr., Suite 308
PO Box 225
Watertown, 57201-6113
(605) 753-0282
(800) 658-4505

Days Inn
2900 Ninth Ave. SE
(605) 886-3500
(800) 329-7466
www.daysinn.com
Moderate

Quality Inn and Suites
800 Thirty-fifth St. Cir.
(605) 886-3010
www.qualityinn.com
Moderate

Traveler's Inn Motel
920 Fourteenth St. SE
(605) 882-2243
(800) 568-7074
Moderate

Where to Eat in Northeastern South Dakota

ABERDEEN

The Flame Restaurant & Lounge
(American)
2 South Main St.
(605) 225-2082
Moderate

Guadalajara Restaurant
3015 Sixth Ave. SE
(605) 229-7555
Moderate

Imperial Chinese Buffet
311 South Main St.
(605) 229-2587
Moderate

Millstone Family Restaurant
2210 Sixth Ave. SE
(605) 229-4105
Inexpensive to moderate

Minervas Restaurant and Bar
(in Best Western Ramkota)
1400 Eighth Ave. NW
(605) 226-2988
www.minervas.net
Moderate to expensive

Red Rooster Coffee House
202 South Main St.
(605) 225-6603
www.myspace.com/red
roostercoffeehouse
Inexpensive

BROOKINGS

Cottonwood Bistro
Brickwood Plaza
1710 Sixth St.
(605) 692-8938
www.cottonwoodbistro
.com

Cottonwood Café
509 Main Ave.
(605) 692-7009
www.cottonwoodcoffee
.com
Inexpensive

HURON

Ida May's Café
1111 Dakota Ave. N
(605) 352-5988
Inexpensive

SISSETON

Lakeland Lanes Steakhouse and Lounge
614 West Hickory St.
(605) 698-7407
Moderate

WATERTOWN

The Grainery
3800 Ninth Ave. SE
(605) 882-3950
Moderate

Guadalajara Restaurant
1509 Ninth Ave. SE
(605) 882-4548
Moderate

SOUTHEASTERN SOUTH DAKOTA →

With more than forty museums and galleries, as well as countless parks, the southeastern corner of South Dakota feels more cosmopolitan than the rest of the state. It deftly proves that the prairie can certainly be urban and hip if it wants to be. Of course, it takes only minutes to get into the countryside, where you can enjoy the parks, small towns, and other gems of southeastern South Dakota. The region is easily accessible via east-west I-90 or north-south I-29.

The Land of Jesse James

Tucked between Lake Madison and Lake Herman, the town of Madison is a popular recreation spot. Formed by melting glacial ice thousands of years ago, the 1,350-acre Lake Herman was named for Herman Luce who settled here in the 1870s with his son. The cabin they built, lived in, and used as a survey office is available for tour in *Lake Herman State Park.*

On Lake Madison the Chautauqua summer program was a pioneer's favorite pastime from 1891 to 1933. People gathered to hear lectures and concerts, watch plays, and engage in lively debates. The *Smith–Zimmermann Heritage Museum*

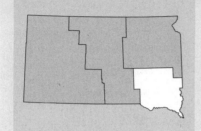

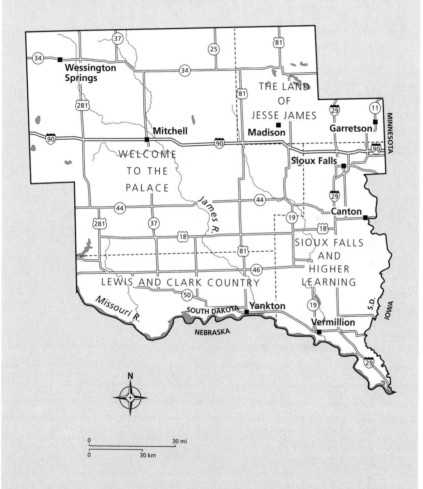

Wessington
Springs

THE LAND
OF
JESSE JAMES

Garretson

MINNESOTA

Mitchell

Madison

Sioux Falls

WELCOME
TO THE
PALACE

James R.

Canton

SIOUX FALLS
AND
HIGHER
LEARNING

LEWIS AND CLARK COUNTRY

Missouri R.

SOUTH DAKOTA

Yankton

NEBRASKA

Vermillion

S.D.

IOWA

N

0   30 mi
0   30 km

SOUTHEASTERN SOUTH DAKOTA'S TOP HITS

Corn Palace

Dakota Discovery Museum's Oscar Howe Gallery

Devil's Gulch

Falls Park

Great Plains Zoo and Delbridge Museum

Heartland Arabians

Minerva's

National Music Museum

Old Courthouse Museum

Prairie Village

Rose Stone Inn

Zandbroz Variety

on Madison's Dakota State University campus is home to the Chautauqua Collection, which is considered one of the most important in the Midwest. While you're here be sure to look at the Civil War memorabilia, the covered wagon, period clothing, and 1880s parlor. The museum is open from 1 to 4:30 p.m. Tues through Fri or by appointment. Admission is free. Call (605) 256-5308 or visit www.smith-zimmermann.dsu.edu.

To the west of Madison, **Prairie Village** is a living museum of an authentic pioneer town. Attractions include antique tractors, an 1893 steam carousel, a sod house, and a log cabin. The annual Threshing Jamboree in Aug embraces an array of pioneer-worthy events that include horse-powered grain threshing, antique tractor pulling, weaving, and quilting. The village is open 10 a.m. to 6 p.m. Mon through Sat and 11 a.m. to 6 p.m. Sun from Mother's Day until Labor Day. Admission is $5 for adults; $2 for children age 6 to 12, and free for children under 6. Call (605) 256-3644; www.prairievillage.org.

The annual **Quarry Days** celebration is held the last weekend in June in Dell Rapids, and the event shows the civic pride this small town has for its quartzite quarries. Located north of Sioux Falls, Dell Rapids is just 3 miles east of I-29 and only 15 miles from the intersection of I-29 and I-90. Dell Rapids calls itself "A South Dakota Treasure," and its awe-inspiring landscapes and fascinating buildings make it a stunning piece in the state's ever-growing patchwork quilt of experience.

The bounty of the **Dell Rapids** quartzite quarries is handsomely displayed as building stone in walls and foundations throughout the downtown district. Many of the buildings, which showcase Victorian, Romanesque revival, and neoclassical revival architectural styles, are listed on the National Register of

Historic Places. The dells were formed more than 12,000 years ago by strong currents of water passing over exposed Sioux quartzite fissures. Native Americans called it *imnizeusteca,* or "canyon."

Winston Churchill once said, "We shape our buildings, and afterwards they shape us," and Dell Rapids' architecture has magnificently primed the community's cultural scene. You can pick up a Dells Rapids Walking Tour guide at the **Dells Rapids History Museum,** 407 East Fourth St., then hit the streets. First stop: Seeing the art deco glamour that oozes from the facade of the 1938 **Dells Theatre** at 511 East Fourth St. It still has its original paint, seats, stage curtain, and light fixtures.

Another fabulous building is the **Grand Opera House,** built in 1888. Located at 425–427 East Fourth St., it is where all special occasions are celebrated in Dell Rapids. With a dining room, lounge, and opera hall, the facility is popular for weddings and traveling performances. Check out the calendar of events on line at www.dellrapidsgrandoperahouse.com and then call for more details at (605) 428-3580.

Stay the night in the 1908 **Rose Stone Inn,** 504 East Fourth St., for another experience of small-town intimacy and the bewitching iridescence of quartzite, which is the inn's main building material. Owners Rick and Sharon Skinner offer guests four themed rooms—the Violet and Ivy Room, the Friends Room, the Garden Room, and the Victoria Rose Room—plus the smaller Peach Blossom Room if additional beds are needed. This beautifully renovated hotel, which is on the National Register of Historic Places,

AUTHOR'S FAVORITES IN SOUTHEASTERN SOUTH DAKOTA

Corn Palace
Mitchell
(605) 995-8430
(800) 289-7469

Earth Resources Observation Systems (EROS)
Sioux Falls
(605) 594-6511

Great Plains Zoo
Sioux Falls
(605) 367-7003

Lewis and Clark Lake Gavins Point Dam
Yankton
(402) 667-2546

National Music Museum
Vermillion
(605) 677-5306

is furnished with loving care and fashionable pieces from the late-19th and early-20th centuries. Room rates range from $95 to $150 per night for two people, including breakfast. Open year-round. Call (605) 428-3698 or visit www.rosestoneinn.com.

Drive southeast of Dell Rapids and walk in the footsteps of the legendary outlaw Jesse James near *Garretson.* At *Devil's Gulch,* a rocky chasm at least 20 feet across and 50 feet deep, the notorious outlaw stymied a posse trying to catch him after the infamous failed bank robbery in Northfield, Minnesota. The story goes like this: The James brothers were chased into eastern South Dakota. When Jesse reached Devil's Gulch, he reined in his horse and stared into the forbidding chasm. Jesse turned, retraced his steps to get a running start, let out a whooping battle cry, and dug his spurs into his horse. The horse bounded forward. Time stood still; then the bandit lurched forward as his mount landed. He had made it. The posse, too dumbfounded by Jesse's daring jump to follow, simply milled about as the outlaw rode off. Today you can stand on a footbridge that spans Devil's Gulch and picture yourself visiting the site in 1876, just like Jesse James.

Stop in the gift shop for a copy of the seven-point walking trail map that provides additional history and insight to the geography in the area. If volunteer Don Schubert is on duty, he'll talk your ear off, but don't dare take him up on his offer to lead your hike on the trail—you might not be able to keep up with this 80-year-old. Take the hike at your own pace, and don't forget your camera. Call (605) 594-6721 for more information.

The Garreston Area Historical Society has been hard at work in recent years making significant improvements to the *Garretson Historical Museum.* If you like agricultural history or need detailed information on local happenings of the past, stop in at 609 North Main Ave. Free admission; (605) 594-6694.

Each June, the escapades of the James brothers are celebrated during the *Jesse James Roundup Days* at Split Rock Park, just north of Garretson off SD 11. A Dutch oven cook-off, craft fair, chuck wagon feed, and theater production commemorate the nefarious, although exciting, James brothers' connection to South Dakota. The park is a perfect place for camping, hiking, and other outdoor sports.

There are two options for getting out on the creek. The first is Zack Hoisington. He and his father operate about the only canoe/kayak outfitter in the region. If you've never kayaked before, this is a great place to give it a try because the creek is quite shallow and has very little current. For more information, call (605) 929-1122.

The second option is Bruce Rekstad. As his name indicates, he's Norwegian, so he offers a "Norwegian Cruise" of Split Rock Creek. His ship is actually a pontoon boat from which he narrates a pretty wild tale while the boat moves slowly up and down the creek. You're not sure whether you should believe or repeat the stories he tells. Bruce grew up in the area and played in a cave that was apparently a hide-out of Frank and Jesse James. Call (605) 594-2225.

Spectacular quartzite chasms are a drawing card, too, in **Palisades State Park,** southwest of Garretson. The view is breathtaking, and the waters here are an inviting and dreamy blue. Colorful red quartzite pinnacles and formations with 50-foot vertical cliffs line Split Rock River, which winds through the park. Please take note of the many posted signs that say DON'T JUMP OFF THE CLIFFS, and then follow that advice, even if you see others doing it. Each summer, someone jumps into the water below onto a big rock under the water line, and the best you can hope for is a broken leg and a $100 fine. Notice, too, the unique architecture of the WPA (Works Progress Administration) of the 1930s, which features a dam with a waterfall, a bathhouse, bridges, and a rock wall with a flower garden. You can camp at the park or stay in the cabins. For reservations, call (605) 594-3824. But at minimum, plan on bringing a picnic lunch with you here and just enjoy the view. Long before this was a state park, it was a popular picnicking destination for people from the area, and it continues to be so. And for an interesting activity, pick up a brochure about the new Lichen Trail. The trail has 30 different kinds of lichen identified, and information about as many as 100 more kinds of lichen found in the park. Who would have thought lichen could be so interesting?

Have you seen the movie *Horse Whisperer* with Robert Redford? That's very much the philosophy of training horses at **Heartland Arabians,** 11 miles north of Sioux Falls. Not only is it a showplace for internationally famous horses (three international champions live here), but clinics focus on communicating with horses in the manner that Robert Redford did so spiritually in that movie.

Nestled in the rolling hills of the Big Sioux River Valley, this all-weather facility is also home to exotic animals like llamas, angora goats, peacocks, and donkeys. You also can see equine art and clothing in Heartland's shop, or take an antique sleigh or buggy ride around the historically authentic 100-acre farm. You must make reservations. Owner Jayne Solberg offers pony parties as well. Heartland is open by appointment at no charge to the public. Call (605) 543-5900; www.heartlandventures.net.

Also near **Baltic** (10 miles north of exit 402 on I-90) is the **Earth Resources Observation Systems (EROS) Data Center** (605-594-6511), which houses the government's central archives for nonmilitary satellite images and aerial photography. The center operates an archive with more than 8 million photographs of the United States taken from aircraft and more than 3 million worldwide images acquired by sensors aboard several satellites. The complex reproduces and disseminates data to scientists throughout the world and assists users in the application of such photographs. Audiovisuals in the lobby will take you on an engrossing thirty- to forty-five-minute self-guided tour. Guided tours are offered at 10 a.m. and 2 p.m. Open Mon through Fri from 8 a.m. to 4 p.m. Free admission.

Sioux Falls and Higher Learning

With a population of more than 148,000, *Sioux Falls* is the largest city in the state. Established in 1865 at the falls of the Sioux River, the town has been like the Energizer Bunny: It keeps going and going and going. Its résumé reads like one of a proud college graduate. The city is consistently listed as one of the Top Ten Best Places to Live in America—a remarkably low crime rate, an abundance of jobs, clean air, and a cordial atmosphere make it a wonderful place to live or visit. The growth of Sioux Falls has been buoyed by its diversified industry and farming as well as by its citizens, who eagerly embrace change and the cultural and economic promises a larger city can bring. Today Sioux Falls is called a mini Minneapolis. It has everything its residents need in terms of shopping, cultural activities, and entertainment, but if they crave a bigger city, Sioux Falls lies within reasonable driving distance from Des Moines, Omaha, Minneapolis, and Kansas City.

The city is rightfully proud of its *Washington Pavilion of Arts and Science* at the corner of Eleventh and Main Streets. It's a place where visitors can be touched by extraordinary artwork or go ahead touch interactive science displays.

The Pavilion's Visual Arts Center features seven galleries of changing exhibits, including Native American artists, regional and national contemporary

Sioux Falls Sculpture Walk

For artists, particularly sculptors, and those who love their work, Sioux Falls is a gold mine. Since 2004, about six blocks of downtown, between Eighth and Thirteenth Streets, has been the exhibition space for 55 outdoor sculptures. New sculptures are placed about mid-May each year, and the public is invited to stroll, look, and vote for their favorite. The People's Choice stays in Sioux Falls, and many of the others are sold or leased to an appreciating public in Apr at the end of the exhibition year. As you walk along Phillips Avenue, look for wooden boxes hanging from street lights. These boxes contain a brochure with a map to all of the sculptures, as well as a ballot to vote for your favorite. It's just such a cool thing for the city to do, don't you think? For information: (605) 339-8359; www.sculpturewalksiouxfalls.com.

TOP ANNUAL EVENTS

Downtown Holidays
Sioux Falls, Nov through Dec
(605) 338-4009

Great Plains Powwow
Sioux Falls, second weekend in
Oct (in conjunction with
Native American Day)
(605) 339-7039

Riverboat Days
Yankton, third weekend in Aug
(605) 665-1657

Sidewalk Arts Festival
Sioux Falls, Sept
(605) 977-2002

Sioux Empire Fair
Sioux Falls, early Aug
(605) 367-7178

visual arts exhibitions, and a hands-on children's gallery. The Visual Arts Center presently has a collection of 300 works, including pieces by noted South Dakota artists Oscar Howe, Lova Jones, and Charles Greener. Other artists represented include Signe Stuart and Robert Aldern. The 300-seat Small Theater is available for performances requiring more-intimate space, such as musical ensembles, lectures, poetry readings, experimental theater, and dance and piano recitals.

The Husby Performing Arts Center brings the best in music, dance, and theater from around the world. The 1,800-seat Great Hall is home to local community groups, as well as the South Dakota Symphony.

If science is more your style, check out the three-story, 45,000-square-foot *Kirby Science Discovery Center,* where you can fly a space shuttle, dig up a dinosaur, or touch a tornado. And if you need just one more friend on Facebook, Stan the Dinosaur keeps Facebook friends up-to-speed on the latest activities at the Science Center. Science adventure films are shown hourly on the four-story dome screen at the Wells Fargo CineDome Theater.

The stunning building is a history lesson in itself. Originally built in 1906 it was the former Washington High School, and it reopened as the new Washington Pavilion of Arts and Science in the summer of 1999. The visually distinctive, 255,000-square-foot building is constructed of native Sioux quartzite. The roof balustrade and dentiled cornices are visible from many downtown Sioux Falls locations. For more information, call (877) 927-4728, or visit www .washingtonpavilion.org.

The downtown district is especially appealing. As America becomes "mall-ified," downtown areas must draw on unique services, products, and history to recapture shoppers, and Sioux Falls has done that commendably. The district extends from Fourth to Fourteenth Streets and includes Dakota, Main, and Phillips Avenues. The congenial people of Sioux Falls have made the downtown area a wonderfully pleasant place—with trolley rides, festivals, and a plethora of history. Before you visit downtown, you might wish to visit Downtown Sioux Falls at www.dtsf.com.

One thing Sioux Falls has learned is that the way to shoppers' hearts is through their stomachs. Gastronomical delights are easily found in elegant restaurants or quirky bistros. **Minerva's,** at 301 South Phillips Ave., is one of the best restaurants in the city. A classy establishment, the restaurant is perfect for special occasions, dates, or any time you just want excellent food and impeccable service. Appetizers such as pheasant ravioli, almond duck strips, coconut shrimp, and crabmeat artichoke pique the taste buds. Main course options include Cajun chicken linguine, and Italian sausage and pepper pasta—musts for carb lovers. Meat-and-potato enthusiasts will find a mouthwatering selection of top sirloin, roast prime rib of beef, rib eye, filet mignon, and New York strip-sirloin steaks. The specialty salad bar at Minerva's is exceptionally well done—and visually satisfying as well—with fresh cheeses, fruits, cold cuts, homemade soups, and breads. Minerva's is open from 11 a.m. to 2:30 p.m. Mon through Sat, from 5:30 to 10 p.m. Mon through Fri, and from 5 to 10 p.m. Sat. (Dinner reservations are suggested.) A children's menu is available. Call (605) 334-0386; www.minervas.net. Minerva's also has a sister restaurant called **Spezia** which is known for its Sun brunch, but also has great pizzas in a more casual setting. Spezia is located at 1716 South Western Ave.; (605) 334-7491.

The **Book Shop** in Sioux Falls (223 South Phillips Ave.) buys and sells used and collectible books in a refreshingly well-organized manner. You'll find paperback and hardcover, fiction and nonfiction, old favorites, and recently published books on a wide variety of topics. The store is located mid-block in the old Carpenter Hotel. Open Mon through Sat from 10 a.m. to 5 p.m. Call (605) 336-8384.

Nostalgic in a happy, New Wave sort of way describes **Zandbroz Variety** (605-331-5137; www.zandbroz.com). Located in the heart of downtown Sioux Falls at 209 South Phillips Ave., the place oozes with a "happening granola" attitude, but it has a universal appeal that even Grandma would like. Candles, books, cards, baskets, jewelry, gourmet foods, and other nifty things for giving (or keeping for yourself) make this shop a heavenly expedition. The real bonanza, however, is located at the back of the store, where the **Soda Falls Fountain & Coffee Bar** is located. It has all the perks: bubbly waitresses, an extensive menu of iced and gourmet coffees, and plenty of room for talking.

Dakota-style Cooking

Looking for a cookbook that reflects the beauty and heritage of the Dakotas while helping a good cause? The Junior League of Sioux Falls sells *Dining Dakota Style,* a 175-page hardcover cookbook for the bargain price of $15. I've been told all of the recipes have been double and triple checked and range from the easy and ordinary to the sophisticated and complex. The home furnishings store called Traditions (320 South Phillips Ave.) has them in stock. Or you can order online at www.jlsiouxfalls .org/fundraisers.

Other treats are the malts, shakes, and old-fashioned sodas. Authenticity is the name of the game here, and even the whipping cream is 100 percent real dairy. Since life is uncertain, eat dessert first, and make it the tiramisu cake or caramel apple tart, both worth every calorie. The Back Room features authors, poets, musicians, and other entertainment.

Several classic structures have been grandly maintained by families and preservationists in the *St. Joseph's Cathedral Historic District,* located between Fourth and Tenth Streets and bordered by Prairie and Spring Streets.

One of the most magnificent is the *Pettigrew Home and Museum,* located at 131 North Duluth Ave. Built in 1889, this was the home of South Dakota's first full-term U.S. senator. A seasoned traveler, Richard F. Pettigrew collected artifacts from all over the world, which are now displayed in his home. These items are shown with natural history and cultural artifacts from the Siouxland area, which include Native American objects and the home's 5,000-volume research library that contains Pettigrew's personal papers. The site is open from 9 a.m. to 5 p.m. Mon through Sat, and from noon to 5 p.m. Sun from May 1 to Oct 1. After that, it's noon to 5 p.m. every day. Admission is free. Call (605) 367-7097; www.siouxlandmuseums.com.

Whet your appetite for history and discover the heritage of Siouxland in the *Old Courthouse Museum* (200 West Sixth St.), a restored structure listed on the National Register of Historic Places. The massive stone building served as the county courthouse from 1890 to 1962. The first-floor exhibits bring to life the history of early settlers and the Plains Indians, along with the art and cultural significance of Siouxland. On the second floor see the restored circuit courtroom and law library. A handsomely laid-out building, the Old Courthouse is decorated with sixteen murals of different sizes, created by the Norwegian artist Ole Running in 1915. The building also houses the Minnehaha County Historical Library and the Sioux Valley Genealogical Society Library, both listed as landmarks on the National Register of Historic Places. The Old Courthouse Museum is open from 9 a.m. to 5 p.m. Mon through Wed, from 9 a.m. to 9 p.m. Thurs, from 9 a.m. to 5 p.m. Fri and Sat, and from 1 to 5 p.m. on Sun. Free admission. Call (605) 367-4210; www.siouxlandmuseums.com.

You also can find the Queen City Mercantile at the museum, where local and regional books, crafts, old-fashioned toys, holiday collectibles, souvenirs, and exhibit-related items are for sale.

The annual **Sidewalk Arts Festival** entertains more than 65,000 visitors each year. The downtown festival along Main and Eleventh Streets showcases artists and vendors from fifteen states. Art Rocks! is the free entertainment stage. The event, which is held the first Sat after Labor Day, is the annual fund-raiser for the Visual Arts Center at the Washington Pavilion of Arts and Science. Call (605) 977-2002, or visit www.siouxempireartscouncil.com.

Sioux Falls' namesake is located 1 mile east of the downtown district. See the waterfalls of the Big Sioux River at **Falls Park.** Walkways give the visitor a magnificent view of the thundering falls. The outdoor museum was the setting for the Queen Bee Mill, built in the late 1800s, which was an effort to harness the power of the falls. R. F. Pettigrew convinced an eastern investor to finance the construction of this huge, seven-story 1,200-barrels-per-day flour mill. The remains of the mill help paint a nostalgic picture of what industry was like in Sioux Falls in its early days. Today the mill is a small cafe serving a fabulous breakfast on weekends, but is most popular in the summer aa a spot to cool off with ice cream or fresh squeezed lemonade. The Falls Park Visitor Information Center offers information on Falls Park and other Sioux Falls attractions, and includes a five-story observation tower and elevator. The Horse Barn Arts Center adds an artsy touch with gallery shows and other activities. The Wells Fargo Park Sound and Light show spectacularly outlines the history of Sioux Falls. You can watch the show nightly during the summer months after sunset. Call (605) 367-7430.

Sioux Falls has more than sixty parks, one of which is **Terrace Park** at Sixth Street. The Shoto–Teien Japanese Gardens are located here next to Covell Lake. Built from 1928 to 1936 the gardens feature a lush array of flowering trees and shrubs, pagodas, and lanterns. The Terrace Park Aquatic Center is a perfect jumping-off point, too, with swimming pools and water slides.

A full-scale cast of Michelangelo's *David* stands in the heart of Sioux Falls at **Fawick Park** (located on Second Avenue between Tenth and Eleventh Streets). Thomas Fawick, a Sioux Falls philanthropist and industrialist who made a fortune as an inventor, gave the city the statue in 1972. The statue of *David,* fully in the buff, created enormous controversy when it first arrived. To mollify public opinion, the statue was placed facing away from traffic, and trees were planted to screen it from the street. (Fawick later gave the city the sculptor's statue of Moses, which was placed on the Augustana College campus.)

Augustana College is the home of the **Center for Western Studies** (located on South Summit in the lower level of the Mikkelson Library). The center is dedicated to preserving and interpreting the history and cultures of both native and immigrant people in the area. Each Feb, the Center hosts an art show featuring artists of the Plains. Open Mon through Fri 8 a.m. to 5 p.m. and Sat from 10 a.m. to 2 p.m., the Center is free of charge. Call (605) 247-4007; www.augie.edu/cws.

At Twelfth and Kiwanis Streets, the **USS South Dakota Battleship Memorial** in Sherman Park is a patriotic sample of World War II naval history. The battleship, which participated in every major battle in the Pacific from 1942 to 1945, was the most decorated of World War II. Parts of the actual battleship punctuate a concrete outline of the ship's width and length. Visitors can walk through the concrete configuration and learn about the military personnel who gave their lives while serving on this vessel. A gift shop is open daily 10 a.m. to 5 p.m. Memorial Day through Labor Day. Call (605) 397-7060.

The **Great Plains Zoo and Delbridge Museum** combines the rugged expanse of a North American plain, the wild recesses of an African veldt, and the quiet beauty of the Australian Outback. Located at 805 South Kiwanis Ave. (0.5 mile east off I-29, exit 79 to Twelfth Street), the Delbridge Museum of Natural History houses one of the largest collections of mounted animals in the world. The zoo is known for its big cat collection, which includes cheetahs and tigers. But there are also wallabies and delicate flamingos, and bears that look more cuddly than they really are. This zoo is recognized nationally for its innovative partnership with the local children's hospital. Cameras in many of the animal habitats stream live video to the patient rooms, entertaining and educating children who otherwise might not visit the zoo for a long, long time. Open daily year-round. Zoo hours are from 9 a.m. to 6 p.m. Tickets are $6.80 for adults, $6 for senior citizens, $3.80 for children ages 3 to 12, and admission is free for children 2 years of age and younger. Call (605) 367-7059; or visit www.gpzoo.org.

More outdoor education is available at **Sioux Falls Outdoor Campus,** an initiative of the state games, fish, and parks department to get people in touch with the outdoors. Classes include everything for the outdoors from canoeing and kayaking to fishing, hiking, gardening, bird watching, rock climbing, you name it. All classes are free and most are just one or two sessions. This is also a place to come and enjoy without taking a class. There's a small museum with wildlife exhibits, camping information, and the like. A butterfly house, four picnic shelters, and a hiking trail are included on the property.

Inside the visitor center, you may hear the sound of a telephone ringing and think "why doesn't someone answer that phone?" Or you may hear the door buzzer without anyone going in or out of the door. The sound comes from Flopper, a blue jay who was blown from his nest as a baby and raised at the center. They've tried to release him to the wild several times, but he just keeps returning, so now he lives permanently in a cage in the visitor center. Somewhere along the line, he has learned to mimic the sound of a telephone ringing, the door buzzing, and even the security alarm. To keep in touch with the world, Flopper tweets daily on Twitter and invites followers. Flopper and the rest of the center are located at 4500 South Oxbow Ave. Call (605) 362-2777; www.outdoorcampus.org.

At *Country Apple Orchard,* 4 miles south of Sioux Falls on Minnesota Avenue, apple seekers can buy bagged red, shiny apples or pick their own during one of the most treasured rites of autumn. You can hop on a tractor-pulled wagon and jump off when you reach the spot where your favorite variety of apple is grown. Just pluck the ripe apples from tree branches already straining from the weight of fragrant fruit. Of course, you can also find pumpkins here each fall. Call (605) 743-2424; www.countryappleorchard.com.

When people think of downhill skiing in South Dakota, they usually think of the Black Hills. *Great Bear Recreation Park,* however, is a natural for schussing a la East River, with twelve runs nearly 1,500 feet long, a 250-foot vertical drop, chairlifts, and a chalet. A tubing hill, outdoor skating, and a terrain park for snowboarders are also offered at the resort. Great Bear

Farming and Faith

As you drive outside Sioux Falls, you can see firsthand the checkerboard pattern of grasses and crops that have been so vital to the area's economy.

South Dakota grows alfalfa, barley, corn, flaxseed (which contains linseed oil, an extract used in paints and varnishes), rye, and sorghum. Sunflowers, unmistakably bright yellow with dark brown centers, put South Dakota second in the nation in the production of sunflower seeds. And who can forget the golden-brown beauty of wheat, which is a major cash crop for the state? That is not to say farming is an easy life. A story passed down through generations illustrates the faith and tenacity of those who till the land: In 1874 swarms of grasshoppers plagued the fields of eastern South Dakota. They tormented cattle and ate the plants. Pierre Boucher, a local pastor, finally appealed to a higher power. The priest led his parishioners in an 11-mile trek from field to field. In each field, the people prayed and erected a giant cross to ward off the grasshoppers and save the crops. Miraculously, the pests disappeared that very day.

(605-367-4309, www.greatbearpark.com) is located 3 miles east of Sioux Falls on Rice Street. Ski instruction and rentals for both downhill and cross-country skiing are available. The park is also open for hiking during the summer.

Just 5 miles east of Sioux Falls on I-90 at exit 406 is Brandon, one of the state's fastest-growing communities. The two city-owned parks, **Aspen Park** and **Pioneer Park,** offer tennis courts, swimming, ice skating, sledding, walking paths, and soccer fields. Two state parks also are located near Brandon: the **Beaver Creek Nature Area** and the **Big Sioux Recreation Area.**

One of the many treasures at Big Sioux Recreation Area is **Bergeson's Homestead**—the park's very own little house on the prairie—which was built in 1869 by Ole and Soren Bergeson. Ole was one of the first settlers in Split Rock Township. The log frame, which is constructed of hand-hewn cottonwood, was inadvertently discovered in the 20th century during the process of razing the entire old Bergeson homestead. Notice the fine dovetailed notchwork. If you want to spend the night in a log cabin of your own, the park now has a number for overnight rentals at $35 a night. They are simple, with just bunk beds and electricity, but that's more than Ole and Soren Bergeson had in the 1860s.

The **Valley of the Giants Trail** at Big Sioux is a one-and-a-half mile hiking trail that passes some of the oldest trees in the state. The cottonwood and ash trees provide a heavy cover, almost blocking out the sun. It's a pleasant hike around a little lake. There are seven more miles of trails in the park, one and a half miles of paved biking trails, a disc golf course, archery range, equestrian trails, and access to the Big Sioux River Canoe Trail. Call (605) 582-7243.

The Brandon's Hometown Days is an annual festival in McHardy Park each July. The three-day event attracts a wide variety of artists and food vendors. There are also games for the kids, musical entertainment, and a tractor pull.

The annual **Homesteader Day Harvest Festival** at Beaver Creek Nature Area (south of Brandon off I-90) offers a glimpse into what life on the prairie was like for the pioneers. First, turn back the clock to the year 1869: John and Anna Samuelson, both Swedish immigrants, were newlyweds, and John bought his bride a 160-acre homestead east of present-day Sioux Falls. For the first three years, they made their home in a dugout carved from a nearby hill. They later moved to a log cabin, which is now the centerpiece of the Homesteader Day Harvest Festival. An interpretive shelter tells the story of the Samuelsons' cabin. As part of the festival, volunteers demonstrate candle making, sheep shearing, tatting, butter churning, wheat grinding, and more. Visitors can try their hand at rope making and can sample fresh-squeezed apple juice made in a sixty-year-old apple press. The festival is held the first Sun after Labor Day and is free. Call (605) 594-3824.

While you're enjoying the fruits of your labor at the festival, explore Beaver Creek Nature Area, an ideal place for hiking, picnicking, fishing, cross-country skiing, and snowmobiling.

Another agricultural product gaining recognition in South Dakota is the grape growing/winery industry. Jeff and Victoria Wilde began planting their vineyard on 40 acres north of Brandon in 1997, and today **Wilde Prairie Winery** produces about five tons of grapes, which translates into about 2,000 gallons or 10,000 bottles of wine annually. They started out with tomato, rhubarb, and dandelion wine. Now they grow Frontenac, La Crescent, and Valiant grapes, all of which has been researched and tested by South Dakota State University and Minnesota State University.

There's a 100-year-old barn at the winery that the Wildes rent out for parties and weddings, but also doubles as a small tasting room. They invite you to stroll through the vineyard with them as they talk about all they have learned about growing grapes in South Dakota. Call (605-582-6471); www .wildeprairiewinery.com.

The magnificent farming operations of the **Wolf Creek Hutterite Colony,** just forty-five minutes southwest of Sioux Falls, off US 18 in Olivet, are worth a visit. Here you can see community members make perfectly pleated skirts or fashion rugs. Explore the schoolhouse and communal kitchen, and experience the ways of these gentle people, whose ingenuity allows them to live in a self-sustaining community. Tours can be arranged through Freeman Community Development Corporation. Call (605) 925-4444. There is a fee.

Vermillion, 56 miles south of Sioux Falls on I-29, best fits the old description of a place where the college is the community. The economy of this town of 9,862 people thrives on the presence of the University of South Dakota (USD), the state's second-largest university, founded in 1862. Vermillion, the seat of Clay County, originally was settled below the bluffs of the Mighty Mo until the flood of 1881 changed the river's course, forcing residents to higher ground. Now it's located in a part of the state that was twice claimed by France and once by Spain before it was sold to the United States. As in any college community, there is a vibrant energy that students and higher education bring. Then there is the cultural life, which is manifested in the university's impressive fine arts college and three distinctly unique museums.

Named for one of its early directors, The **W. H. Over State Museum** (1110 Ratingen St.) is a tribute to state and natural history. Exhibits include a life-size diorama of a Teton Dakota village. The museum's Clark Memorial Collection includes pre-reservation and reservation Lakota art, as well as pioneer artifacts, costumes, firearms, and the Stanley J. Morrow collection of historic photographs. The Lewis and Clark/Spirit Mound Learning Center sheds light on the explorers' famous journey, especially through the region. The artifacts include a map drawn in 1806 from Lewis's notations and journal entries. The gift shop features Native American and Scandinavian crafts, as well as Oscar Howe and Robert Penn prints and note cards and lithographs by other regional artists. Best of all, there is no admission charge, not even to the Sat morning classes and special events. The museum is open from 10 a.m. to 4 p.m. Mon through Sat. Call (605) 677-5228; or visit www.whovermuseum.org.

On the University of South Dakota campus, you will find more than 13,500 musical instruments from all over the world in the *National Music Museum* (414 East Clark St.). Exhibits include a 1693 Stradivarius violin, a 9-foot-tall slit drum from the South Pacific, Civil War band instruments, Elizabethan ivory lutes, and a 1785 French harpsichord. A guitar autographed by B. B. King is displayed here as well. The museum is the only place in the world where one can find two 18th-century grand pianos with the specific type of action conceived by the piano's inventor, Bartolomeo Cristofori. One of these, built in 1767 by Manuel Antunes of Lisbon, is the earliest signed and dated piano by a maker native to Portugal; the other, built by Louis Bas in Villeneuve les Avignon in 1781, is the earliest extant French grand piano.

This is a must-see museum that continues to expand, with such stellar acquisitions as two guitars and a banjo from the Johnny and June Carter Cash estate. The 1971 Martin D-28 guitar, known as the Bon Aqua, was kept at Johnny's 100-acre farm near Bon Aqua, Tennessee, outside Nashville. Returning from extensive tours in the United States and abroad, Johnny would go there alone, as he wrote in his autobiography, "to cook my own food, read my own books, tend my own garden, water my own land, and think, write, compose, rest, and reflect in peace." As such, the guitar, which Johnny used while writing songs during the last thirty years of his life, was more intimately connected with him than the hundreds of other guitars that came and went through his hands on the road.

The National Music Museum also acquired the 1967 Gibson "Hummingbird" guitar that was one of June Carter Cash's favorite guitars, according to Marshall Grant, bass player with Johnny's show from 1955 to 1980. She was still playing it when she posed for the September 18–24, 1999, issue of *TV Guide*. The third acquisition is a 1980 Gibson five-string banjo that was given to Johnny by Earl Scruggs, the bluegrass legend, who wrote on the head of the banjo, "To my friend Johnny Cash/Earl Scruggs." Johnny and Scruggs collaborated often throughout their careers.

This one-of-a-kind facility is open daily, and suggested donations are $7 for adults and $3 for students. Admission is free for USD students and faculty. Also make sure you get your parking ticket validated or you could

get a good fine, ruining an otherwise perfect visit. Call (605) 677-5306; www
.usd.edu/smm.

The last building in Vermillion's museum trio is the **Austin–Whittemore
House,** an impressive Italian villa-style structure that also houses the **Clay
County Historical Society Museum** (15 Austin Ave.). The museum, built in
1882 on a riverside bluff overlooking Vermillion, is best known for its Victorian
displays and settings. Call (605) 624-8266; or visit www.historicclaycounty.org.

The campus of the University of South Dakota (www.usd.edu) is a stately
one, with historic buildings and grand shade trees. The Dakota Dome sports
facility includes an indoor football stadium, where the USD Coyotes meet
other colleges for competition. The school's strongest rival is the South Dakota
State University Jackrabbits. USD, whose alumni include NBC news anchor
Tom Brokaw, is considered one of the best liberal arts colleges in the state.
Accordingly, there are fine productions to see on campus, including dance,
theater, and fine arts. Slagle Auditorium is often home to concerts by the USD
Chamber Singers and Chamber Orchestra and the USD Men's and Women's
Chorus Concert. You also can see a play at the Fine Arts Building theater, or
enjoy a piano concert at the Colton Recital Hall.

The South Dakota Tourism Department has put together a helpful brochure—aptly named *Lewis and Clark Trail: The South Dakota Adventure*—that
includes a map of the explorers' journey highlighting 15 significant sites,

An Excellent Adventure

Like North Dakota, South Dakota takes great pride in its close relation to explorers
Meriwether Lewis and William Clark, who set out to explore America's newest land
acquisition—the Louisiana Purchase—in 1804.

The Lewis and Clark National Historic Trail follows Highways 1804 and 1806, which
hug the Missouri River and trace the route that Lewis and Clark traveled. Indeed,
some parts of the vast Missouri shoreline remain as wild and breathtaking as they
were in the explorers' days.

On August 25, 1804, they were intrigued by a cone-shaped mound of land the
Sioux claimed was bewitched. Undaunted by such stories, the pair traveled to **Spirit
Mound,** one of the highest points in the county, where they did not find 18-inch devils, as legend claimed, but instead found the beautiful landscape and a herd of buffalo most intriguing. The hiking trail leads visitors about three-quarters of a mile from
the parking lot to the summit. Interpretive signs along the trail tell the story of Spirit
Mound. Spirit Mound Historic Prairie (now part of the state park system) is 8 miles
north of Vermillion on Route 19.

excerpts from their journal, and a complete list of campgrounds and other accommodations along the way.

Once you get your nose out of the books or museums, stop by **The Roadhouse** and enjoy a prime-rib dinner amid an early-Western gambling hall atmosphere. Located at 911 East Cherry St., the restaurant is open from 11:30 a.m. to 11 p.m. Mon through Sun. Call (605) 624-4830.

Be sure to check out **Valiant Vineyards Winery,** too, at 1500 West Main St., which hosts the annual Great Dakota Wine Fest in Sept. Valiant Vineyards offers winery tours and tastings daily (except Christmas). Tours include a tour of the winemaking facility, cask room, and bottling area with an expert guide and conclude with a wine tasting. Tours last about thirty minutes. And you don't have to leave, as the Buffalo Run Resort at Valiant Vineyards also offers five elegant guest rooms. The Native American, the USD, the Frontier, the Queen Anne, and the Honeymoon Suite are all uniquely decorated. Rates run from $95 to $105. Call (605) 624-4500; www.buffalorunwinery.com.

The **Union Grove State Park,** located 11 miles south of Beresford off I-29, offers hiking and bridle trails, picnicking, camping, and a playground on 500 beautiful acres. Call (605) 987-2263.

Newton Hills State Park, just 6 miles south of Canton on County Road 135, is a wooded oasis where plants and animals thrive. This southern tip of the Coteau des Prairies was spared the plow, and its grassy knolls and wooded ravines today shelter deer, wild turkey, and more than 200 species of birds. Explorers can make their way along several hiking trails, while horse riders and all-terrain bikers can enjoy a 6-mile multiuse trail. To add a little excitement, hike those trails by candlelight during FestiFall the first Sat of Oct. The annual Sioux River Folk Festival (www.fotm.org) attracts music aficionados from all over and is held the first weekend in Aug. Call (605) 987-2263.

History runs deep in **North Sioux City,** which is located at the farthest tip of southeastern South Dakota on SD 29 and pokes into Iowa and Nebraska. Charles Lindbergh chose North Sioux City as his landing site for the *Spirit of St. Louis* in 1927.

Known as the Las Vegas of the Heartland, **North Sioux City's strip, Military Road,** features more than thirteen casinos that buzz with the sounds and flash of video games and entertainment. Here you can test your luck at a variety of games: keno, bingo, blackjack, draw poker, and joker poker.

If bright lights and the sound of gambling machines aren't your style, head for peace and solitude at the 1,500-acre **Adams Homestead and Nature Preserve,** located 2 miles southwest of McCook Lake (take exit 4 off I-29). This land was the property of three generations of Adamses, who later donated to the state. In addition to several restored buildings, including the Adams' homestead, the nature preserve has 10 miles of hiking and biking trails. The town of McCook was the first homesteaders' settlement in the state, and the McCook Cemetery, plotted and registered in 1869, is regarded as the first homesteaders' cemetery. The visitor center is open from 8 a.m. to 4:30 p.m. Mon through Fri and from 10 a.m. to 6 p.m. Sat and Sun. Call (605) 232-0873.

Lewis and Clark Country

Less than 30 miles west of Vermillion, *Yankton* (population 13,767) today is a small town. Yet it once bustled as the capital of the Dakota Territory in the 1860s. In 1889 it was passed over as the state capital. That honor went to the more centrally located town of Pierre.

The *Dakota Territorial Capitol Replica* in Yankton's Riverside Park stands as a reminder of the glory days when Yankton served as the capital, from 1861 to 1883. The simple white structure is located on the banks of the Missouri River.

One of the most famous events to take place here was the trial of Jack "Crooked Nose" McCall who shot Wild Bill Hickok in Deadwood, South Dakota. The trial was held in what is now the *Charles Gurney Hotel* (corner of Third and Capital Streets). He was found guilty in December 1876 and hanged here on March 1, 1877. His was the first legal execution in the Dakota Territory. McCall is buried in the Yankton Cemetery. A historic marker in the parking lot at the corner of US 81 and SD 50 marks the spot of the hanging.

While in Riverside Park, learn about the area's history and contributions at the Dakota Territorial Museum at 610 Summit St. The Yankton County Historical Society has lovingly preserved and displayed rare memorabilia from early Yankton and Dakota Territory days, including a rural schoolhouse, a blacksmith shop, a Burlington Northern caboose, and an American LaFrance fire engine. There's a nice exhibition on old fishing lures and equipment as well. Free admission. Call (605) 665-3898; www.dakotaterritorialmuseum.org.

Yankton Daily Press & Dakotan

The Yankton Daily Press & Dakotan is the oldest daily newspaper in South Dakota. It was the first in Dakota Territory—founded in 1861 as a weekly and then as a daily in 1875. The paper's annual *Lake Guide* and *Visitors Guide* are wonderful resources for travelers. The free *Yankton Magazine*, too, is published by the *Daily Press & Dakotan*. The offices are located at 319 Walnut; (605) 665-7811.

Yankton boasts some of the finest historical homes in the Midwest. The Architectural Walking and Auto Tour of Historic Yankton Homes offers visitors at least a curbside glimpse at the exteriors of some homes, most of which are clustered on Douglas, Capital, Pine, and Mulberry Streets, between Fifth and Sixth Streets. Pick up brochures at the Yankton Chamber office at 803 East Fourth St. or at the Dakota Territorial Museum.

The **Cramer Kenyon Heritage Home** and **Dorothy Jencks Memorial Garden** at 509 Pine St., is an outstanding example of Queen Anne architecture. The home, erected in 1886, is open to the public from Memorial Day to Labor Day from 1 to 5 p.m. Tues through Sat and by appointment year-round. Admission is $5 adults; $2 for children. Call (605) 665-7470.

After your tour, stop in at **The Pantry** at 215 West Third St. for an espresso or cappuccino. Pastries and chocolate wafers are also available, the perfect companion to a steaming cup of java. Call (605) 665-4480.

Or if you want something a little stronger, try **Ben's Brewing Company** at 222 West Third St. Ben's last name is Harten and you'll often find him sitting in the front patio, enjoying the fruits of his labors that he opened in 2005. This is the first and only brewpub in Yankton, of that he is quite proud. In addition to four homemade beers, he also serves a homemade pizza, grilled sandwiches, and brats. The most popular brew is Mt. Martian Amber, named for the students at nearby Mount Marty College. Ben's is open 2 p.m. until 2 a.m. seven days a week and often has a live band. Call (605) 260-4844; www.bensbrewing.com.

The **Bistro at the River Rose** at 214 West Third St. is also a nice place to eat. It's located in the basement of what was originally the Yankton National Bank, built in the 1880s. Featuring Italian cuisine, the Bistro is a cozy little place with just ten tables, but the food selection and the wine menu are huge. Call (605) 665-0993.

Yankton's **Riverboat Days and Summer Arts Festival** is the perfect event to witness firsthand the strong community pride and cooperation of small towns, especially those in the Dakotas. The citywide event is held annually the third full weekend in Aug. A fireworks display and dance mark

thelawrencewelk legend

In 1928 a young accordionist and his novelty band from Strasburg, North Dakota, arrived in Yankton, South Dakota, and asked a new radio station, WNAX, if they could perform. Audience reaction was so tremendous that the manager offered to add the band to the station's roster of entertainers. That brief stop lasted almost nine years and began the career of the great Lawrence Welk.

Fri evening. A parade kicks off the Sat activities, which include an antique tractor pull, a 5K walk/run, an arm-wrestling competition, an outdoor dance, and children's programs. Sun is celebrated with a pancake feed, a kids' tractor pull, a classic car show, and a golf tournament. More than 150 artists and craftspeople, too, peddle their wares during Riverboat Days. Foodies will enjoy fajitas, chili dogs, *lefse* (yes, that is the Norwegian flatbread), burritos, homemade ice cream, funnel cakes, and teriyaki sticks. Call (605) 665-1657, or visit www.riverboatdays.com.

Straddling the South Dakota–Nebraska border, **Lewis and Clark Lake** brims with large- and smallmouth bass and offers postcard-perfect opportunities for sailing. Situated 5 miles west of Yankton on US 52, the lake is actually a man-made reservoir above Gavins Point Dam on the Missouri River, and it covers more than 30 square miles.

And if you have a penchant for dams, by all means stop by the **Gavins Point Power Plant.** The Gavins Point Dam, part of the 1944 Pick–Sloan Plan, is vital to the successful operation of six main-stem dams and reservoirs on the Upper Missouri River Basin. The dam was completed in 1957 at the cost of $51 million.

Free tours are given daily Memorial Day through Labor Day. During the thirty-minute tour, visitors can examine such areas as the control room, generator housing, and high-voltage cable areas. For more information call (402) 667-2546.

Anchoring the area's water sports is Lewis and Clark Marina, on the lake's northeast corner. The marina is home to hundreds of boats from Apr to Oct. Slips are available by the night, week, or season, and boats and personal watercraft can be rented. A boat-up gas dock, convenience store, and full-service dealer will keep you well provisioned. Call (605) 665-3111; www .lewisandclarkmarina.com.

OTHER ATTRACTIONS WORTH SEEING IN SOUTHEASTERN SOUTH DAKOTA

Bede Art Gallery
Yankton
(605) 668-1574

Warren M. Lee Changing Gallery
Vermillion

Wild Water West Family Amusement Park
Sioux Falls
(605) 361-9313

Enjoy the view of the beautiful limestone bluffs across the river in Nebraska while enjoying a leisurely meal on the waterfront ***Magilly's Lakeside Marina,*** at 43497 Shore Dr. It's a family-owned business with a Jimmy Buffett-kind of feel to the place, but the food ranges from casual burgers and chicken wings to Pork Osso Bocco. Open year-round; (605) 668-5181; www .magillyslakesideeatery.com.

Lewis and Clark Resort located near the marina and restaurant, offers moderately priced motel rooms and two- and three-bedroom cabins. There's also an outdoor pool. Call (605) 665-2680 or visit www.lewisandclarkpark .com/resort.html.

If you're more in the mood for roughing it, the ***Lewis and Clark State Recreation Area,*** 4 miles west of Yankton on US 52, has more than 370 campsites and cabins, all available by reservation. You'll find all the amenities here—from hot showers and electric hookups to paved pads. For reservations, call (800) 710-2267 or visit www.campsd.com. For other information at the park, call (605) 668-2985.

The latest addition to Yankton's sports scene is the headquarters of the ***National Field Archery Association.*** The NFAA is the largest archery association in the world. The headquarters had been in Redland, California, for more than 60 years, but a combination of high real estate prices in California, the low cost of living in South Dakota, and the presence of the Easton Aluminum Company in Yankton, which makes arrows, resulted in the headquarters moving here in 2008. Members are optimistic that this will soon become an Olympic training center. The property is 20 acres and includes 28 stations outside and 17 stations inside, appropriate for hosting world-class tournaments. But you don't have to be a competitive archer to enjoy this center. For a simple $5, you can come in and shoot at targets all day. There's also a museum on the history of archery, which is surprisingly interesting. It includes, among other items, artifacts from the Battle of the Little Big Horn and souvenirs from major movie sets. The center is just east of town at 800 Archery Lane. Call (605) 260-9279.

If you want to pick your own berries in South Dakota, head for ***Garritys' Prairie Gardens,*** an orchard and berry farm just 7.5 miles east of Yankton near Mission Hill. Pluck strawberries or raspberries, pick apples or pumpkins, or just buy some that other folks have picked. Hayrides are offered too. Call (605) 665-2806 or go to www.garritys.com.

Welcome to the Palace

Located 60 miles west of Sioux Falls on I-90, ***Mitchell*** is home to 14,588 people and the world's only ***Corn Palace*** (604 North Main St.). Every year thousands of bushels of native, naturally colored corn, wheat, grain, and grasses are used to create beautifully decorated mosaics on the outside of the building. The look is the Taj Mahal of the Great Plains—an ode to agriculture, as was first intended by city founders. Mitchell's first Corn Belt Exposition was opened to the public in 1892. Nowadays more than 750,000 people visit annually. Every year by late Sept, old decorations have been removed and new corn and grain have been applied. Throughout the summer crews are busy applying the corn; they must follow precise instructions, which are printed on roofing paper that is attached to wood panels on the exterior of the building. The Corn Palace is open year-round daily 8 a.m. to 9 p.m. Memorial Day through Labor Day, daily 8 a.m. to 5 p.m. in Apr, May, Sept, and Oct, and Mon through Fri 8 a.m. to 5 p.m. Nov through Mar. Free admission. Call (800) 289-7469 or (605) 995-8430; www.cornpalace.org.

The Corn Palace serves as a multiuse center for the community and region. The facility hosts stage shows as well as sports events in its arena. Every third weekend in July, thousands of people gather here to attend the nightly PRCA rodeo performances, as well as the many other activities that are provided throughout Rodeo Week.

The corn craze peaks in late Aug with the Corn Palace Festival, a week-long celebration with marching bands, country music concerts, a polka fest, and carnival rides. The highlight comes when the new mural is officially presented. These murals require thousands of bushels of corn, grain, grasses—including bromegrass and bluegrass—wild oats, rye, straw, and wheat each year. Most years, themes are agricultural or nature related, although previous designs have celebrated the space race, the youth of America, and the Internet.

Not surprisingly, the Corn Palace makes a mighty fine bird feeder. After Corn Palace Week ends and winter arrives, local pigeons and squirrels devour the murals.

The area around the Corn Palace is touristy, but farther away you'll find some interesting, and less visited, attractions.

Mitchell's **Dakota Wesleyan University** campus (which proudly claims Oscar Howe, a Native American artist, as one of its alumni) houses the state's largest museum, the **Dakota Discovery Museum,** located at 1300 McGovern Ave. More than 100,000 Native American and pioneer artifacts are displayed in the building complex. Sites include a restored 1886 Victorian home, built for the cofounder of the Corn Palace; the 1909 Farwell Methodist Church; the Sheldon School, an 1885 one-room territorial school; and a 1914 railroad depot. The **Case Art Gallery** is best known for its display of the oil painting *Dakota Woman,* by Harvey Dunn. Over the years this classic of plains art, depicting a young woman basking in the sunshine in an open field while her baby rests under a parasol, has become synonymous with prairie life and prairie people.

Three other art galleries (Oscar Howe, Charles Hargens, and one for changing exhibits) feature original works by Howe, Dunn, and Hargens, James Earle Fraser, Gutzon Borglum, and others. The changing exhibits gallery features one-person shows, emphasizing American Indian artists of the Northern Plains.

A great source of pride and cultural identity for the community, the **Oscar Howe Gallery** features a permanent collection of original paintings by one of South Dakota's most revered artists. Howe was born on the **Crow Creek Indian Reservation** in South Dakota. As an artist and a teacher, his influence and inspiration provided a living legacy. In 1940 the painter was commissioned to create the dome mural, *Sun and Rain Clouds Over Hills,* for the Mitchell Public Library as a WPA project. In 1972 Howe was widely recognized as one of America's preeminent Native American artists.

The Howe Gallery boasts a collection of drawings and paintings that traces the history of Howe's development as an artist from when he was a student of the Santa Fe Indian School. His later work reflects a highly stylized interpretation of his heritage, using the formal elements of line, color, and space to create vivid, abstract designs.

The most recent addition to the museum is DiscoveryLand, an interactive center that allows children to experience life on the prairie from a number of different perspectives. The gallery's gift shop features the work of area artists and artisans, including original works on canvas and paper, sculpture, pottery and ceramics, quilts, jewelry, and reproductions.

The museum is open Oct through Apr, Mon through Sat from 10 a.m. to 4 p.m. and Sun 1 to 4 p.m. From May through Sept the center is open Mon through Sat 9 a.m. to 6 p.m. and Sun 1 to 4 p.m. Admission is $5 for adults, $4 for senior citizens, $2 for teens, and free for children 12 and under. Call (605) 996-2122 or visit www.dakotadiscovery.com.

Another prominent alumnus of Dakota Wesleyan University was 1972 presidential candidate George McGovern and his wife Eleanor. The **McGovern Legacy Museum** at 1201 McGovern Ave. tells the story of their years at the university, followed by his service in World War II, the 22 years he represented South Dakota in Congress, and his work to end world hunger as an ambassador to the United Nations. The museum is open year-round, Mon through Fri 8 a.m. to 5 p.m. Free admission. Call (605) 995-2935 or go to www.mcgoverncenter.com.

Just north of town on the shores of Lake Mitchell is the state's only National Archaeological Landmark. The **Mitchell Prehistoric Indian Village,** which dates to about 900 BC, reveals the lives of prehistoric people who vanished from the Great Plains in the 13th century, most likely after a great drought. Here as many as 800 seminomadic hunters and gatherers stalked buffalo, built lodges, and dwelled within a protective community. Highlights include a swinging bridge, a full-scale, walk-through lodge, and a complete buffalo skeleton. The site is open daily from 8 a.m. to 8 p.m. Memorial Day through Labor Day. Admission is $6 for adults; $4 for those between 6 and 18 years old. Call (605) 996-5473 or visit www.mitchellindianvillage.org.

A drive through the hinterlands of South Dakota may seem lonely at first, but it can be the best way to see a generous slice of Americana. That's why it's worth a trek up SD 37 from Mitchell to Forestburg. Along the way you'll drive through the lovely James River Valley. If you happen to be in the area from mid-Aug through the end of Oct, you'll see the old-fashioned produce stands that display a colorful harvest bonanza: watermelon, pumpkins, squash, Indian corn, sweet corn, and gourds. Apparently the local melon rage began in the grim 1930s, when Ernie Schwemle and Harold Smith planted a few seeds in the sandy soil west of the James River. The fruits of their labor soon appeared, and the melon harvest has been an autumnal tradition ever since. There are several stands in the area, which are usually open every day, so the out-of-towner may savor the bounty.

From Forestburg, travel west on SD 34 to Wessington Springs and step back in time to the Renaissance and the enchanting **Shakespeare Garden and Anne Hathaway Cottage** in Wessington Springs. Shakespeare and Anne Hathaway in rural South Dakota? In 1926, Mrs. Emma Shay, English teacher at Wessington Springs Seminary, borrowed $1,000 to travel throughout England. Her purpose was to increase her knowledge and ability to teach English literature. She collected flowers, leaves, grasses, and bits of bark from the homes of famous literary figures. These were later mounted in portfolios and sold to pay the debt. The diary of her trip is published in *Mrs. Shay Did It*, by Grace Abrahamson.

On April 23, 1927, Shakespeare's birthday marked the beginning of efforts toward the construction of the Shakespeare Garden in Wessington Springs. An alfalfa patch west of the administration building was the chosen site. The work was done by Professor and Mrs. Shay, other faculty, and students. Shrubs, trees, and flowers of all kinds were donated by the city, the May Seed Company, Henry Field Company, and private citizens. The summer house was built by the boys of the English department, and the sophomore class of 1928 made the lily pond. A sundial and gazing globe were also donated. By the end of 1928, the Shakespeare Garden, South Dakota's first, was a noted attraction with many visitors.

The Anne Hathaway Cottage was built by Professor Shay and Mrs. Shay when they retired in 1932. The builders drew the plans from a postcard of the original at Stratford-on-Avon. In observance of the state's centennial in 1989, the Shakespeare Garden Society of Wessington Springs purchased the Shakespeare Garden and Anne Hathaway Cottage. Listed on the National Register of Historic Places, Anne Hathaway Cottage is the only thatched-roof building in South Dakota.

The cottage and garden host teas, tours, a Maypole dance, one-act plays, Christmas events, and weddings. Located at 501 Alene Ave., North, the garden is open during daylight hours and the cottage is open daily 1 to 5 p.m. from June to Aug or by appointment. Admission is free. Tours and English tea reservations can be made at (605) 539-1529 or visit www.shakespearegarden.org.

Wessington Springs also is fabled for its excellent pheasant hunting in the fall. The town is located in the draws of the Wessington Hills, surrounded by wooded gulches, fertile farmland, and rolling prairie. Two large springs that still provide water for the town first attracted native tribes, French fur traders, and settlers.

Where to Stay in Southeastern South Dakota

DELL RAPIDS

Rose Stone Inn
504 East Fourth St.
(605) 428-3698
Moderate

SIOUX FALLS

Country Inn & Suites
200 East Eighth St.
(605) 373-0153
(800) 456-4000
Moderate

Courtyard by Marriott
4300 Empire Place
(605) 444-4300

Days Inn—Empire
3401 Gateway Blvd.
(605) 361-9240
(800) DAYS-INN
Moderate

Kelly Inn
I-29 at West Russell St.
(605) 338-6242
(800) 635-3559
Moderate

VERMILLION

Buffalo Run Resort
1500 West Main St.
(605) 624-4500
Inexpensive

Comfort Inn
located just west of I-29
on Highway 50
701 West Cherry St.
(605) 624-8333
Inexpensive

YANKTON

Best Western Kelly Inn
1607 East Hwy. 50
(605) 665-2906
(800) 528-1234
Moderate

Lewis and Clark Resort
Lewis and Clark Marina
(605) 665-2680
Moderate

Where to Eat in Southeastern South Dakota

MITCHELL

Chef Louie's
(American)
601 East Havens St.
(605) 996-7565
Moderate

The Depot Pub & Grill
(American)
210 South Main St.
(605) 996-9417
Moderate

SIOUX FALLS

Minerva's
301 South Phillips Ave.
(605) 334-0386
Expensive

SELECTED CHAMBERS OF COMMERCE

Brandon Valley Chamber of Commerce
109 Pipestone Ave.
Brandon 57005
(605) 582-7400
www.brandonvalleychamber.com

Mitchell Convention and Visitors Bureau
P.O. Box 1026
Mitchell 57301
(605) 996-6223
www.visitmitchell.com

Sioux Falls Convention and Visitors Bureau
200 North Phillips Ave.
Suite 102
Sioux Falls 57104
(605) 336-1620
www.siouxfallscvb.com

Vermillion Area Chamber of Commerce
116 Market St.
Vermillion 57069
(605) 624-5571 or
(800) 809-2071
www.vermillionchamber.com

Yankton Convention and Visitors Bureau
803 East Fourth St.
Yankton 57078
(800) 888-1460
www.yanktonsd.com

Monk's House of Ale Repute
420 East Eighth St.
(605) 338-2328
Moderate

Spezia
(Italian/American)
1716 South Western Ave.
(605) 334-7491
Moderate

Tea Steak House
on 215 South Main St.
Tea, SD
(5 miles north of Sioux Falls on I-29)
(605) 368-9667
Moderate

Touch of Europe
(Eastern European)
337 South Phillips Ave.
(605) 336-3066
Moderate

VERMILLION

The Roadhouse
911 East Cherry St.
(605) 624-4830
Moderate

YANKTON

Bistro at River Rose
(Italian)
214 West Third St.
(605) 665-0993
Moderate

Ben's Brewing Company
(American)
222 West Third St.
(605) 260-4844
Inexpensive

JoDean's
(American)
2809 Broadway
(605) 665-9884
Moderate

Magilly's Lakeside Marina
(American)
Lewis and Clark Marina
(605) 668-5181
Moderate

ALONG THE
MISSOURI RIVER

→

For sheer wanderlust and a love of the outdoors, travel the *Missouri River* section of South Dakota. It's a hunting and fishing paradise, rich in water, wildlife refuges, and parks. Beyond the capital, there are few communities along this central strip—except those of Old World and Native American heritage which proudly share their culture. The Missouri River winds through central South Dakota for 453 miles, offering not only a spectacular ribbon of blue water but also shore land rich in history, mystery, and adventure. Sliding past forts, monuments, ruins, reservations, and pioneer towns in South Dakota, the Missouri River ultimately flows into the Mississippi River and then to the Gulf of Mexico.

The powerful Missouri neatly divides the state into two dissimilar geographic and cultural regions. Along the west side of the river, wide stretches of prairie are broken by low hills and cut by ravines. Trees are sparse, and great cattle ranches fill the expanse of land. In the extreme west rise the forested Black Hills, one of the primary sources of the nation's gold. Fertile farmlands stretch out east of the Missouri River. Culturally speaking, East River is the well-heeled cousin who needs to be sent away to the spirited West River once in a while to

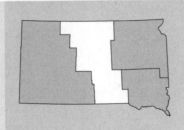

NORTH DAKOTA
SOUTH DAKOTA

Lake
ON Oahe
LAKE-
OAHE

THE NORTH-CENTRAL
RESERVATIONS

PIONEERS
AND
WALLEYES

Mobridge

Gettysburg

Missouri R.

THE CAPITAL

Pierre

THE CENTRAL
RESERVATIONS

Chamberlain

Winner

PHEASANTS
AND A LAKE

SOUTH DAKOTA
NEBRASKA

N

0   30 mi
0   30 km

get a good grasp of terra firma in his hand and in his soul. Likewise, this East River gentleman could rein in the wild Westerner.

The Mighty Mo, as residents like to call the river, served as the first highway into the region at a time when fur trappers pulled keelboats up the river by hand. Later, fur traders arrived in steamboats, beginning with the arrival of the *Yellowstone* in 1831. They sang the now-familiar folk song "Oh, Shenandoah," and you can almost hear the strain of ". . . across the wide Missouri."

River traffic became a thing of the past as the railroad reached the area at the turn of the century, and the number of settlements increased rapidly thereafter. The river in those days was known as the Muddy Mo, and the standard joke was that a person didn't know whether to plow it or drink it. Stand-up comedy had its last laugh under the Pick–Sloan plan and the construction of four dams across the Missouri, which created Lewis and Clark Lake, Lake Francis Case, Lake Sharpe, and Lake Oahe. These reservoirs have transformed Old Muddy into a series of crystalline blue lakes that have become popular recreation areas for South Dakotans and nonresidents alike.

Today life along the Missouri River isn't as bustling as life in East River or as animated as that in West River. But isn't new geography or culture what we crave? Feel doubly blessed along the Mighty Mo.

On Lake Oahe

South Dakota's claim to a portion of the Missouri River begins at the north-central edge of the state. The river was formed when glaciers to the east blocked the flow of western rivers, and the town of **Mobridge** enjoys the

TOP HITS ALONG THE MISSOURI RIVER

Al's Oasis

Grand River Casino & Resort

Indian Creek Recreation Area

Karl E. Mundt National Wildlife Refuge

Oahe Dam

Pierre Historic Homes Driving Tour

Scherr Howe Arena

Sitting Bull Monument

South Dakota Cultural Heritage Center

South Dakota Discovery Center and Aquarium

Vérendrye Monument

West Whitlock Recreation Area

prosperity that the river has afforded. Mobridge calls itself the Walleye Capital of the World, and no one is likely to dispute that moniker, since both the Missouri and the Oahe Reservoir envelop this town of 3,400. In 1906 the Milwaukee Railroad built the first bridge to cross the Missouri River in South Dakota, at what was formerly the site of an Arikara and Sioux village. A telegraph operator used the contraction *Mobridge* to indicate his location, and the name has stuck.

Lake Oahe, with a shoreline of more than 2,250 miles, is the longest lake on the main stream of the Missouri River, stretching 231 miles from Pierre to Bismarck, North Dakota. Begun in 1948, it is the largest of the four impoundments. The shoreline is virtually devoid of trees, making it a curious earthbound moonscape. The lake's azure waters and native stands of grass on the bluff, however, make it appealingly endless and warm.

The genuinely down-to-earth people of Mobridge are eager to accommodate the visitors who flock to the town during hunting, fishing, and boating seasons. The choices in lodging are appropriate for both the serious-minded and casual sportsperson. The sparsely furnished but clean rooms of the **Mo-Rest Motel** on US 12 are perfect for no-frills fishermen. Owners Denny and Glenda Palmer have ensured that there are special amenities for anglers such as aerial river maps. The motel is across the street from two bait shops with

Mobridge's Mystical Stones

One of the biggest mysteries in Mobridge can be found in City Park on North Main Street. It's here that what was called the Conqueror's Stones were discovered. No one knows why or when they were put here on the north side of the park, platted in 1910. The original inscription once said:

NOTE THE GROOVES
ACCORDING TO TRADITION, DEFEATED INDIAN WARRIORS WERE REQUIRED TO PLACE
THEIR HANDS IN THESE GROOVES AS A SIGN OF SUBMISSION

SHETAK CAPTIVES RESCUED HERE
NOVEMBER, 1862
BY FOOL SOLDIER BAND

Continued research revealed a more hopeful meaning. The stones were commonly referred to as prayer rocks. Native Americans would place their hands in the grooves in the rocks when taking an oath as part of initiation ceremonies. Some believe the grooves are the handprints of the Thunderheads, the powerful gods displayed on totem poles. According to this belief, by putting their hands in the prints before they died, the Indians would be taken to the Sky World, or heaven.

AUTHOR'S FAVORITES ALONG THE MISSOURI RIVER

Akta Lakota Museum
Chamberlain
(800) 798-3452

Grand River Casino & Resort
located 2 miles west of Mobridge on
US 12
(800) 475-3321

Oahe Dam
4 miles north of Pierre

Samuel H. Ordway Jr.
Memorial Prairie
50 miles northwest of Aberdeen on
US 281

South Dakota Cultural
Heritage Center
900 Governors Dr., Pierre
(605) 773-3458

---

boat repair. Denny himself is a veteran Missouri River guide, tournament fisherman, speaker, and outdoor writer. The Palmers' MoPro Guide Service offers on-the-water instruction using the latest fishing techniques and boat control. Call the motel at (605) 845-3668.

For more luxurious surroundings, the **Wrangler Motor Inn,** 820 West Grand Crossing (0.5 mile west on US 12), offers civilized respite for the evening along with the Windjammer restaurant and bar. While kids may head to the indoor swimming pool, adults will want a seat on the deck with its stunning view of the river. Here, too, you'll find fish and game storage and access to local guides. Call (605) 845-3641 or (888) 884-3641; www.wranglerinn.com.

Adjacent to the Wrangler Inn is the **Grand Oasis Restaurant** (906 West Grand Crossing), with a noon buffet and evening salad bar, homemade pies and soups, and even fruit smoothies. For more information, call (605) 845-7474 or (877) 363-5884.

The **Oahe Hills Country Club,** 3 miles north of Mobridge on SD 1804, has a nine-hole golf course. Call (605) 845-2307 for hours.

History buffs will find a profusion of items to marvel at in the **Scherr Howe Arena,** or the city auditorium, on Main Street. Colorful murals by the late Oscar Howe, a highly esteemed Dakota Indian and art professor at the University of South Dakota, depict both the history and ceremonies of Native Americans. Each mural measures about 16 feet high by 20 feet wide. For instance, one mural depicts the Social Dance, a prenuptial ceremony common among the Sioux. Custom prescribed a well-established routine for courtship and marriage, but the marital relationship was mostly the result of an agreement between the parties. Since marriage involved being taken into the families of the contracting parties, there were usually group meetings of the relatives with feasting, dancing, and ceremonies that sometimes lasted four or five days. Members of the family wishing to pay tribute to the bride and groom brought appropriate gifts. The bride was suitably honored, her hair combed and braided, and she was given face paints and beautiful garments. Earthenware vessels and other household goods also were common wedding presents.

The groom's father also brought gifts that he bestowed upon his son. Spirited horses and weapons used in the chase and in battle were among the gifts given to honor the new union. Songs of praise about the newlyweds were sung, and small gifts were distributed to the elderly and needy people of the camp. Admission to the center is free. Open 8 a.m. to 5 p.m. Mon through Fri. Call (605) 845-2387 for more information.

For more history on the Arikara and Sioux Indians, head 2 miles west on US 12 to the *Klein Museum* at 1820 West Grand Crossing. Arikara and Sioux artifacts share space with relics of the pioneer past, such as old farm machinery and a restored schoolhouse. This museum was the dream of an early homesteader, Jake Klein, long before the building was ever designed. His goal was to have a top-notch museum that would represent the counties of Campbell, Corson, Dewey, and Walworth, where he traded, homesteaded, and finally retired.

The museum building, with its native stone front, was Klein's gift to Mobridge and the surrounding area with the help of a $15,000 grant from the South Dakota Bicentennial Commission. The museum displays focus on prairie and Native American artifacts. More than twenty pictures of Sitting Bull are featured, along with stone and bone artifacts. The culture of the Sioux and Arikara Indians is reflected in the many articles of clothing, beadwork, pottery, tools, and implements that are on display.

The daily tasks of the early pioneers also come alive through the room scenes. For instance, the 1900s pre-electric kitchen features a wood/coal stove, large doughmaker, berry press, kraut cutter, and wooden icebox. A one-room

TOP ANNUAL EVENTS

Capitol Christmas Trees
Pierre, Dec

German–Russian Schmeckfest
Eureka, the third weekend in Sept

Sitting Bull Stampede Rodeo
Mobridge, July

schoolhouse and the original Glencross post office are also located on the museum grounds.

The museum is open Wed through Mon Apr 1 through Oct 31, from 9 a.m. to noon and from 1 to 5 p.m. It is open from 1 to 5 p.m. Sat. Admission is $3 for adults, $2 for students (605-845-7243; www.mobridgekleinmuseum.com).

The *Fool Soldier Band Monument* is located at the Klein Museum. On August 20–22, 1862, a group of young Teton Sioux negotiated for white captives of the Santee Indians and returned the captives to their families. They expected no rewards or reimbursement, and their actions seemed to be motivated by purely humanitarian concerns. This act of heroism took place in what is now Walworth County.

In Mobridge the Missouri River and Lake Oahe are the center of outdoor leisure. Fishing isn't the only sport in town; the Mobridge area is also a hunter's paradise, with open seasons on pheasant, grouse, turkey, deer, and antelope. Water-skiing, swimming, boating, or just soaking up the brilliant South Dakota sun can easily fill an afternoon.

Indian Creek Recreation Area (located 2 miles east on US 12, then 1 mile south) on the Oahe Reservoir offers fishing and water sports, along with picnicking, playgrounds, and tent and trailer sites. For more information call (605) 845-7112.

Some 135 million years ago, the area around Mobridge was covered by a great shallow sea, teeming with marine mollusks and shellfish. Clues to their prehistoric existence have turned up along the shores of Lake Oahe in the form of fossil ammonites, baculites, and belemnites that range from 1 to 6 inches long. If you look hard enough, you might find one of the ancient treasures.

Sitting Bull Monument, in Dakota Memorial Park, west of Mobridge on US 12, marks the burial site of the famous Hunkpapa medicine man. Like many chapters in the collective Plains Indian story, Sitting Bull's is one of a fascinating, enigmatic man who met an untimely death. Sitting Bull was born in 1834 on the Grand River, a few miles west of Mobridge, and his tragic demise years later occurred in the same place. The last known leader of the *Cante Tizna,* an elite warrior society, Sitting Bull also helped to defeat General George Custer's troops in 1876 at the Battle of the Little Big Horn. Sitting Bull met his own death, however, after he was arrested and then shot at his camp on the Standing Rock agency near Fort Yates in North Dakota.

The bodies of Sitting Bull and his men were buried in the corner of a post cemetery at Fort Yates. On April 8, 1953, descendants, with the help of the Dakota Memorial Association, moved Sitting Bull's remains to the present location and dedicated the memorial.

The giant granite bust of Sitting Bull was carved by Korczak Ziolkowski, who also started the Crazy Horse Memorial in the Black Hills. The marker today seems desolate and rather forgotten. Sitting Bull's remains, encased in a steel vault, are embedded in a twenty-ton block of concrete on which the monument stands. The grave site is open to the public free of charge.

It is also fitting that a memorial to Sakakawea (an alternate spelling of Sacagawea), the indomitable guide of Lewis and Clark, is located near the Sitting Bull Monument. Sakakawea, or Bird Woman, was a Shoshone Indian princess of the Big Horn Mountains of Montana. She was captured and taken to North Dakota. There she married a French fur trader, and together they were hired by Lewis and Clark for their first trip west in 1804.

Sakakawea guided the expedition over seemingly insurmountable obstacles. Much of the credit for the venture's success is given to her. She died later of "putrid fever," in 1812, at the age of 25, at Fort Manuel in Corson County, a short distance north of Mobridge.

In 1929 Mobridge schoolchildren donated pennies to erect a monument to honor this illustrious Indian woman. On September 27, 1929, a graceful cement shaft with a bronze plaque was erected at the Dakota Memorial Park in her memory.

siteselection

Founded in 1901, Pollock, northeast of Mobridge in Campbell County, thrived until the early 1950s, when construction of the Oahe Dam threatened to leave the town underwater. For several years the people of Pollock struggled with whether to move, abandon their town, or consolidate with nearby Herreid. After much consideration the town decided to move. But in what direction? A vote was held and ballots cast, some with a touch of humor. One vote called for Pollock to be put even deeper under the waters of Lake Oahe. Groundbreaking ceremonies for the "new" town were held on June 4, 1955. Today Pollock is surrounded on three sides by water and enjoys its reputation as one of South Dakota's most mobile cities.

The North–Central Reservations

Two of the state's more sparsely populated Indian reservations abut Mobridge to the west. The **Standing Rock Indian Reservation** covers 562,366 acres in South Dakota (it extends into south-central North Dakota). The **Cheyenne River Indian Reservation** covers 1.4 million acres, making it the second-largest reservation in the state.

In Eagle Butte southwest of Mobridge, the **H. V. Johnston Cultural Center** (605-964-2542) displays traditional beadwork and murals that depict the Lakota way of life. You also can buy beadwork and paintings by contemporary artists here. The center is located on US 212 near SD 63 on the Cheyenne River Indian Reservation. Free admission.

One of the area's more famous residents is Arvol Looking Horse, a 19th-generation keeper of the Sacred Pipe of the Great Sioux Nation. In this position he cares for the Sacred Pipe, presented by the White Buffalo Calf Woman many years ago. Looking Horse leads the annual Sacred Pipestone Run, which was formed to stop the sale of sacred pipestone. He holds an honorary degree from the University of South Dakota and has been profiled many times by local and national media. Looking Horse also is featured in the book of portraiture, *Visions Quest,* the story of contemporary Lakotas, Dakotas, and Nakotas who have chosen to carry on the traditions and culture of their people. The book was a collaborative project between Jesuit Don Doll and prominent Native American men and women. This handsomely arranged book features fifty contemporary members of the Sioux nation from five states and fifteen reservations, as well as Sioux lands, sacred sites, and photographs of dancers in traditional costume.

Pioneers and Walleyes

While Native American history swells from the central plains of the state, the tiny town of *Eureka* (www.eurekasd.com), northeast of Mobridge on SD 10, shows the Old World's contribution to America's melting pot.

Cheyenne River Tribe Flag

Color is magically represented in the Cheyenne River Sioux tribe's flag. The tribe's name appears in a banner framed by color. Blue represents the thunderclouds above the world where the thunderbirds that control the four winds live. The rainbow is for the Cheyenne River Sioux People, who are keepers of the Most Sacred Calf Pipe, a gift from the White Buffalo Calf Woman. The eagle feathers at the edges of the rim of the world represent the spotted eagle, which is the protector of all Lakota. Underneath the banner, two pipes fused together represent unity. One pipe is for the Lakota, the other for all the other Indian nations. Behind the pipes are yellow hoops symbolizing the Sacred Hoop, which shall not be broken. The Sacred Calf Pipe Bundle in red, in the center, represents *Wakan Tanka*—the Great Mystery. Adjacent to the Sitting Bull Monument on the west bank of the Missouri River is the *Grand River Casino & Resort,* with more than 15,000 square feet of gambling fun, as well as a lounge, an outdoor amphitheater, and a restaurant, perched high on a bluff overlooking Lake Oahe. The Grand River casino, owned by the Standing Rock Sioux tribe, features slots, blackjack, and poker. The casino walls are decorated with the artwork of Del Iron Cloud. The casino is located 2.5 miles west of Mobridge on US 12. For more information call (800) 475-3321 or go to www.grandrivercasino.com.

For more than a hundred years, beginning in the late 1700s, German colonists had been permitted to live in Russia and retain their culture, customs, and language; then, in 1871, Czar Alexander II revoked the agreement, which spurred a mass exodus. Thousands of German–Russian immigrants made their way to Dakota Territory, and eventually to Eureka.

You can find German influences throughout Eureka. Many of the 1,101 residents still speak German, often slipping between English and German without a thought. The Lutheran church had two pastors—one English-speaking and one German-speaking—well into the 1960s. Appropriately, the town celebrates its heritage with the annual **German–Russian Schmeckfest** during the third weekend in Sept. It's an ideal opportunity to enjoy the local cuisine, from savory sausages to the famed state dessert—*kuchen*. The town even has a kuchen factory, so you're sure to find a wide variety of the sweet, custardy dessert.

You can learn more about the area's German–Russian roots and its frontier past at the **Eureka Pioneer Museum of McPherson County** on SD 10 at the west edge of town. Open Wed through Sun Apr 15 to Nov. 1, its exhibits encompass military memorabilia, furniture, household items and antique farm machinery. There is no admission charge, but donations are always appreciated. Call (605) 284-2711 for hours.

Lakeview Motel, overlooking Eureka Lake, offers thirty-three rooms and knows how to cater to guests who need a bird-cleaning room and a pheasant freezer. The motel is located at 49 West Hwy. 10 (605-284-2400; www.motellakeview.com).

lewisandclark

Like many other points along the Missouri River, the stretch in central South Dakota swells with the historical exploits of Lewis and Clark. Near Greenwood in the south-central part of the state, for instance, Captain Lewis wrapped a newborn Sioux in a United States flag and predicted the babe would always be a friend of the whites. The child grew up to become Chief Struck by the Ree. Farther upstream, at Mobridge, the explorers camped with the Arikara Indians and met with French fur traders.

Neuharth is a common name in this part of the country, and it's also the last name of Al Neuharth, one of its most famous natives. Founder of Gannett Newspapers, Al Neuharth recalls his impoverished youth in his book, *Confessions of an S.O.B.* The town's information booth on the west edge of town, is dedicated to Al Neuharth's father, Daniel J. Neuharth.

For the dauntless explorer, the **Samuel H. Ordway Jr. Memorial Prairie** (50 miles northwest of Aberdeen on US 281) offers a rare, unspoiled pocket of native America, albeit an out-of-the-way jaunt. On the 7,600 acres of pristine land here, wild grass and more than 300 species of plants flourish, thanks to the foresight of the Nature Conservancy. See big bluestem, needle-and-thread, and other native grasses weave through colorful patches of wild-flowers. Waterfowl and shorebirds nest on the waters, while buffalo, deer, antelope, coyotes, and other animals populate the uplands. But hang onto your hat, as it's awfully windy here.

If you drive on US 83 south from Eureka, you'll come to tiny towns such as Selby and Akaska, which, like so many others in rural America, are small enough to become instant acquaintances of the traveler. If you take US 212 east for just a few miles, you will have a formal introduction to **Gettysburg** (population 1,154), located in the Whitlock Bay area on the eastern shore of Lake Oahe. The Forest City Bridge spans Lake Oahe at Whitlock Bay, and the Potter County seat of Gettysburg is near the intersection of US 212 and 83.

Gettysburg was settled in 1883 by 211 veterans of the famous Civil War battle after which the town was named. Many of the streets, townships, and communities in the area share names intrinsically associated with the Civil War.

The town's most popular historic exhibit is the mysterious 40-ton Medicine Rock on display at the **Dakota Sunset Museum,** 205 West Commercial St. The rock—considered sacred by local Native Americans—is embedded with footprints believed to have been made by the Great Spirit. The museum also includes a Civil War exhibit, big game exhibition, and a painting of the Battle of Shiloh. The local historical society also takes care of the **G. L. Stocker Blacksmith Shop,** which served as the Grand Army of the Republic Hall during the post–Civil War years and later became a blacksmith shop. Renovated to its original condition from the early part of the 20th century, it includes an interpretive center. Dakota Sunset museum is open 1 to 5 p.m. daily during summer months and Tues through Sat the rest of the year. For more information call (605) 765-9480.

The **Potter County Courthouse,** built in 1910, is a splendid example of a classical revival courthouse building. It is located on Exene Street 1 block east of Main Street. For more information, call the chamber of commerce at (605) 765-2528. Other noteworthy historic sites include the **National Hotel** and the **Odd Fellows Re-Echo Lodge,** which was moved to its present site by eighty teams of mules. The 1908 **Holland House** reflects a combination of colonial and Queen Anne styles of architecture.

Just outside Gettysburg at 31230 153rd St., innkeepers Norma and Don Harer promote privacy at their five-room bed-and-breakfast, the **Harer Lodge,** which also features a separate honeymoon cottage. The lodge sells South Dakota-made products in its country store, and visitors can try horseback riding as well. For more information call (605) 765-2167 or visit www.bbonline.com/sd/harerlodge.

For a look at how farming can contribute to the world's architectural style, visit **Sloat's Round Barn,** 13 miles north on Old US 83, then 2.5 miles west. C. B. Sloat designed this round barn as a college mechanical-drawing and carpentry project, and it was built after he graduated from college in 1915. The 100-foot-diameter barn was designed to house hogs, beef, and dairy cattle. A track is located inside the barn around the top and bottom of the wall to facilitate feeding and cleaning.

If you like camping, Gettysburg offers free sites in its city park, and you'll find both state-run and privately operated camping facilities

wheatkings

From 1887 to 1902, Eureka was known as the greatest primary wheat market in the world. As many as thirty-two grain buyers worked day and night, storing and shipping wheat brought in by horses and oxen. In 1892, 3,330 freight-car loads of wheat were shipped from the town.

nearby. One of the most popular destinations for campers, boaters and anglers is **West Whitlock Recreation Area** with its 100 sites and two camping cabins (800-710-2267; www.campsd.com). Just 15 minutes west of Gettysburg on US 212, its beautiful setting on giant Lake Oahe began as a campsite for the Arikara and Mandan people. The replica of an Arikara earth lodge found in the park is a reminder of the many lodges that the Lewis and Clark expedition saw as they traveled this area. Each lodge, made of cottonwood logs, willow branches, and grass, could house up to twenty people. The Arikara people were farmers and grew crops such as corn, beans, squash, sunflowers, and tobacco.

When the area became a park, it was named for Mrs. J. F. Whitlock, whose pioneering family once owned the land. Whitlock Crossing was the name given to a small settlement that operated a ferry across the river near the area. Although a thirty-six-pound northern pike was caught from shore in 1993, the main sport fish here is walleye. The annual **Whitlock Bay Walleye Tournament,** which is held each summer, offers competitors big prizes and lots of action. The reservoir's newest sport fish is the Chinook salmon. Each year thousands of eggs are taken from adult salmon at **Whitlock Spawning and Imprinting Station;** after hatching, fingerling salmon are returned to the lake. When adult salmon return in the fall, these fast and furious swimmers will test the skills of even the most avid fishermen.

You can download a copy of the current *South Dakota Fishing Handbook* by visiting the Web site at www.sdgfp.info/publications/fishinghandbook.pdf. Or request the *South Dakota Hunting and Fishing Guide* by logging on to www.travelsd.com.

History buffs and mountain bikers will find their own adventure schools in this rugged land, first explored by Lewis and Clark. West Whitlock is open year-round. Call (605) 765-9410 or go to www.sdgfp.info for more information. Admission is $6 per day or $28 for the year.

Hunters will feel right at home on the 10,000-acre **Paul Nelson Farm.** Half the acreage is dedicated to pheasant hunting. They offer different hunting packages, corporate retreats, shooting schools, fly-fishing schools, and more. For more information, call (605) 765-2469 or visit the Web site at www.paul nelsonfarm.com.

As you head south along the Missouri, grasslands and the sparse landscape give way to the capital of South Dakota and a cultural hub.

The Capital

The easiest way South Dakotans can spot a newcomer is by how he or she pronounces **Pierre,** the state capitol. French class will be no help. Here, they say *"pier."* The ruggedly autonomous forefathers were perhaps trying to down-play the très français beginnings of the state, but it was indeed a Frenchman who started South Dakota's first permanent white settlement in 1832. American Fur Company agent Pierre Chouteau Jr. piloted his steamboat, the *Yellow-stone,* to the mouth of the Bad River and established Fort Pierre Chouteau. Representatives from nine Sioux tribes brought their furs to trade, principally buffalo, which were valued at the time from $3 to $4 per hide. An average of 17,000 buffalo robes were traded each year. The site of the settlement is now a designated landmark on the National Register of Historic Places. Pierre is the nation's second-smallest capital with a population just over 14,000, but its central location in the middle of the state makes it neutral when it comes to East River–West River favoritism.

Merry Christmas

The nation's capitol building received a special gift from South Dakota for Christmas in 1997: a 60-foot white spruce tree from the Black Hills. After the Nov 14 tree-cutting ceremony, the spruce was carefully wrapped and secured on a semitrailer for its 2,500-mile journey to Washington, D.C. The tree was appropriately adorned with thousands of ornaments crafted by South Dakota students and groups.

South Dakota artist Jon Crane captured this momentous occasion in his painting, *America's Holiday Tree,* which depicts the snow-flecked spruce in the forest before all the holiday fanfare.

The **Oahe Dam,** 4 miles north of Pierre on SD 1806, is the nation's largest rolled-earth dam. It creates the fourth largest manmade reservoir in the United States, running 231 miles from Pierre to Bismarck. With 2,250 miles of shoreline, it claims a longer coast than the state of California and boasts 51 recreational areas. The power plant, dedicated by President Kennedy in 1962, houses seven of the world's largest generators. You can tour the plant at 28563 Powerhouse Rd. three times a day Memorial Day through Labor Day. Call (605) 224-5862 or go to www.recreation.gov for more information.

Overlooking the Oahe Reservoir, the Oahe Visitor Center offers information on anything from recreation to local hotels and restaurants. The center has numerous informational displays, which include Lewis and Clark, the Oahe Chapel, Oahe intake structures, and a Kid's Korner. The center is open from Memorial Day through Labor Day.

The lake takes its name from the Oahe Mission, started in 1874 by the Reverend Thomas L. Riggs, a Congregational minister, and his wife, Cornelia Margaret Foster, to serve the Dakota Indians. The mission was originally located on the site of an old Arikara Indian village, about 5 miles from the location of the modern-day chapel.

In the 1950s, when it became evident that the completion of the Oahe Dam would flood the mission location, the chapel was given to the South Dakota Historical Society. In 1964 it was relocated at the eastern end of Oahe Dam, where it stands today. Nondenominational Sun services start at 8 a.m. Memorial Day through Labor Day. The chapel is also a popular wedding location.

Fishing on Lake Oahe or Lake Sharpe is legendary. The Walleye Capital of the World also is known for its trophy northern pike. Chinook salmon, white and smallmouth bass, brown and rainbow trout, and catfish also are caught here. Eminent filmmaker Ken Burns, creator of the popular PBS documentaries *Baseball* and *The Civil War,* made a documentary of the Lewis and Clark expedition along the Missouri River system. His crews visited Pierre in the summer of 1995 to capture sections of the river and to film buffalo near the Lower Brule Indian Reservation. "We're looking for stretches of river that represent how it really was," Burns told the *Lincoln (Nebraska) Star Journal.* "We want to see it as [Lewis and Clark] might have seen it."

The French connection is underscored at the **Vérendrye Monument** in Fort Pierre, just off US 83 across the Missouri River. The two French brothers Vérendrye were the first white people to set foot in South Dakota in 1743. They buried a lead plate on a bluff that overlooks Fort Pierre to claim the area for King Louis XV of France. Safely covered by dirt for generations, the plate was accidentally unearthed by schoolchildren in February 1913. Now

The Oyate Trail

The concept of a scenic route to the Black Hills of South Dakota has been around since before the Missouri River was dammed and before Mount Rushmore was even finished. Since the day the state could boast of having a "fully improved road" along its southern border, South Dakotans have been promoting this 388-mile stretch of highway as an educational alternative to Interstate travel. Travelers will discover diverse geography, as well as the cultural and historical contributions of both the Sioux Nation and European immigrants.

The Oyate Trail of today turns off I-29 at Vermillion and heads west on SD 50 and US 18 to Edgemont near the Wyoming border. For local attractions along the way and suggested itineraries, call the Southeast Tourism Association, (888) 353-7382 or visit www.oyatetrail.com.

the artifact is on display at the Cultural Heritage Center (900 Governors Dr.; 605-773-3458). A monument in Fort Pierre marks the spot where the plate was discovered. The lead plate is only ⅛-inch thick. Scratched onto the back with the tip of a knife are these words: PLACED BY THE CHEVALIER DE LA VÉRENDRYE WITNESSES LOUIS, LA LONDETTE, AMIOTTE 30 OF MARCH 1743. Interestingly, a second plate was found by a man who was canoeing on the Cheyenne River in the summer of 1995. It also was dated 1743 and presumably was buried by the Vérendrye party. The plate was much sought after by museums, various government agencies, and individuals. The man eventually became so overwhelmed by all the attention that he took an airplane over the river and dropped the plate back where he had found it.

For a walk on the historic side, the Pierre Historical Society has prepared a pamphlet, *Pierre Historic Homes Driving Tour,* that lists homes of historic interest. Several homes are listed on the National Register of Historic Places: For instance, a Georgian revival home built by a physician later served as the governor's mansion during Peter Norbeck's term from 1917 to 1921. Now an apartment building, this stately home can be seen at 106 East Wynoka St. Queen Anne, Tudor, neoclassic, Victorian, Dutch colonial, and Gothic revival styles also are represented on this list of twenty-four homes. The number-one home, located at 119 North Washington St., is the governor's mansion, which was built in 1936 as a WPA project. Although the eighteen-room private residence of South Dakota's first family is not open to the public, visitors are welcome to drive by or walk along the south lawn, which adjoins Capitol Lake. For a copy of the tour pamphlet or for more information, call the Historical Society at (605) 773-3458.

During the Thanksgiving and Christmas seasons, the Capitol Rotunda is awash in the lights and color of beautifully hand-decorated trees. The annual *Christmas at the Capitol* was begun more than twenty years ago by Dottie Howe, who is now retired from state government. Dottie and her friends couldn't find a perfect tree to display in the rotunda, so the group took a dozen or so and bunched them together—kind of like an exaggerated version of Charlie Brown's Christmas tree. Now the display has grown to include more than ninety trees—Black Hills spruce, pine, and other evergreens—that are decorated with a holiday theme. See a teddy bear tree, a Victorian Christmas tree, a music tree, even a pheasant tree. More than 50,000 people visit the striking display each year. *Capitol Christmas Trees* is open 8 a.m. to 10 p.m. daily the week of Thanksgiving until just after Christmas. For more details, call (800) 962-2034.

The Capitol, which more than casually resembles the Capitol in Washington, D.C., is dazzling. You can see for yourself by scheduling tours with volunteer guides or taking your own self-guided tour Mon through Fri. Call (605) 773-3765 or stop by the Capitol Lake Visitor Center for more information. Built on a foundation of South Dakota granite, the graceful building features terrazzo floors, coolly elegant marble staircases, stained-glass skylights, and a solid copper dome. This striking limestone structure, which looks much as it did when it was completed in 1910, is one of the most fully restored capitols in the United States. The state seal, which bears the motto "Under God the People Rule," symbolizes the way of life in South Dakota and the resources that keep it vital: farming, ranching, industries, lumbering, manufacturing, and mining. The seal was adopted in 1885, four years before the state was admitted to the union, and it is repeated on the state flag. A blazing sun encircles the seal, and the state's motto encircles the sun.

Fed by a warm artesian well, *Capitol Lake* never entirely freezes. It has become a winter haven for Canada geese, mallards, wood ducks, and many other varieties of migratory waterfowl. The *Flaming Fountain* perpetually glows as a memorial to all veterans, while the *South Dakota Korean & Vietnam War Memorial* stands as a tribute to the valiant South Dakotans who lost their lives in those two wars. The names of these slain veterans are carved in granite next to the Flaming Fountain.

A reproduction of Korczak Ziolkowski's *Fighting Stallions* also stands on the capitol grounds. It was erected in remembrance of the late governor George S. Mickelson and seven staff members and state leaders who died in a plane crash in 1993.

While the goings-on of state government present a busy and intriguing scene in Pierre, this town has more to offer than just politics.

Start with the ***South Dakota Cultural Heritage Center*** at 900 Governors Dr. for a look at the state's multifaceted personality. *Oyate Tawicoh'an* ("The Ways of the People"), a permanent exhibit at the center, showcases Native American history with more than 300 Native American artifacts, including an eagle feather headdress, a full-sized tepee, and a mounted buffalo. The museum, gallery, and gift shop are open 9 a.m. to 4:30 p.m. Mon through Sat and until 6:30 p.m. during the summer. It's open Sun 1 to 4:30 p.m. For more information call (605) 773-3458 or go to www.history.sd.gov. Admission is $4 for adults; $3 for seniors; free for children under 18.

Pierre also has a long military history from the Civil War to the Iraq War. You can learn more about it and get up close to a Sherman tank, General Custer's sword, a Civil War horse-drawn gun, and an A-7D jet fighter at the ***South Dakota National Guard Museum,*** 301 East Dakota St. It's open 9 a.m. to 4 p.m. Mon through Fri. Tours can be arranged by calling (605) 224-9991. There is no admission charge.

Another hot spot is the ***South Dakota Discovery Center and Aquarium*** (805 West Sioux Ave.), a former Pierre power plant that now houses hands-on science and technology exhibits and much more. Three aquariums feature native species of fish. Visitors can experience the universe through astronomy in the Sky Lab planetarium or test their reflex skills in the reactionary car. The center is open Sun through Fri 1 to 5 p.m. and Sat 10 a.m. to 5 p.m. Summer hours are from 10 a.m. to 5 p.m. Mon through Sat, 1 to 5 p.m. Sun. Admission is $4 for adults and $3 for children 3 and older (605-224-8295; www.sd-discovery.com).

If you've worked up an appetite, settle into ***La Minestra,*** which was touted for its crostini with sun-dried-tomato tapenade in a 2002 *Bon Appetit* feature on great neighborhood restaurants of the Midwest. Owners Stacey and Mark Mancuso restored the 1886 tavern at 106 East Dakota, revealing wainscoting and original pressed metal walls and ceiling. They might wish the walls could talk. The building has been a funeral parlor, pool hall and card room, and a country-western bar. As a popular Italian restaurant, it's now known for freshly made pasta dishes and hand-cut steaks (605-224-8090).

Much of the Academy Award–winning movie *Dances with Wolves* was filmed 25 miles northwest of Pierre, on a private ranch along SD 1806. The 53,000-acre ***Triple U Buffalo Ranch*** is home to a herd of some 3,500 buffalo (605-567-3624; www.tripleuranch.com).

Birds of a feather flock together, and in Pierre, the residents unite through annual festivals that spotlight the area's charm and scenic landscape.

The Lewis and Clark ***Goosefest,*** held every Sept at Steamboat Park, celebrates both the journey of Lewis and Clark and the return of migrating geese to the Pierre area. The three-day event celebrates crisp autumn days, South Dakota Arts Showcase, craft booths, children's activities, and live entertainment along the shores of the Missouri River. Vendors also sell a variety of unique products, including South Dakota honey, Arikara-style pottery, dried flower arrangements, and Indian tacos. Entertainment in the park's band shell ranges from goose-calling demonstrations to folk music. Aug visitors can join in the three-day *Riverfest* with a water-ski show, car and air shows, a Kiddie Parade, kids carnival and fishing events, a buffalo chip flip, and paddleboat and kayak rides along the Mighty Mo. Call (800) 962-2034 for details on either event.

Fort Pierre was the stomping ground of rodeo legend *Casey Tibbs,* who was born in a log cabin on the family homestead outside Fort Pierre in 1929. A life-size statue of Casey, riding the famous bronc "Necktie," is on display at the Fort Pierre community park and historical turnout. By fifteen, he was in nationwide competitions, and in 1949, at age 19, Casey became the youngest man ever to win the national saddle bronc-riding crown. Between 1949 and 1955, he won a total of six PRCA saddle-bronc-riding championships, a record still unchallenged, plus two all-around cowboy championships and one bareback-riding championship. You can learn more about his colorful, spirited life (including a couple of movies and stunt work) and celebrate South Dakota's rich rodeo history at the new *Casey Tibbs Rodeo Center* overlooking Pierre and Fort Pierre. Exhibits spotlight the work of Mattie Goff Newcombe, a spectacular trick rider of the 1920s, and the work of rodeo clowns, cowboys, entertainers, and rodeo queens. Hours are 10 a.m. to 4 p.m. Mon through Fri; 10 a.m. to 3 p.m. Sat; and noon to 3 p.m. Sun. Admission is $5, adults; $4, seniors; and $3, kids 6 to 18 (605-494-1094; www.caseytibbs.com).

To the south of Pierre is the *Fort Pierre National Grassland,* 200 undulating square miles of grasslands bisected by US 83. It's a hotspot for birders who come to see the greater prairie chicken, burrowing owls, and raptors, which are especially easy to see during the winter months. This is part of the national grassland that ranges across Nebraska and central and western South Dakota. Call headquarters in Chadron, Neb., for more information: (308) 432-0300.

The Central Reservations

One of the easiest ways to explore central South Dakota's reservations is to follow the 101-mile stretch of SD 1806, known as the Native American Scenic Byway, from Pierre to Lower Brule, Fort Thompson, and Chamberlain.

Driving through the area, you can appreciate the beauty of Lake Sharpe or Lake Francis Case, or catch a glimpse of a buffalo herd on the way through

Lower Brule. For a more modern-day indulgence, test your luck at the **Golden Buffalo Casino.** To get there, take I-90 to exit 248 at Reliance; then turn north for a fifteen-minute drive to **Lower Brule.** Slot machines and live blackjack and poker in the 9,000-square-foot casino keep the adrenaline flowing. The 38-room resort motel and convention center, restaurant, lounge, and gift shop overlook Lake Sharpe. Call (605) 473-5577 or go to www.lbst .org for more information.

The **Lode Star Casino** in **Fort Thompson** is accessible from the Native American Loop just north of Chamberlain. Owned by the Crow Creek Sioux tribe, the Lode Star boasts 250 slot machines, 6 game tables, and bingo. A 50-room hotel and restaurant also are on-site (888-268-1360; www.lodestarcasino.com).

nativeamericanfacts

A self-guided driving tour starts in Chamberlain and covers the nearby **Crow Creek** and **Lower Brule Indian Reservations.** Highlights include the Akta Lakota Museum, the Big Bend Dam, and the Lower Brule Game Lodge. In the summer the Lower Brule and Crow Creek tribes hold powwows, and visitors are welcome. The tribes also operate casinos. Maps and audiotapes of the Native American Loop are available from the Chamberlain Area Chamber of Commerce (605-734-6541; www.chamberlainsd.org).

Considered the gateway to the Old West, **Chamberlain** lies just east of the Missouri River. Its vast shoreline was surveyed by Lewis and Clark. Their adventurous spirit continues in this modest-sized town of 2,252. Chamberlain was named for Selah Chamberlain, who was director of the Milwaukee railroad in 1880, when the town was started. Rumor has it that, before 1880, natives called Chamberlain *Makah Tepee,* or "mud house," because a hermit had a dugout there.

When traveling from the Black Hills to Sioux Falls (or vice-versa), one of the most popular stops is **Al's Oasis,** off exit 260 on I-90. A great almost-halfway-there point (or over-halfway-there, depending on which way you're traveling), the restaurant has been a respite for weary travelers for more than seventy-five years. They come for the homemade pie, buffalo burgers and 5-cent coffee. Owners Albert and Veda Mueller moved the Oasis to its present location in the 1950s when it was a grocery store and ten-stool lunch counter. Since then Al's Oasis has expanded into a full-menu, 325-seat restaurant and lounge with moderate prices. The Oasis Trading Post and General Store has anything and everything you forgot or need on your trip—from food and toiletries to men's, women's, and children's clothing, and cowboy boots—as well as a campground and an eighty-six-room inn if you need to crash for the night (605-734-6054; www.alsoasis.com).

The **Cedar Shore Resort** (888-697-6363; www.cedarshore.com) is the first resort erected on the shores of the Missouri River. The 80,000-square-foot facility, on 164 acres, features a marina breakwater, a ninety-nine-room hotel, a day spa, a full-service convention center, and a 200-seat restaurant with lounge, art gallery, and more. The marina facility is one of a kind, with 100 boat slips and a floating concession. The interior design centers on themes indigenous to the area such as buckskin, the pasqueflower, yucca, coyotes, horses, and prairie wind.

Cable's Riverview Ridge Bed & Breakfast, 24383 SD Hwy. 50, is a contemporary home that overlooks a scenic bend on the Missouri River about 3.5 miles north of downtown Chamberlain. Innkeepers Frank and Alta Cable promise country peace and languorous quiet. They start the day off right by serving a full breakfast for visitors (605-734-6084; www.bbonline.com/sd/riverviewridge).

Founded by the Priests of the Sacred Heart in 1927, **St. Joseph's Indian School,** nestled on the banks of the Missouri River, is surrounded by prairie, rolling hills, and blue waters. St. Joseph's fosters the spiritual and educational growth of more than 200 Lakota and Dakota Indian children and young adults of all religious backgrounds. The school uses the concept of *tiospaye,* or "extended family," in its four communities. In recognition of the Native American heritage, St. Joseph's opened the **Akta Lakota Museum and Cultural Center** on its campus, which features exhibits and art that represent the past and present Lakota way of life. The museum rightly lives up to its name, which means "to honor the people."

On display at the museum are extraordinary hand-painted winter "counts," which provided a record of history. For generations, Plains Indians drew pictographs to document their daily experiences and to record time. A historian appointed by the tribal community drew one pictograph on a buffalo or deer hide at the end of each winter season. The pictograph represented a significant event that happened within that year. The Akta Lakota Museum (1301 North Main St.) hosts one of the finest collections of artifacts and contemporary Lakota art in South Dakota. Summer hours are 8 a.m. to 6 p.m. Mon through Sat and 9 a.m. to 5 p.m. Sun; winter hours are 8 a.m. to 5 p.m. Mon through Fri. For information on the school or museum, call (800) 798-3452 or visit www.stjo.org.

Pheasants and a Lake

Winner, a community of 3,357 residents on the east-west Oyate Trail (Trail of Nations), is internationally known as a hunter's paradise, and justifiably so.

The wily ring-necked pheasant, grouse, prairie dog, and big game lure hunters from around the world. Fishing in the many stocked dams and lakes of Tripp County is also excellent.

Each fall thousands of hunters aim for Gregory County on the western edge of the Missouri River in central South Dakota, accessible via SD 44 or SD 47. Hunting ranks as the second-largest industry in the county, behind agriculture. Appropriately, a large, artificial pheasant greets visitors at the west entrance to the town of Gregory.

In the heart of pheasant country, the *Circle H Ranch,* located 8 miles south of Gregory, is a working ranch known throughout the region for its fine crops, superb grassland, and excellent natural game habitat. In 1992, the ranch was opened as a private retreat to accommodate hunters and guests for business retreats and vacations. The quiet serenity, along with the breathtaking natural beauty of the land, makes a visit to the Circle H Ranch a perfect getaway. Lodging options include a guest house with five rooms or a renovated pioneer church with six bedrooms (605-731-5050; www.circlehranch.com).

If you want to travel across the longest bridge this side of the Mississippi, head 15 miles west of Platte to cross the Missouri River. The bridge stretches just over a mile long on SD 44.

To reach the tiny town of Pickstown, go east on SD 44, then southeast on SD 50 for about 30 miles. This community of just 170 people boasts the mammoth-sized *Fort Randall Dam–Lake Francis Case.* A part of the Missouri River Basin project, Fort Randall Dam is 10,700 feet long and 165 feet high. You can learn more about it at the visitor center and take a self-guided tour or set one up by calling (605) 487-7603. At the base of the huge earthen dam is the Fort Randall Historic Site, which commemorates a military outpost established in 1856 to keep peace between white settlers and the Sioux. Its visitors list reads like a Who's Who in plains history: George Custer, Philip Sheridan, and Hunkpapa Sioux leader Sitting Bull (who was held prisoner at the fort for two years). At present the only visible sign of the fort's existence is the *1875 Fort Randall Chapel,* which looks like a crumbling Gothic ruin. You can tour the dam's powerhouse daily from Memorial Day through Labor Day.

Many recreation areas along the reservoir have swimming, fishing, boating, picnicking, and camping. Randall Creek Recreation Area has a bonus: an eagle roost that's a designated National Natural Landmark. You can quietly walk in or ski in to see the eagles roosting in cottonwoods about 50 feet from shore. The nearby *Karl E. Mundt National Wildlife Refuge* is the nation's first federal eagle sanctuary and marks the end of the trail for this region. Call (605) 487-7603 for more information.

Where to Stay Along the Missouri River

CHAMBERLAIN-OACOMA

Cedar Shore Resort
I-90, exit 260,
1500 Shoreline Dr.
(605) 734-6376
(888) 697-6363
Moderate

EUREKA

Lakeview Motel
1307 J. Ave., Hwy. 10
(605) 284-2400
www.motellakeview.com
Inexpensive

MOBRIDGE

Wrangler Inn
820 West Grand Crossing
(605) 845-3641
(888) 884-3641
www.wranglerinn.com
Inexpensive

PIERRE

Best Western Ramkota River Centre
920 West Sioux Ave.
(605) 224-6877
www.pierre.ramkota.com
Moderate

Comfort Inn
410 West Sioux Ave.
(605) 224-0377
www.comfortinn.com
Moderate

Governor's Inn
700 West Sioux Ave.
(605) 224-4200
www.govinn.com
Moderate

Where to Eat Along the Missouri River

CHAMBERLAIN

Al's Oasis
(American)
take exit 260 off I-90
(605) 734-6054
Inexpensive to Moderate

MOBRIDGE

Grand Oasis Restaurant
906 West Grand Crossing
(605) 845-7474
(877) 363-5884
Inexpensive to Moderate

SELECTED CHAMBERS OF COMMERCE

Chamberlain–Oacoma Area Chamber of Commerce
115 West Lawler St.
P.O. Box 517
Chamberlain 57325
(605) 734-6541
www.chamberlainsd.org

Mobridge Chamber of Commerce
212 Main St.
Mobridge 57601
(605) 845-2387
www.mobridge.org

Pierre Convention and Visitors Bureau
800 West Dakota Ave.
P.O. Box 548
Pierre 57501
(800) 962-2034
www.pierre.org

WESTERN SOUTH DAKOTA →

While glaciers flattened the eastern half of South Dakota, the west kept its ruggedness in more than just geography. Strength and a sense of individualism thrives in the lifestyles of its residents, from its early visionaries, explorers, and miners to modern cowboys and Plains Indians who also embrace centuries-old traditions. This is a land so rich in natural wonders, you'll find something fresh to experience no matter how many times you visit. There are few other places where you can go deep into a jeweled cave and enjoy top-of-the-world views in the same day. No wonder there's a tangible spirit here in this often sacred landscape known as *"Paha Sapa,"* or Black Hills.

Western South Dakota boasts one of America's best road trips, from wide-open grasslands and the eerie moonscape of the Badlands to the patriotic pride of Mount Rushmore and fragrant, thick pine forests. The Black Hills in particular buzz with activity from Memorial Day to Labor Day as seasonal shops and attractions hit full swing. Visitors stream in from across the globe, especially for the famed Sturgis bike rally. It's surprisingly easy, though, to dodge crowds and find overlooked places or fresh ways to experience favorite attractions. Give yourself time for quiet hikes along the Black Hills'

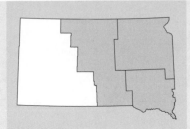

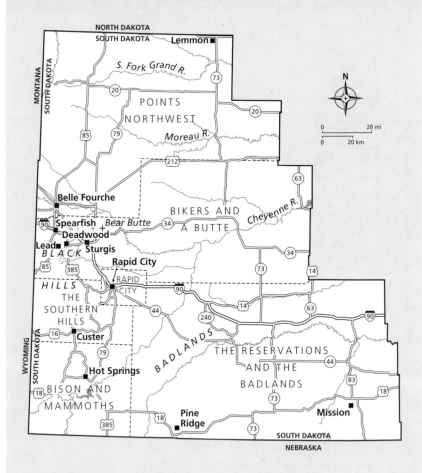

NORTH DAKOTA
SOUTH DAKOTA
Lemmon ■

S. Fork Grand R.

(73)

(20)

POINTS

NORTHWEST

MONTANA
SOUTH DAKOTA

(85)

(79)

Moreau R.

(20)

N

0   20 mi
0   20 km

(212)

(63)

Belle Fourche ■

BIKERS AND

A BUTTE

Cheyenne R.

(34)

Spearfish ■ Bear Butte
Deadwood +
Lead ■   Sturgis ■

(90)

B L A C K

Rapid City ■

(34)

(73)

(14)

RAPID
CITY ■

(90)

H I L L S
THE
SOUTHERN
HILLS

(85)

(385)

(44)

(14)

(63)

(240)

(90)

(16) Custer ■

BADLANDS

THE RESERVATIONS

(44)

(79)

AND THE

(83)

WYOMING
SOUTH DAKOTA

Hot Springs ■

BADLANDS

(18)

BISON AND
MAMMOTHS

(18)

(73)

Mission ■

(18)

(385)

Pine
Ridge ■

(18)

(73)

SOUTH DAKOTA
NEBRASKA

TOP ANNUAL EVENTS

Black Hills Powwow and Art Expo
Rapid City, Oct

Buffalo Roundup
Custer State Park, late September

Central States Fair
Rapid City, every Aug

Days of '76 (rodeo and parade)
Deadwood, first full weekend in Aug

Gold Discovery Days
Custer, late July

Native American Day
Crazy Horse Memorial, Oct

glittering trails where you can hear the wind singing through the pines. Or walk across wide-open prairies to imagine the lives of Native Americans more than a century ago.

The Reservations and the Badlands

To truly get off the beaten path, explore some of South Dakota's reservations where towns are few and far between, but history and tradition remain deeply rooted in the rolling hills and grasslands. Nine federally recognized tribes call South Dakota home. Rosebud Reservation, home of the Rosebud Sioux, and Pine Ridge Reservation, home of the Ogala Sioux, are among the largest.

Start at **Rosebud Indian Reservation** in southcentral South Dakota. The state's most populated reservation covers 882,416 acres with headquarters in Rosebud. Most visitors head to St. Francis, home of the **Buechel Memorial Lakota Museum** (350 South Oak St.).

Far away from the noise of more prominent attractions, the towns here are few and far between. Yet visits here and to other Dakota reservations offer an authentic glimpse at the state's Native American culture, both its past and present. The museum in St. Francis displays many Lakota items, ranging from traditional dress to hunting tools, as well as historic photographs of Sicangu Sioux Chief Spotted Tail, who strove for peace between Native Americans and

what'sinaname

The term Sioux, short for *nadoues-sioux,* or "little snakes," actually came from the Chippewa, a longtime foe. The people of the Great Sioux Nation, however, prefer to be called Dakota, Nakota, or Lakota, according to their language group. (*Dakota* means *"friends"* or *"allies."*)

Famous Sons

The late Ben Reifel, a five-term U.S. congressman, was born near Parmelee on the Rosebud Reservation in 1906. During his lifetime he worked for the Bureau of Indian Affairs, served in the U.S. Army, and received a doctoral degree from Harvard University. Reifel ran for office in 1960 and served until his retirement in 1971. He died in 1990.

White Eagle, a member of the Rosebud Sioux tribe, was the first Native American to sing leading tenor roles in American musical theater and opera. He graduated from the prestigious Merola Opera program at the San Francisco Opera and performed with the Pennsylvania Opera Theatre, Florentine Opera, and Cleveland Opera, among others.

the white settlers during the turbulent 1800s. Spotted Tail selected this land for his people in 1877.

The museum was named for another spiritual leader of the times, although he was not a Sioux. Father Buechel was a Jesuit priest assigned to the St. Francis Mission. Intrigued by the native culture, he collected photographs and artifacts and wrote several books in Lakota. His collection is the heart of the museum. Located on the grounds of the St. Francis Mission, the museum is open seven days a week from 8 a.m. to 5 p.m. Memorial Day through Labor Day. Admission is free. You may be able to visit in the off-season by making at appointment Call (605) 747-2361 for more information or visit www.sfmission.org.

The **Red Cloud Heritage Center** (100 Mission Dr.; 605-867-5491; www .redcloudschool.org), at Red Cloud Indian School in Pine Ridge, features a Native American art collection that is considered one of the finest in the Northern Plains. It includes more than 2,000 graphics, paintings, and sculptures from the annual Red Cloud Indian Arts show, a large national competition for native artists from all over North America. The show runs from June through mid-Aug and attracts more than 11,000 visitors who enjoy discovering up-and-coming Native American artists. Leave time to browse the gift shop with its locally crafted star quilts, bead and quill work, Dakota dictionaries, pottery, and music recordings. The Heritage Center is open from 8 a.m. to 6 p.m. Mon through Fri and from 8 a.m. to 5 p.m. Sat and Sun. Free admission.

You can explore the area's backcountry on a scenic drive through **Crazy Horse Canyon,** southwest of Rosebud. This canyon entices visitors with 50,000 acres of magnificent views. Guides are available to lead travelers through the canyon or any other area of the reservation. Call ahead for guide service, which is strongly recommended, as this area is remote and has no developed roads. The Rosebud Sioux tribe can be reached at (605) 747-2381 or go to www.rosebudsiouxtribe-nsn.gov.

About 2 miles west of Rosebud on BIA 7, you can enjoy a picnic along the Little White River, which flows through Ghost Hawk Park, 50,000 acres of raw beauty.

Pine Ridge Indian Reservation is the second-largest reservation in the United States. Among its members are runner Billy Mills, who won the 1964 Olympic gold for the 10,000-meter race, becoming the first American to win it.

Pine Ridge is most famous for the tragedy of Wounded Knee, a massacre of innocents in the winter of 1890. Chief Big Foot and his Minniconjou band had set out for Pine Ridge following the death of spiritual leader Sitting Bull on Dec 15. They were intercepted by the Seventh Cavalry and were brought, under a white flag of truce, to Wounded Knee. On the morning of Dec 29, soldiers prepared to search the band for weapons. A rifle was fired, setting off intense shooting that killed more than 250 natives, most of them unarmed. Bodies of women and children were found as far as 3 miles from the site, apparently shot as they fled into the plains.

The ***Wounded Knee National Historic Landmark*** is located 8 miles east of Pine Ridge on US 18, then 7 miles north on an unnumbered paved road to Wounded Knee. A solitary stone monument stands on the mass grave site. The Native American community, the National Park Service, and the state of

South Dakota Mixtape

Liven up a long road trip with downloads, audio books, and compact discs from South Dakota authors and artists:

- *Dakota: A Spiritual Geography* by Kathleen Norris

- *Little House on the Prairie* by Laura Ingalls Wilder

- *A Long Way from Home: Growing up in the American Heartland, The Greatest Generation,* and *Album of Memories* from long-time *NBC Nightly News* anchor Tom Brokaw

- *The Wizard of Oz,* by Frank L. Baum, who was apparently inspired by a tornado that he saw in Aberdeen.

- "A Few Small Repairs" or "Fat City" from singer/songwriter Shawn Colvin

- "We the People" or other recordings by Brule, one of the nation's best-known and most award-winning Native American musical groups

South Dakota are working to create a national memorial park in honor of the victims of the Wounded Knee massacre. In 1973, as a way of drawing attention to grievances, some 200 armed Native Americans occupied Wounded Knee for 70 days. *Bury My Heart at Wounded Knee,* by Dee Brown, is an excellent book on what is often called the last major conflict between the U.S. Army and the Great Sioux Nation.

About 120,000 acres of the Pine Ridge Indian Reservation lie within ***Badlands National Park.*** Farther from the Interstate, this less-crowded South Unit was added to the park in 1976. Ogala Sioux Parks and Recreation Authority runs the White River Visitor Center here, open 10 a.m. to 4 p.m. from June 1 through mid-Sept. It includes cultural exhibits and a videotape program on Oglala history. Call (605) 455-2878 for more information.

Heading into the Badlands

If you're approaching the ***Badlands*** from the east, take exit 131 off I-90 and go half a mile south. On the right will be the ***Minuteman Missile National Historic Site*** next to the Conoco Station. Opened in 2004, this is one of the newest additions to the national park system. A new 12-minute film will get you oriented to South Dakota's Minuteman Missile Field, which included 150

AUTHOR'S FAVORITES IN WESTERN SOUTH DAKOTA

Badlands National Park
62 miles east of Rapid City on I-90
(605) 433-5361
www.nps.gov/badl

Black Hills National Forest
(605) 673-9200
www.fs.fed.us/bhnf

Crazy Horse Memorial
5 miles north of Custer
(605) 673-4681
www.crazyhorsememorial.org

Custer State Park
(605) 255-4464
www.sdgfp.info

Jewel Cave National Monument
(605) 673-2288
www.nps.gov/jeca

Mammoth Site
Hot Springs
(605) 745-6017
www.mammothsite.org

Mount Rushmore National Memorial
25 miles southwest of Rapid City
(605) 574-2523

silos and cost $56 million in the early 1960s. By today's dollars, the Cold War national defense would be well over $9 billion.

Visitors can look through a glass enclosure at the Delta-09 missile silo, catch a ranger talk, or choose a cell-phone or self-guided brochure tour. The best option, though, is to plan ahead and get a coveted spot on the in-depth 90-minute tours that go into Delta-09 and the Delta-01 launch control facilities. South Dakota's missiles were decommissioned after a 1991 treaty.

Due to confines within the missile areas, only six spots are available and can be reserved up to three months in advance. The site is now open year-round, with spring and fall the ideal times to secure a tour. Call (605) 433-5552 or go to www.nps.gov/mimi for more information. Admission and tours are both free.

Spearfish Canyon Drive

At the east entrance of Badlands National Park, the **Prairie Homestead Historic Site** is the only original sod building on public display in South Dakota. Located 0.5 mile from the east entrance of the park on SD 240, it is furnished in the style of the original homesteaders, and letters and photographs of the original homesteader's family and neighbors offer riveting insight into the hardships they endured. Many of the early homes on the plains and prairies of the Dakotas were built of sod. The homes were efficient—cool in the summer and warm in the winter—but also dark, dirty, and often infested with mice, bedbugs, and other unsavory houseguests. It is open daily, sunrise to sunset, from May through Sept. For more information call (605) 515-0138 or go to www.prairiehomestead.com. Admission is $4.50 to $6.50 per person. Kids 11 and under are free with a parent.

Badlands National Park (605-433-5361; www.nps.gov/badl) is as otherworldly as land can be; soft clays and sandstones were deposited as sediments 26 to 37 million years ago by streams from the Black Hills that left vast plains. This once rich landscape attracted a community of ancient creatures. Remains of three-toed horses, dog-sized camels, and saber-toothed cats have been discovered here in the Oligocene beds. They're considered some of the world's richest vertebrate fossil sites. More than a 250,000 of the discovered fossils have been collected by the Museum of Geology in Rapid City while others have gone on to museums such as the Smithsonian. Protecting these fossils from the golden age of mammals was one reason the park expanded to include the White River unit.

Eventually humans stumbled upon this seemingly hostile land. Upon arriving in the Badlands, native tribes called it *mako sica,* meaning "land bad." French Canadian trappers who traveled through its rugged terrain in the early 1800s dubbed it *les mauvaises terres à traverser,* or "bad lands to travel across."

At present, Rocky Mountain bighorn sheep, antelope, mule deer, prairie dogs, bison, and the re-introduced black-footed ferret and swift fox live among the Badlands. Keep your eyes peeled and the binoculars handy while driving the 32-mile **Badlands Loop,** which begins at exit 131 off I-90. Leave plenty of time to stop at numerous scenic points for photos and hikes. The Badlands may look barren from the highway, but a closer look lets you see some of the 200 kinds of wildflowers and 50 grasses.

As you wind down the road, you'll pass the **Ben Reifel Visitor Center,** which offers the best all-around introduction to the park from 8 a.m. to as late as 7 p.m. in peak season. It re-opened in 2006 with new exhibits and an air-conditioned theater that shows "Land of Stone and Light." You can camp in the park or check into **Cedar Pass Lodge** or **Badlands Inn** within a few miles of the visitor center. Both are run by Forever Resorts (877-386-4383) and moderately priced at $95 to $125. You can also dine at Cedar Pass, which includes Indian fry bread and buffalo tacos.

Even if you've seen the Badlands once or several times, they're still worth another look. Like a fine wine, they improve with time as every rainstorm and windstorm gnaws at the sediments and accentuates each ravine and ragged pinnacle. Shifting light constantly repaints the landscape in new colors. If you're lucky enough to see the Badlands when heat lightning crackles up from the horizon or when a rainbow follows a sultry storm, it's a sight you'll never forget.

fifteenminutes offame

Scenes from *Starship Troopers,* the Paul Verhoeven movie based on Robert A. Heinlein's classic 1959 science-fiction novel, were filmed in the Badlands. Although the movie didn't win an Oscar for best acting or script writing, it gets two thumbs-up for best natural location that is as otherworldly as it gets.

As you leave the Badlands at exit 110, you might be parched. The Hustead family built its iconic, campy **Wall Drug Store** empire banking on that theory and first luring Depression-era travelers with free ice water. Curiosity is the other draw after seeing countless hyped-up billboards spool past on the Interstate. It's the kind of place where people playfully pose with statues of cowboys and showgirls posed on benches or sitting atop the famous 6-foot jackalope. My kids barely give it any notice—not with a snarling, roaring, smoke-snorting animatronic T-Rex that comes to life about every 15 minutes. There's also a water show with jumping jets of water that tempt kids to get playfully soaked. Beyond the gimmicks and souvenirs, the tale of this sprawling 72,000-square-foot emporium and how it became famous is in itself interesting. You also can enjoy displays with more than 600 cattle brands, hundreds of historical pictures, and a collection of Native American artifacts. The cafe still serves 5-cent coffee. You might want a homemade donut or hot beef sandwich to eat with it. Wall Drug Store is open year-round. Call or go online for current hours (605-279-2175; www.walldrug .com). Two blocks south of Wall Drug Store is the National Grasslands Visitor Center where you can explore the four main ecosystems of the High Plains and learn more about one of the country's largest protected mixed-grass prairies.

Just a minute away from Wall Drug Store, **Wounded Knee Museum** (605-279-2573) shares harrowing and heartbreaking details of the Wounded Knee Massacre through vivid graphics and photographs. Indian gifts, jewelry, books, and T-shirts are also sold here.

As the Badlands disappear into the rear view mirror, it's just an hour to Rapid City and the foothills of the Black Hills National Forest. About seven miles before you reach the city, you'll hit exit 66 and the Ellsworth Air Force Base. It's home to the **South Dakota Air & Space Museum** (605-385-5188; www.sdairandspacemuseum.com). The free museum includes historic bombers, fighters, missiles, and utility aircraft, as well as many indoor exhibits of aviation memorabilia June 1 through early Sept. Here you can see a three-fifths-scale model of the Honda Stealth bomber and General Eisenhower's personal Mitchell B-25 bomber. Ellsworth is home to the 28th Bomb Wing and B-1B bombers, and it's not uncommon to see the sleek, low-level bomber graze the skyline. The museum is open seven days a week from 8:30 a.m. to 4:30 p.m., with expanded hours until 6 p.m. during the summer. Visitors can also take an official 50-minute bus tour of the base and a Minuteman Missile silo for $4 to $7 per person after passing through security. Once you hit the Hills, the number of places to go and things to do can be overwhelming. The $3.2 million **Black Hills Visitor Information Center** can help with their excellent maps, on-site trip counseling, free Wi-Fi, video theater and brochures galore. Exhibits and displays preview national parks, state parks, and every community in the Black Hills and Badlands region. To reach the center, take exit 61 (Elk Vale Road) north off I-90. Open year-round from 8 a.m. to 6 p.m. daily, with extended hours from May through Sept. Call (605) 355-3700 for more information.

Head west again on I-90 and you'll reach Rapid City. With a population of more than 67,000, it's the state's second-largest city.

Rapid City

To "lay out a Denver" was what the city founders—a group of unlucky miners—had in mind for **Rapid City,** founded in 1876. The city hasn't reached the population base of Denver, Colorado, but that's okay with its residents today.

Four Seasons

There is a saying about the climate in South Dakota, which is part deadpan humor and part reality: "Summer is three months in South Dakota, and winter lasts nine months." That is an exaggeration, of course, but you could see a few rare snowflakes in June. In general, here's what you can expect from South Dakota's four seasons:

Summer—Warm (sometimes hot) days and cool nights are the norm from mid-June to mid-Sept.

Fall—Comfortable warm weather through Sept and crisp cool weather into Nov is typical.

Winter—Dastardly cold from Dec to early Mar, alternating with milder weather. Snowfall is prevalent, providing excellent conditions for winter sports.

Spring—Mostly sunny days late Mar to mid-June with scattered rain showers or the more rare snow showers through early May.

Growth has been steady, and Rapid City is large enough to lure a variety of cultural attractions but small enough to be laid-back and welcoming.

Rapid City's most remarkable museum, ***The Journey,*** at 222 New York St., blends local history with the nature of the universe. Its excursion through time unifies collections from five sources: the Museum of Geology, the South Dakota State Archaeological Research Center, the Sioux Indian Museum, the Minnilusa Pioneer Museum Collection, and the Duhamel Collection. The museum tour begins with a twenty-minute video, which details pioneer and Native American history. The self-guided tour begins with 1,000 points of light that represent the immense nature of a universe deep in space and time. The time line takes you from the formation of the Black Hills billions of years ago to the present day. Visitors are given sound sticks so they can listen to historical stories and descriptions at each exhibit. Open daily from 9 a.m. to 6 p.m. during the summer, and 10 a.m. to 5 p.m. during winter, except Sun, when hours are 1 to 5 p.m. Admission is $7 for adults, $6 for seniors, $5 for children 11 to 17, and free for children 10 and under.

Call (605) 394-6923 or www.journeymuseum.org for updates on the Storyteller Series, Family Fun Days, teas, and other events that bring to life the colorful and sometimes infamous characters of the Dakota past.

At nearby Rushmore Plaza Civic Center you'll hear the drums and jingle of dancers during the ***Black Hills Pow Wow*** each fall. Lakota, Nakota, and Dakota nations come together for this celebration and competition which highlights the Native Americans' vast cultural heritage and pageantry. It is an unforgettable and mesmerizing experience to witness more than 700 dancers in colorful regalia, 35 drum groups, singers and representatives from nearly 60 tribes. For more information, contact the Black Hills Pow Wow Association at (605) 341-0925 or www.blackhillspowwow.com.

Follow Omaha Street east and see why folks from Rapid City are so crazy about dinosaurs. It seems they're everywhere. The **Museum of Geology** at the South Dakota School of Mines and Technology campus exhibits some of the best local fossils giant fish, prehistoric mammals, and dinosaurs, including the state's official dinosaur, a triceratops skeleton found in Harding County in 1927. The school boasts the largest paleontology program in the country. It's no wonder with major digs and discoveries in western South Dakota and eastern Wyoming. Dioramas tell the story of the Badlands and the strange and wild creatures that once lived there. Rock hounds can find a collection of minerals, ores, and local agates, including the state gemstone: the beautiful Fairburn agate. The Museum of Geology should be moved into its new $8 million campus building and research center scheduled to open by summer 2010. Call (800) 544-8162 or go to http://museum.sdsmt.edu for current hours and special programs. Admission is free.

Take St. Joseph Street west and you can see more museums in Rapid City's historic downtown district. Like so many other communities across the nation, the city's downtown has been on an economic seesaw as malls have redefined where America shops. Rapid City's downtown wholeheartedly met the challenge and lined its streets with restaurants, galleries, one-of-a-kind boutiques, and a movie house. Before you browse in the shops, take a good look at the architecture. Each building is unique, and as one adjoins another, you get a

navigatingrapidcity

The downtown district basically spreads from two one-way streets: Main and St. Joseph Streets. Be mindful of this, for during summer many near-collisions and several fender benders have occurred as newcomers try to go against the flow of traffic on a one-way street.

mini lesson in architecture. Notice the ornate Italianate facades, as well as the European onion-shaped domes. A walking-tour guide of the historic downtown district is available at the Rapid City Area Convention and Visitors Bureau (605-718-8484; www.visitrapidcity.com).

At 512 Sixth St., the 1911 Elks lodge and opera house is now the **Elks Theatre,** the grandest, cushiest spot to nuzzle next to a date over a bucket of popcorn, especially if you're in the balcony with the most sweeping view of the screen. Movies start at just $3 (605-343-7888; www.elkstheatre.com).

Rapid City Park & Art Sampler

- **President's walk,** downtown, lets visitors see eye-to-eye with life-sized bronze statues of American presidents.

- **Memorial Park & Garden,** north of downtown along Omaha Street, is dedicated to the 239 people who died in the devastating flood of 1972. Stroll fragrant rose gardens, catch a concert at the bandshell, and see one of America's largest sections of the Berlin Wall.

- **Dinosaur Park,** along Skyline Drive, geographically divides the town in half and offers some of the city's finest scenic views. Not that your kids will. Let them loose among seven life-size replicas of dinosaurs, including a triceratops and a Tyrannosaurus rex, all on the National Register of Historic Places.

- **Storybook Island,** 1301 Sheridan Lake Rd., is another nostalgic (and free) family favorite.

- **Wilson Park,** located on Mount Rushmore Road, a main drag that runs parallel to West Boulevard, is small, but its charm is enormous. An outdoor skating rink sets a Currier-and-Ives scene during winter, and arts festivals in summer continue the neighborly feeling as visitors flock around the flower gardens and gazebo.

Across the street at 523 Sixth St. looms the stately *Hotel Alex Johnson* (605-342-1210; www.alexjohnson.com), built in 1925. Listed on the National Register of Historic Places, this is where celebrities and politicians congregate while in the city. "The Alex" recently wrapped up an extensive renovation of the guest rooms, lobby, and *Paddy O'Neill's Pub* as it becomes an Ascent property. A *Seattle's Best Coffee Shop* replaced venerable restaurant, The Landmark.

The dining scene, too, is changing with visionary chefs such as M. J. Adams, who opened the *Corn Exchange* a few years ago. The small restaurant with wood floors and a copper ceiling at 727 Main St. feels big-city yet intimate and has drawn the attention of several national magazines. The menu constantly changes with what's in season and available and mostly organic. It's the kind of place to sit back and savor the meal—and enjoy the break from buffalo burgers and fries you'll find elsewhere. Here you might dine on pheasant dumplings with a Japanese dipping sauce, locally raised steak in a mushroom-cream sauce, or savory buttermilk white corn and scallion pancakes with house-smoked South Dakota trout as an appetizer. Leaving room for dessert—whipped up by a New York City–trained pastry chef—is mandatory (605-343-5070; www.cornexchange.com).

Enigma also has drawn praise. While it's located in the Radisson at Main Street and Mount Rushmore Road, it doesn't feel anything like a typical hotel restaurant. Diners slide into dark-wood booths beneath blue pendant lights and choose from menu items that may include lime-curried shrimp, filet mignon with truffled mashed potatoes, and free-range chicken cooked in port wine, served with mushrooms, bacon, and spatzle. Follow up with hot Dutch apple cobbler (605-348-8300; www.enigmarestaurant.com).

Both places are perfect for couples seeking a romantic evening out and willing to splurge a little.

For a more casual night out or hearty lunch, head to the popular *Firehouse Brewing Co.* at 610 Main St.; (605) 348-1915, which bears the distinction of being the first brewpub in the state. It features great beer and food. And yes, it's located in an honest-to-goodness 1915 firehouse, complete with historic photos and memorabilia.

As you stroll through downtown's shops, the one don't-miss destination is *Prairie Edge Trading Co. and Galleries* (800-541-2388; www.prairieedge .com) at 606 Main St. It's jaw-dropping to see the vast arrange of American Indian art, much of it museum quality. When I was there, a massive cast-paper, ghostly white powwow scene was going for $72,000 and had to be transported across the country. You'll find large art galleries, handiwork such as intricately woven leather-and-quill clothing and traditional drums to paintings and a music collection with more than 500 Native American titles. One of the biggest sellers is music by Brule, a band that lives in central South Dakota. Don't miss the Indian bead and craft supply area or the elegant bead museum in the loft, which showcases some of the nine tons of glass beads the gallery bought from Venice, Italy. It's easy to get lost in this store, whether you love art, books,

Take a Spin Through the Hills

Biking has soared in popularity in the Black Hills. Rapid City has a 13.5-mile bikeway along Rapid Creek, but most riding is done on the area's wide-shouldered highways. Some of the favorite routes are Rapid City to Mount Rushmore, the Needles Highway, Iron Mountain Road, Spearfish Canyon, and the Badlands Loop Road. All feature some steep grades and long climbs, but the spectacular scenery along the way makes the effort worth it.

Mountain bikers can explore 6,000 miles of fire trails, logging roads, and abandoned railroad grades that crisscross the backcountry ridges, wind down canyons, and climb to mountaintops. Or they can join the fun at the Black Hills Fat Tire Festival (www.bhfattirefestival.com) in late May.

jewelry, or fine leather. There's really something to appeal to everyone, and you'll walk away feeling like you've been to a museum.

A few blocks away, at the corner of Seventh and Quincy Streets, the **Dahl Fine Arts Center** (605-394-4101; www.thedahl.org) is another great place to admire local talent. It houses three art galleries, including one that brings in world-class artists; the Cyclorama Gallery, a unique 180-foot oil-on-canvas panorama spanning 200 years of United States history; and an interactive children's area. The Dahl Theater Black Hills Community Theatre stages five productions in the 170-seat theater during the fall and winter. The Dahl is open 9 a.m. to 5 p.m. Mon through Fri, with extended evening hours Thurs. Weekend hours are 1 to 5 p.m. Admission is $2.50.

If you travel south on **West Boulevard,** you'll see the grand homes that have made it possible for this street to bear the designation of a historic district. The best way to see it is to take a leisurely stroll down its tree-lined median. The boulevard is so stately that it's common to see walkers, joggers, daydreamers, and artists getting wrapped up in its turn-of-the-20th-century grandeur. Tudor revival, neoclassical, Queen Anne, Federal revival, and many more styles are represented on this street. Residents take great pride in their homes, and it shows through their vigilant upkeep of the properties and some fantastic flower gardens. If you're here in wintertime, take a slow drive up and down the boulevard to see some ornate Christmas-light displays that make the area shine like an enchanted village.

Chocoholics have nowhere to run—and nowhere to hide—once they enter the doors of **Mostly Chocolates** (1919 Mount Rushmore Rd.). The charming store features more than twenty-three kinds of truffles, including chocolate raspberry, Black Forest, apricot brandy, Irish crème, lemon chiffon, and rum. If you happen to be at the store during Christmastime, you can sample such red-and-white treats as the candy-cane truffles. To keep the sugar buzz going, the store has added a gelato bar. The fudge is equally tempting, especially in such seasonal themes as pumpkin pie and fresh strawberry. For more information call (605) 343-9426.

Located 5 miles west of the downtown district at 3788 Chapel Lane is **Chapel in the Hills** (605-343-9426; www.chapel-in-the-hills.org). Stavkirke, as it also is known, is an exact replica of the famous 12th-century Borgund Church in Norway. Wood carvings, Christian symbols, and Norse dragon heads adorn the building, which features pegged construction. It's a favorite and most romantic place for couples to exchange their wedding vows. Evening vespers are at 7:30 p.m. daily during the summer months. The chapel itself is open dawn to dusk May 1 to Oct 1. While you're there, check out the nearby **Norwegian Log Cabin Museum.** Admission is free; donations are welcome.

For the most part, western South Dakota has taken advantage of its handsome surroundings, and tourism is vital. The tourist trappings are evident in Rapid City—sometimes elegant, sometimes cheesy—but to get a true snapshot of what South Dakota's second-largest city is like, just get in the car, drive, and go wherever the wind takes you.

The Southern Hills

If you take US 16 west, you'll find tourist attractions and small towns threaded throughout the **Black Hills National Forest.** Actually a domed mountain region, the **Black Hills** extend about 6,000 square miles. They often are described as intimate because they don't loom above you like the Rockies and other mountain ranges. Ingenious scenic roads, hiking and biking trails all tug you into the landscape, threading through thick pine forests, tunneling through rocks, ambling along cold, clear streams, or through prairie wildflowers. Round out your adventures with fishing, camping, skiing, mountain climbing, rock hunting, and daydreaming, and you have an outdoors-lover's menu for magic. Where else can you hike across trails where mica sparkles like glitter beneath your feet and hillsides are studded with pink quartz?

South Dakota's Badlands and Black Hills region ranks among the top five places in the United States for its variety of minerals and rocks.

Tunnel Mania

There are a lot of tunnels in the Black Hills, and children will especially love them if you honk the horn while passing through. There are several narrow tunnels you should be aware of, however, particularly if you're driving a recreational vehicle, camper, truck, or bus. Here are the locations of these tunnels:

ROUTE	LOCATION	WIDTH	HEIGHT
US 16A	6 miles SE of Keystone	13'6"	12'6"
US 16A	4 miles SE of Keystone	13'7"	12'7"
US 16A	3 miles SE of Keystone	13'6"	12'10"
US 16A	1 mile N of Keystone	47'	18'
SD 87	6 miles SE of Sylvan Lake	10'4"	12'8"
SD 87	2 miles SE of Sylvan Lake	9'	12'
SD 87	1 mile N of Sylvan Lake	11'4"	10'

The Black Hills are obviously famous for gold, but also copper, silver, iron, lead, tin, zinc, feldspar, spodumene, and more than 140 other minerals. Expansive surface outcroppings of all three major rock types—igneous, metamorphic, and sedimentary—yield not only rock specimens, but embedded crystals, ores, and fossils. Beds of alluvial outwash on the perimeter of the Black Hills offer a colorful mix of all kinds of stones.

While it's a no-no for rock hounds to go collecting at Badlands National Park, the surrounding public lands—***Buffalo Gap National Grasslands***—hold some fine rock beds that produce Fairburn agates, funny eye, gay prairie, and bubblegum agates, red jasper, blue chalcedony, and petrified wood.

Most visitors beeline to the most famous rock of all: the carved-granite faces upon **Mount Rushmore National Monument.** In this one parking lot, you'll likely see license plates from almost all 50 states—testimony this truly is an All-American road trip. The monument's located 25 miles southwest of Rapid City on US 16A; follow the signs. If you follow Mount Rushmore Road you'll effortlessly be on US 16A.

You'll hit **Keystone** on your way to the Four Faces. Its carnival atmosphere will stand out as one of the most raucous and cluttered displays of tourism in the Hills. Either you embrace the fudge and taffy shops and old-time photos, or you keep driving. Breathing room is just minutes away.

The Four Faces are one of the most recognized and beloved national symbols. The 60-foot granite images of George Washington, Thomas Jefferson, Abraham Lincoln, and Theodore Roosevelt were carved by Gutzon Borglum. Mount Rushmore was commissioned as a national memorial by Congress in 1929, although work actually began in 1927. The project was not always the media darling of its time. Back east, a newspaper blasted: "Borglum is about to destroy another monument. Thank God it is in South Dakota, where no one will ever see it." Fortunately, Borglum and others had more foresight. When President Calvin Coolidge dedicated the project in 1927, he proclaimed that Mount Rushmore was "decidedly American in its conception, magnitude, and meaning. It is altogether worthy of our country."

Over the next twelve years, Borglum and his crews, using pneumatic drills and dynamite, carved four massive heads out of the mountaintop. Although the sculptor died before the project was finished, his son, Lincoln, made sure his father's vision continued. At present, more than two million visitors each year see the Borglums' legacy to America and the four men who inspired it.

A walk down the ***Avenue of the Flags*** with all 50 states plus territories colorfully frames Mount Rushmore as you approach Grandview Terrace and the amphitheater. Go below ground to the ***Lincoln Borglum Museum*** and see what the mountain would have looked like if the sculptors had finished the project down to the presidents' waistlines. Kids and adults love pushing a mock detonator and seeing a virtual blast. Two movies tell tales of the monuments, but you can go even more in-depth with the award-winning audio tour that's considered one of the best in the national parks system. It blends narration, music, sound effects and historic recordings and runs 30 to 120 minutes. It comes in multiple languages, including Lakota.

One of the park's newer attractions is a **Lakota, Nakota and Dakota Heritage Village** on the first section of the half-mile Presidential Trail loop. It's also a good place to look for mountain goats. They're not native from the area, but they have thrived here since 1924 when Canada gave six of them to Custer State Park as a gift. You might even spot one on the presidents' heads if you have binoculars handy.

On the far side of the trail, you'll find the **Sculptor's Studio,** built in 1939, with winches, jackhammers, and pneumatic drills that date from the time of construction. Borglum's original model of Mount Rushmore also can be viewed here. During summer months, there's also a sculptor-in-residence nearby, creating works using many of the techniques that created Mount Rushmore. You can catch 15-minute ranger talks at the studio or 30-minute talks at Grandview Terrace throughout the day. Check times when you arrive. If you're traveling with children, have them get a Junior Ranger workbook to make the most of their visit and earn a cool badge before leaving.

Carver's Café serves food and drinks with great views of the mountain, plus the chance to cool off or warm up, depending on the weather.

A patriotically fitting end to a day at Mount Rushmore is watching the 45-minute evening lighting ceremony from the outdoor amphitheater. Evenings can be downright chilly, so bring a light jacket. The ceremony is held nightly at 9 p.m. late May through mid-Aug and at 8 p.m. through the end of Sept. Mount Rushmore National Memorial is open year-round, and while admission is free, plan on $10 for a parking pass that's good for a year (605-574-2523; www.nps.gov/moru).

As you make your way from Rapid City to Mount Rushmore, you can watch bear, elk, wolves, bighorns, and other North American wildlife roam at **Bear Country USA,** 8 miles south of Rapid City on US 16. Bear cubs, wolf pups, and other park offspring are featured in the walk-through Wildlife and Welcome Center at the end of the driving tour. Bear Country is open daily, from 8 a.m. to 6 p.m. in the summer months and 9 a.m. to 4 p.m. in May and Sept through Nov. Tickets are $8 for children, $15 for adults (605-343-2290; www.bearcountryusa.com).

For the shopper who plans ahead for the holidays or just enjoys unique gift items, **Mistletoe Ranch & The Quilt Corral** (605-574-4197; www

.mistletoeranch.com or www.quiltcorral.com), a half mile south of the US 385 and US 16 junction, is a must-see. The bi-level 1890 home is peacefully nestled in the pine trees. The staff likes to celebrate Christmas every day and does so with holiday ornaments, decorations, porcelain dolls, specialty foods, and collectibles to fit almost any holiday theme. Open daily year-round.

Wine lovers will enjoy sipping samples at the stylish, multistory **Prairie Berry Winery,** just 3 miles northeast of Hill City on US 16. The patio offers fabulous views of Harney Peak, making it easy to linger and savor the flavors. Among their 15 wines are Pheasant Reserve, a dry red made with Marechal grapes and wild chokecherries; Blue Suede Shoes, a sweet wine with hints of blueberries; and a semisweet rhubarb-raspberry wine that earned silver in the *San Francisco Chronicle* wine competition. It's also a good lunch stop with flat-grill sandwiches and soups. One of the most popular ways to visit is by boarding the 1880 train for fall's Wine Express weekend. The December Fezziwig Festival also is popular featuring wine, live music, and food prepared with wine, along with self-guided tours of the winery (605-574-3898; www.prairieberry.com).

Twelve miles north of Hill City off US 385, you can taste a little bit of Europe while nestled into the forest. Swiss-born Hans Peter and Christine Streich run **Coyote Blues Village Bed and Breakfast,** a cedar-lodge haven they built more than a decade ago. Guests pick from themed rooms: European Antique, Mediterranean, Turkish, Swiss, Lakota, African, or Celtic. Each is equipped with a deck, a hot tub, and a private bath. There are three smaller rooms, as well. Rates range from $85 to $160 during the summer (888-253-4477; www.coyotebluesvillage.com).

Hill City, with a population of 871, is affectionately considered one of the most unpretentious towns in the Black Hills (800-888-1798; www.hillcitysd .com). The attitude is whatever goes. If you're looking a bit disheveled after three days of camping, don't fret. You can visit any of the Main Street establishments, and no one will make you feel out of place.

The oldest town in Pennington County, Hill City was a bustling region when gold first was discovered in the Palmer Gulch area. Bigger strikes in the Deadwood area left the town almost deserted, but when the Burlington Railroad ran its Hot Springs–Deadwood line through Hill City in 1892, the town reclaimed its place as gateway to the central Black Hills. It's hard to imagine that the town had a population of 3,000 in the 1890s.

Despite being a small town, Hill City has an impressive cross-section of galleries, shops and attractions. Its galleries in particular stand with places such as **Warrior's Work Studio and Ben West Gallery,** 363 Main St. (605-574-4954; www.leatherframegallery.com). Randy Berger creates leather frame designs for Native American and other fine art. They're covered in deerskin, buffalo hide, or elk leather and accented with embossing or beadwork. Randy will tell you about the Native American artists whose works are showcased and describe the latest art trend or technique—like the fancy-sounding gicleé (French for "spraying in ink")—in plain terms for the layperson.

At 208 Main St., *Jewels of the West* (605-574-2464, www.jewelofthewest .com) presents jewelry, Western art, pottery, and more. You can find great stuff here, including handcrafted jewelry, art by Karen Noles, pottery by Susan Davy, beautiful silk jacquard Western print scarves, and sculpture from Mill Creek Studios. The Old World Plaza features a collection of shops, including Vintage Cowboy, the Coffee Garden, and Snow Creek Gallery.

Jon Crane Watercolors (800-288-1948; www.joncranewatercolors.com) nearby is filled with watercolors by one of South Dakota's favorite artists. Crane's trademark is capturing the landscape of the region, and his work readily evokes the gentle yet determined spirit of the pioneer. Collectors will enjoy trolling through Heart of the Hills Antiques, Firearms and Collectibles, also on the main drag.

One of the best-kept secrets in the Black Hills is the *Black Hills Museum of Natural History,* 117 Main St. These are the folks who discovered the famous Tyrannosaurus rex named Sue in Faith, S.D., but lost the lengthy court battle to keep her when the Field Museum of Chicago bought her for millions. This museum does, however, have Stan, another stellar South Dakota T. rex find. The original bones are on display in Hill City, but he's been reproduced for the Smithsonian, Oxford University, and 28 other museums worldwide. You'll get a great cross-section of dinosaurs, mammals, birds, minerals, and other fossils here. Their Everything Prehistoric shop is a great place to buy native fossils and minerals, plus resin and bronze casts of dinosaur teeth. Admission is $4 for kids 6 to 14, $6 for seniors and military folks, and $7.50 for adults (605-574-3919; www.bhmnh.org).

If you've worked up an appetite, try Main Street's *The Bumpin' Buffalo Bar & Grill.* Its extensive menu includes Italian entrees, prime rib, seafood, specialty pizzas, and pub cuisine such as burgers and chicken, shrimp, and fish-and-chips baskets. For libations, choose from microbeers, wine, and espresso. The three-story historic building is tastefully decorated with hardwood floors, high ceilings, historic photos, an incredibly large bar, antiques, and mounted buffalo heads. Call (605) 574-4100 or visit www.bumpinbuffalollc.com.

Another good place to eat is the *Alpine Inn Restaurant* (605-574-2749), located in the classic 1886 Harney Peak Hotel. The lunch menu has a European flair, whereas the affordable filet mignon dinners with salad, baked potato, and Texas toast rule the dinner menu. The homemade dessert menu is famous with more than 30 to choose from—including apple cheese strudel. Open

Mon through Sat. Moderately priced bed-and-breakfast arrangements also are available.

With a nostalgic chug and blast of a whistle, the *1880 Train* is one of Hill City's most familiar and endearing tourist attractions. Years ago, the iron horse pulled cars carrying equipment and ore from Hill City to Keystone. The movie industry has tapped the historical significance of both the railroad and the area for productions such as *Orphan Train* and *Gunsmoke*. Modern-day travelers can board the train for a two-hour round-trip excursion that will take them from the Hill City Depot or the Keystone Junction several times a day from mid-May through early Oct. Look for special events, such as the barbecue with Teddy Roosevelt, the costumes-encouraged Fright Train for adults ages 21 or older on Halloween, or the family-oriented Holiday Express. For more information call (605) 574-2222 or go to www.1880train.com.

Not far from Hill City on US 16A, you can better appreciate the accomplishment of Mount Rushmore by seeing an even larger undertaking—*Crazy Horse Memorial*—painstakingly progressing, blast by blast (605-673-4681; www.crazyhorse.org). The late Korczak Ziolkowski began the project more than 60 years ago when several chiefs asked him to create a sculpture of the famous Oglala Lakota leader. Chief Henry Standing Bear's invitation said, "My fellow chiefs and I would like the white man to know the red man has great heroes, too." Although Ziolkowski died in 1982, his wife, Ruth, and their ten children continue the sculptor's dream, guided by his scale models and detailed plans. The process has been slow but steady and precise; Ziolkowski insisted that no federal or state monies be used to fund the project. The nine-story-high face of Crazy Horse was completed in 1998. The horse's head, which measures 219 feet (or twenty-two stories), is the focus of current work on the mountain. You can get the most amazing (and rare) up-close view of Crazy Horse by joining in the annual 10K Volksmarch in June. The strenuous two- to four-hour hike up the mountain has drawn up to 15,000 people eager to see the carving face to face. Stay after dark (or return later in the day) to see the evening laser show May through early Oct. They use some of the world's largest lasers and slide projectors for a multimedia blend of Native American music and stories with the mountain providing a 500-foot backdrop.

Beyond the fascinating story of the monument and the work that will be underway for generations to come, the site also is noteworthy for its Indian Museum of North America and Native American Cultural Center, the sculptor's studio; and a 40,000-square-foot Orientation Center and theaters. Many Native American artists and craftspeople create their artwork and visit with guests at the memorial during the summer season. Chances are good you'll also see Ruth Ziolkowski, too, who's in her 80s and still passionate about her family's mission. Surprisingly down-to-earth for someone leading the charge on sculpting a mountain, she still lives in the cabin she and her husband built.

There are two dramatic night blasts scheduled: one to commemorate Ruth's birthday and the Battle of the Little Bighorn in late June, and one to celebrate the death of Crazy Horse and Korczak's birthday over Labor Day weekend. There also is one during early Oct's Native American Day, a celebration of art, music, dancing, and storytelling, plus free buffalo stew. Crazy Horse is open year-round; admission is $10 per adult (children under age 6 free), $27 a carload. Off-season admission is three items for a local foodshelf.

Heading south on US 16/385, head west at *Custer* and the intersection of US 16A. It's a 13-mile trip to *Jewel Cave National Monument,* the second-longest cave in the world. The latest exploration in January 2010 brought its length up to 148 miles—most of it beneath just three square miles of land. Jewel Cave also is considered one of the prettiest caves with calcite crystals glittering along the walls. Guides will point out other formations such as moonmilk, scintillites, and hydromagnesite balloons. Prospectors discovered the cave around 1900 when they heard wind rushing through a hole in the rocks in Hell Canyon. It became part of the National Park System by 1908. There are four ways to see the cave with the easiest being a 20-minute Discovery Talk and a look at one of the larger caverns. Reservations are highly recommended for the longer tours, including an 80-minute scenic tour and the historic 105-minute Lantern Tours. If you don't mind belly crawling through a few tight spaces while wearing a hard-hat and headlamp, the Wild Caving/Spelunking Tour provides a three- to four-hour adventure that's essentially an underground obstacle course with climbing, sliding, and a chance to experience rarer parts of the cave such as feeling the wind at Hurricane Corner. Go to www.nps.gov/jeca for full details and schedules of tours and what to wear. Call (605) 673-8300 to make reservations. The visitor center and trails are open year-round, but lantern tours are only in the summer months.

Trailside Bikes

One of the best ways to see the spectacular scenery of the Black Hills is pedaling along the 114-mile George S. Mickelson Trail. It follows the historic Burlington Railroad line from Deadwood to Edgemont, putting bicyclists right in the heart of the Hills. It's easily accessed in Hill City and Custer. If you prefer a more rugged journey, the Centennial Trail spans 111 miles from Bear Butte State Park to Wind Cave National Park. You can swing into Rabbit Bikes, 175 Walnut Ave., Hill City (605-574-4302) to rent bikes of any variety.

Just west of Custer on US 16, the **National Museum of Woodcarving** celebrates the art in grand fashion. Here, visitors can see the work of nationally recognized woodcarvers and twenty-five of the nation's top caricature carvers. Sure to entertain all ages, this unique museum also features The Talking Woodcarvings, more than thirty scenes created by an original Disneyland animator. The museum is open daily May 1 through late Oct. For details call (605) 673-4404.

Heading back east on US 16, breathe in the local history at the **1881 Custer County Courthouse Museum and Bookstore,** 411 Mount Rushmore Rd. Residents and businesses have lovingly contributed pieces of the past to fill this commanding brick Italianate building. Visitors see slices of early Custer life, from artifacts of the timber and farming industries, which made the town prosper, to Victorian apparel and furnishings. On the museum grounds, printing equipment from Custer's 1879 first continuously operated newspaper and blacksmith forge and tools are on display. A self-guided tour brochure takes visitors through the expansive collections. The first stop is a room dedicated to rocks and minerals and native birds and animals, which were mounted by a local taxidermist in the 1920s. The Custer room depicts photographs of the 1874 Custer expedition when General George A. Custer entered the Black Hills. Custer hunted antelope at Fort Hays, Kansas, with the gun on display here. Custer's epaulets and a first edition of his book, *My Life on the Plains,* are also displayed. Upstairs is the courtroom with the original cherry furniture and judge's chamber. Admission is $5 for adults, $4 for seniors, $1 for students 12 and older, and free for children under 11. Open 9 a.m. to 8 p.m. Mon through Sat, and 1 to 8 p.m. Sun May to Sept (605-673-2443; www.1881courthousemuseum.com).

Custer boasts a growing number of stores and cafes, but beeline a block from the museum to 529 Mount Rushmore Rd. for the best one-stop shopping. The former hardware store became home to **Adzukibean, Surroundings,** and the **Black Hills Pie & Bistro** in 2009. Adzukibean lures kids of all ages with funky children's clothes, retro games and toys, kitchen gadgets, and tasty foods, while Surroundings tempts shoppers with women's clothing, handbags, eclectic home decor, make-you-laugh cards, and artsy jewelry. The bistro makes a great gathering spot, too, with its rock-n-roll jukebox and 1959 chrome soda fountain. They serve ice cream, of course, but also coffee, pie, Panini sandwiches, and caramel rolls. The stores are open Mon through Sat. Call (605) 673-2278 for more information.

Bison and Mammoths

East of Custer the city you'll enter **Custer State Park** (605-255-4515). At 71,000 acres, it rivals many national parks. Be prepared to spend at least a day or two here, honking through one-way tunnels, circling pigtail bridges, and admiring the amazing rock formations along the Peter Norbeck Scenic Byway.

"It's a phenomenal place to view wildlife," says Craig Pugsley, park superintendent. "It's unmatched anywhere in the U.S."

Get on the Wildlife Drive early in the morning or close to evening for the best chance to view the park's famed bison herd (one of the largest in the country), along with elk, mule deer, white-tailed deer, pronghorn antelope, burros, and coyotes roaming the prairies. Bighorn sheep and mountain goats can be spotted at the higher elevations, especially near Sylvan Lake or Blue Bell Lodge. Viewing is particularly good in the late spring when animals seek tender roadside grasses as snow melts or in the fall during breeding season. During the summer, the park is so popular its more than 300 campsites ($16–$25/night) and camper cabins ($45/night) book up. Plan ahead. Call (800) 710-2267 or go to www.campsd.com.

Entering from the west on US 16A, detour south on SD 87 for two of the park's best scenic views. You can drive up to Mount Coolidge (elevation 6,000 feet) to see the fire tower or stop at the peaceful Heddy Draw overlook for a picnic. On a sharp, blue-sky day, you can see clear to the Badlands from both. On the return to Highway 16A and heading toward Legion Lake, keep an eye out for the Badger Clark Historic Trail on the right. The **Badger Hole** was home of the state's first poet laureate, Charles Badger Clark (1883–1957), whose most popular poem is "A Cowboy's Prayer," which, incidentally, is frequently misprinted and rarely attributed to its author. After a tour of the four-room cabin where Clark spent most of his literary career, hike the trail and read his poetry at quiet stops amid the pines. The Badger Hole is open from Memorial Day to Labor Day. Hours are 10 a.m. to 5 p.m. weekdays and 1 to 4 p.m. on Sat and Sun.

The **Black Hills Playhouse** (605-255-4551), nestled in Custer State Park, offers top-drawer entertainment. You can dress up or dress down for performances, because your presence is valued much more than your attire at this nonprofit professional theater and training program. The summer troupe works, lives, eats, and breathes theater at this rustic site. A visit here can be a fun expedition for the theatergoer, especially kids who will love seeing a chipmunk scurry by or hearing soothing sounds from a nearby stream. As bucolic as this might seem, the performances are anything but homespun. The professionally trained cast and crew present five productions each summer, and the schedule can include anything from *Greater Tuna* to *Hello, Dolly!* Shows begin at 7:30 p.m. Tues through Sat with matinees on Sat and Sun at 2 p.m. Tickets are more than reasonable, ranging from $5 to $10 for kids to $15 to $23 for adults. Call (605) 255-4141 or visit www.blackhillsplayhouse.com for more information.

Buffalo Rock Lodge bed-and-breakfast sits between the playhouse and Keystone, two miles outside the state park and tucked onto Playhouse Road. Guests can enjoy a distant but clear view of Mount Rushmore while eating a hearty Western breakfast on the deck among the pines. Owners Art and Marilyn Daniels trace their family's roots in the Black Hills to Marilyn's grandfather who helped build *Custer State Park's State Game Lodge.* The fireplace, inset with a variety of local stones they've collected, provides the centerpiece of this spacious yet homey lodge. The three rooms range from $150 to $200 per night, with two large enough for families (888-564-5634; www.buffalorock.net).

A simple drive through Custer State Park can raise the adrenaline with electrifying spins around and through majestic granite spires on the brilliantly planned 14-milelong *Needles Highway.* Take your time. You'll want to pull over and drink in the views. And like the Iron Mountain Road and the rest of the 66-mile Peter Norbeck Scenic Byway, drivers aren't meant to go more than 20 mph. (In winter the Needles Highway is closed to allow snowmobiling and cross-country skiing.)

If you want to slow down the scenery even more, head to *Sylvan Lake Lodge & Resort* (605-574-2561), one of four historic lodges in the park and a hub for many of the park's best hikes. Guests can choose from cozy lodge rooms starting at $135/night or cabins that top out at $375/night for one that sleeps 10. This magnificent mountain resort overlooks Sylvan Lake and the granite outcroppings of Harney Peak. It's considered Custer State Park's crown jewel and a favorite romantic destination, attracting weddings throughout the summer and anniversary visits ever after. You'll need to book early. Call (888) 875-0001 for reservations.

Sylvan Lake was created in 1881, when Theodore Reder built a dam across Sun Gulch. By 1895 a Victorian-style hotel opened along its shores and

Custer Resorts

All of Custer State Park's resorts feel steeped in history, especially Sylvan Lake Lodge and the State Game Lodge, which has served as a summer White House. Bluebell Lodge and Legion Lake are more family and budget-oriented. Check rates and make reservations for all of them at (888) 875-0001, www.custerresorts.com.

AUTHOR'S FAVORITE HIKES

Harney Peak

Cathedral Spires

Little Devils Tower

Sunday Gulch

Roughlock Falls near Spearfish Canyon

remained popular until it burned to the ground in 1935. The current hotel opened in 1937, and the new wing was added in 1991. The hotel features cozy lodge rooms, a lobby, a lounge, and a restaurant, the Lakota Dining Room, which specializes in native game entrees and seafood and gorgeous views of Harney. If you look closely, you'll just make out the historic stone fire tower on the top.

Feeling adventurous? Hike to **Harney Peak,** which is the state's highest point at 7,242 feet and the highest elevation east of the Rockies. Be prepared, though. This 6-mile trek is a challenge and a workout. The first time I hiked it, gasping up the last set of stairs, a smiling Kansas dad with kids strapped to his chest and his back put me to shame. The second trek was easier, and both were well worth the chance to gaze across a spectacular 60-mile view of undulating forest and rocky peaks. Stand atop the historic stone fire tower to breathe in the clean, rarefied air and feel it ripple across you. Without question Harney Peak has inspired people of all faiths. When he was only nine years old, the Oglala holy man Black Elk had his first vision here. "Then I was standing on the highest mountain of them all, and round about beneath me was the whole hoop of the world," he said. Harney Peak is part of the Black Elk Wilderness.

If you head south on US 385, you will enter the wonderful wild kingdom of **Hot Springs.** This small town known for its woolly mammoths, fascinating architecture, commendable bistros, and healing springs—ranked as our three kids' favorite destination on a 2,400-mile road trip one summer. Chalk it up to mammoth bones and the fascination of exploring underground. Following US 385, you'll reach **Wind Cave National Park** before hitting city limits. Keep an eye out for the amazing urban sprawl of prairie dogs. While some consider them pests, kids will find them entertaining with their chunky, cheery shapes and social nature.

Wind Cave's claims to fame include being the nation's seventh oldest national park and the fourth-longest cave in the world with a labyrinth of levels. It also has great examples of boxwork, gridlike formations as delicate

The Black Hills Rock

My first rock-climbing experience was near the shores of Sylvan Lake in the capable hands of Daryl Stisser, who runs Hill City-based **Sylvan Rocks Climbing School** with his wife Cheryl. We were there just a few weeks after they had set up camera crews and stunt folks for the dizzying action scenes in *National Treasure 2: The Book of Secrets.*

The outfitters get their share of adrenaline junkies and people who want multiday trips and the opportunity to climb Devils Tower, but many customers are first-timers. They range in age from preschoolers to gung-ho grannies.

"Most of climbing is from the neck up. It's achievable by many, many people," Stisser says. "And it's very empowering."

The Hills also are ideal for beginners because the rocks are easy to reach with tapering summits that let you power a climb with leg muscles and balance rather than upper body strength.

We learned quickly to scrutinize granite grays for tiny toe holds and bits of quartz and feldspar to gratefully grab onto as we ascended. It was an amazing experience: scary, exhilarating, and surprisingly satisfying to be standing high above ground surrounded by the gentle whoosh of pines. You can find more information about Sylvan Rocks Climbing School & Guide Service at (605) 484-7585 or www.sylvanrocks. com or stop by the Hill City outdoors store, Granite Sports (605-574-2121), on Main Street.

as potato chips on the ceiling. Popcorn and frostwork formations also can be seen. Visitors can choose from five different tours. Each highlights different sections of the cave and ranges from an easy quick look to lantern tours and a four-hour wild caving adventure. The tours require admission, but there is no fee to enter the park and explore the several hiking trails threading through the 28,000-acre wildlife preserve above ground. Look for bison, antelope, elk, and deer roaming the grassland and forests (605-745-4600; www.nps.gov/wica).

In the late 1800s Hot Springs and its mineral springs attracted trainloads of wealthy visitors who sought the therapeutic benefits of "healing water." Although springs continue to flow up through the pebble bottom of *Evan's Plunge* at 1145 North River St., the focus here is more on fun. Admission is $9–$11. Call (605) 745-5165 or go to www.evansplunge.com for hours.

If you want more of a healing and pampered experience, head to the historic downtown with its thirty-nine Romanesque revival sandstone buildings in soft shades of pink, tan, and red. It's a beautiful setting tucked along the bluff and Fall River and a great location for the *Red Rock River Resort,* a four-story hotel and spa at 603 North River St. Rooms are decorated in earth tones, and beds heaped with down comforters. Minnekahta Spa, open to hotel guests and day visitors, offers a full menu of massages. There is even one for kids. Hotel and spa packages, which run from $95 to $165 a night, include full use of the spa with its whirlpool, tea room, and Norwegian spruce sauna. If you still haven't reached that limp noodle nirvana, you can sprawl out in the Korean style heat rooms, including one with a four-inch layer of Cheyenne River sand heated to 115–120 degrees (888-306-8921; www.redrockriverresort.com).

History buffs in will enjoy the **Fall River County Historical Museum** at 300 North River St. in a 1893 building that was once a school. Admission is free. The museum is open 9 a.m. to 5 p.m. Mon through Sat May 15 to Oct. 15 (605-745-5147; www.pioneer-museum.com).

A Dakota Dream Bed & Breakfast is a four-story octagonal bed-and-breakfast that sits high on a bluff at 801 Almond St. overlooking Hot Springs. The beautiful home, established in 1891, is listed on the National Register of Historic Places.

Fine furnishings and antiques beautifully appoint this 1891 bed-and-breakfast, which features spectacular panoramic views of Hot Springs, its town, the rugged canyons, and pine-covered hills. This site was selected in 1891 as the location of the **Sioux City Gentleman's Gaming Club.** This exclusive club had several elegant suites and featured a two-story octagonal great room, topped with the Gentleman's Poker Room. In the 1920s, Chicago multimillionaire F. O. Butler purchased the property and converted it into a guesthouse for his affluent friends. In 1990, the house was totally renovated and opened as a bed-and-breakfast. The inn has six bedrooms, each with a queen-size bed and private bath. For information call (605) 745-4633 or visit www.adakotadream.com.

The Other Black Hills

Ninety percent of the Black Hills are in South Dakota, but the mountains also grace Wyoming for 10 to 40 miles. Even though they cross the South Dakota state line, the towns of Devils Tower, Hulett, Upton, Newcastle, and Sundance are very much part of the Black Hills community.

The Wyoming segment of the Black Hills includes a distinct branch known as the Bear Lodge. This is the site of the nation's first national monument, Devils Tower. The tower is actually a solitary, stump-shaped igneous rock formation that looms 1,267 feet above the Belle Fourche River in northeastern Wyoming like a skyscraper against the rural landscape. The tower is popular with rock climbers and movie makers. Devils Tower was a location for Close Encounters of the Third Kind.

Hot Springs' biggest attraction is mammoth in every sense of the word. More than 26,000 years ago, more than 100 mammoths were trapped and died in a sinkhole on the town's southeastern edge. Mark the **Mammoth Site** as a must-see on your Dakota travel agenda. It was built atop the excavation, which began when a 1974 housing project uncovered the white bones and tusks. Visitors can walk around this mass graveyard and see paleontologists still at work excavating bones or preparing bones and casts in a downstairs laboratory. There also is a great museum with bones of other prehistoric creatures such as camels, short-faced bears, antelope, gray wolf, minks, white-tailed prairie dogs, and frogs. The Mammoth Site is the only *in situ* (bones left as found) display of fossil mammoths in the United States. It's especially exciting for kids ages 4 to 13, who can sign up for the Junior Paleontology program June 1 to Aug 15. The 1- to 1½-hour program lets them experience a simulated dig, excavating casts of different mammoth bones and then trying to identify them. You'll never see a group of kids concentrating this hard and being this quiet anywhere. Digs are popular and limited to 16 participants, so reservations are highly recommended. Younger children can do a free dig in the visitor center, using brushes to sweep away sand from casts of mammoth teeth, which look a lot like the bottom of sneakers. The site is open daily 8 a.m. to 8 p.m. daily in summer, 8 a.m. to 5 p.m. daily Sept and Oct, 9 a.m. to 3:30 p.m. Mon through Sat, and 11 a.m. to 3:30 p.m. Sun Nov through Feb, and 8 a.m. to 5 p.m. daily Mar 1 through May 14. Call (605) 745-6017 or go to www.mammothsite.com for more information.

See the Dakota prairie as it must have looked 300 years ago at the **Black Hills Wild Horse Sanctuary.** More than 500 wild horses roam free at this 11,000-acre private wilderness area. Two-hour guided bus tours are offered twice a day from May 1 through May 31 and Sept 1 through Oct 31. Three tours are offered daily June 1 through Aug 31 at 9 a.m., 11 a.m., 1 p.m., and 3 p.m. Closed Sun. Prices are $50 for adults, $45 for senior citizens, $15 for teens, and $7.50 for children 5 to 12. Other options: a three-hour cross-country tour that's $100 per adult and $75 per child, or the new four-hour photography tour for $250 per person.

In addition to viewing the mustangs, visitors will also see 10,000-year-old Indian petroglyphs, an authentic Native American Sun Dance site, and the movie sets for Ted Turner's classic, *Crazy Horse* (1996) and Disney's *Hidalgo* (2003).

For the serious lover of wild horses, the six-hour adventure tour takes no more than three guests at a time in a four-wheel-drive vehicle along steep, primitive roads and across the dark waters of the Cheyenne before reaching a part of the sanctuary simply known as Up-Top. Adventure Tour is a remarkable opportunity to meet some of the wildest and most beautiful animals at the sanctuary. Travel through wild horse herds, and then have a picnic lunch overlooking a spectacular canyon. The six-hour tour is $750 for one to three people.

From Hot Springs, take SD 71 South and turn right, just past the Cheyenne River Bridge. For more information call (800) 252-6652 or visit www.wild mustangs.com.

If cruising the Southern Hills in pursuit of wild mustangs and woolly mammoths leaves you feeling understandably parched and/or famished, then definitely stop by the *FlatIron Coffee Bar & Guest Suites,* 745 North River St.). This joint has definitely taken the architectural splendor of the building to flattering heights. The first floor has a dining area and lounge, while the second floor boasts four wonderfully prepared guest suites. Rates range from $85 to $175. It's a favorite place for locals, too, with creative casual food and fun with themed entrees each weekend when it shows movies. Even better is the chance to sit outside, where they often have live music in this charming setting on balmy summer evenings. For more information, call (605) 745-5301 or go to www.flatiron.bz.

You wouldn't think that there would be much difference between north and south in the Black Hills; after all, we're not talking about the state of the Union, but a small area in the grand scheme of things. The Northern Hills, however, are distinct from the Southern Hills. The Northern Hills area is more entrenched in tourism and not surprisingly turns a lot colder and snow-covered in the winter. If you take I-90 west from Rapid City, you'll be on your way to an all-seasons wonderland. Sometimes half the fun is getting there, so don't be in a hurry—this stretch of Interstate has lots to offer.

Bikers and a Butte

Even if you're not into motorcycles, the mass of people and machinery that roll through the Hills during the legendary *Sturgis Motorcycle Rally* presents a spectacle like no other. It's a full-blown, hard-core party during the first full week of Aug, drawing more than 600,000 people and vendors. The agenda can include anything from AA meetings and Miss Buffalo Chip Beauty Pageants to wine tastings, Harley shows, and live bands. The rally attracts weekend warriors and biker gangs such as the Bandidos, and fuels a few romances as well. In peak years, local officials have issued close to 200 marriage licenses during the rally. Naturally, the legendary event attracts its share of celebrities, too. Peter Fonda, Emilio Estevez, Mickey Rourke, and Neil Diamond are just a handful of the rich and famous cruising into *Sturgis* for this festival of chrome, leather, and heavy-metal thunder.

J. C. "Pappy" Hoel, probably never pictured this when he started the Sturgis Rally in 1938 with only nine races and a less-than-capacity grandstand crowd. Sturgis, fortunately, has learned to handle the crowds that are far beyond its population of only 6,442 residents. There are thousands of campsites available for the event, but anyone planning to travel through the Black Hills that week in Aug will need to make lodging reservations well in advance and be prepared to hear engines rumbling and echoing through tunnels and along scenic byways.

For information about the rally, call (605) 720-0800 or visit www.sturgis motorcyclerally.com.

You can sample the spirit of the rally without the mania year-round at *Sturgis Motorcycle Museum & Hall of Fame.* Located at 999 Main St., it displays rally memorabilia, antique motorcycles, and bikes that are just plain unique. Admission is $5; (605) 347-2001; www.sturgismuseum.com.

If you prefer a quieter event and love classic cars, time your visit with the Black Hills Overdrive in June when a parade of colorful classic cars, hot rods, and trucks wind through the hills (605-430-8223; www.bhoverdrive.com).

The normally quiet community of Sturgis also is home to *Fort Meade Museum & Old Post Cemetery,* located 1 mile east of Sturgis on SD 34. Fort Meade was built in the shadows of the majestic Bear Butte, a landmark that made it possible for early-day travelers to find the fort. Cavalry and infantry stationed here were assigned to keep the peace in those turbulent years, and so the fort gained the nickname "The Peacekeeper Fort." The site is open daily 9 a.m. to 5 p.m. Memorial Day through Labor Day. Admission is $4 for anyone 12 and older.

OTHER ATTRACTIONS WORTH SEEING IN WESTERN SOUTH DAKOTA

Broken Boot Gold Mine
Deadwood

Fife & Drum Corps Concerts
Main Street in Hill City
(free performances every Mon evening
Memorial Day through Labor Day)

Li'l Nashville Dinner Theatre
Custer

Old Style Saloon No. 10
Deadwood

Parade of Presidents Wax Museum
Keystone

Reptile Gardens
Rapid City

Springs Bath House
Hill City

The Fort Meade Back country Byway winds between Fort Meade near SD 34 and the Black Hills National Cemetery near exit 34 on I-90.

Colonel Samuel D. Sturgis, a Union general during the Civil War, was commander of the Seventh Cavalry and the first permanent post commander at Fort Meade. He was a member of the company that founded the nearby town that bears his name. It was at Fort Meade that "The Star Spangled Banner" was first ordered to be part of the evening military retreat ceremony, long before it became the national anthem.

The Bureau of Land Management manages approximately 6,700 acres of the former Fort Meade Military Reservation, now the Fort Meade Recreation Area. Approximately one-third of this area is on the National Register of Historic Places, due to the numerous historical sites at Fort Meade, mostly remnants of early cavalry life, and the post cemetery. The area accommodates grazing, forestry, wildlife, and a variety of recreational uses that include camping, picnicking, horseback riding, and hiking. The 110-mile multiuse Centennial Trail also winds through this area.

Mato paha (bear mountain) is the name the Indians gave what is now **Bear Butte State Park** (605-347-5240), an outstanding geological formation located 6 miles northeast of Sturgis. Artifacts from 10,000 years ago have been found here, the volcanic laccolith is still used today by Native Americans for religious ceremonies and vision quests. Visitors are asked not to disturb the bits of cloth and offerings of tobacco that have been left on trees in prayer. An easy hike will take you around Bear Butte Lake while the Summit Trail offers more of a challenge. The reward for climbing the summit and gaining about 1,000 feet in elevation is an expansive view of four states. The park is open year-round, but the visitor center is open 9 a.m. to 5 p.m. May 1 through mid-Sept. Because of its natural and historical significance, Bear Butte was designated a National Natural Landmark in 1965.

The abundant snowfall in the Northern Black Hills makes it a veritable mecca for winter sports. Snowmobiling, cross-country skiing, and downhill skiing are popular choices, but gambling, theater, and a good choice of restaurants provide entertainment year-round.

Ghost towns are a common theme in the Black Hills, but **Mystic** is one that still exists in an authentic, noncommercial manner, thanks to the pristine forest that surrounds and protects its remote location (9 miles off US 385, south of Lead–Deadwood; take the Rochford turnoff next to Trout Haven). Originally named Sitting Bull, the town was populated by miners, loggers, and railroaders hell-bent on profiting from the area's natural wealth. Today visitors can enjoy beautiful hiking and biking areas.

Eighteen miles northwest of Sturgis, **Spearfish's** downtown district is bustling with the passion of local businesspeople who still believe that Main Street is vital to a small-town economy. Where else could you find dress shops, thoughtfully planned gift shops, and an opera house, all within the expanse of three city blocks?

The **High Plains Heritage Center Museum,** a five-state regional museum honors old west pioneers with art and artifacts from North and South Dakota, Montana, Wyoming, and Nebraska. Outdoor displays include antique implements, a log cabin, a sod dugout, a one-room schoolhouse, live buffalo, longhorns, miniature horses, and an original Spearfish-to-Deadwood stage-coach. You can hear cowboy poetry and music in the 200-seat theater with a view of three states from the upper balcony. The museum is open year-round 9 a.m. to 5 p.m. The center is located at 825 Heritage Dr., off I-90 at exit 14 (605-642-9378; www.westernheritagecenter.com).

Back in downtown Spearfish (population 12,000), you can visit the **Matthews Opera House** at 614 Main St. The opera house was built in 1906, and although it sometimes veered from its original intent (it was once a dance hall), Spearfish residents returned it to its original charm. Summer community theater performances and concerts at the 250-seat opera house draw audiences from throughout the Hills. Productions always have strong support from the college theater department. For a complete schedule of performances and art events, call (605) 642-7973 or visit www.spearfishartscenter.org.

There are women's fashions for every taste in Spearfish, and if you like a little flash, upscale labels, or just denim and lace, stop by **Kathleen's Boutique** (605-642-3843) at 622 Main St. and see what fine fashions the shop carries.

Once you open the antique door to the **Bay Leaf Cafe** (126 West Hudson; 605-642-5462), you've also entered one of the most refreshing eateries around. Serene and sensitive describe the ambience of the cafe and the attitude of its staff. First, they've put together a healthful menu that tastes good, too. Second, they've made reading the menu fun. Each entree is described in detail and with good humor. A list explains what the more exotic foods are, like seitan, hummus, and tabbouleh. You can also whet your appetite with such local delicacies as buffalo, elk, or trout. The cafe is open for lunch and dinner.

For a place to toss a Frisbee, enjoy a steak hot off the grill, or just relax, **Spearfish City Park,** earns its role as one of the most beloved parks in the Northern Hills. Walk across the footbridge over Spearfish Creek and discover the **D. C. Booth Historic National Fish Hatchery and Archives** (considered the premier facility of its kind). It introduced trout to the Black Hills and had coordinated all federal fisheries in the United States at one point. The underwater viewing area lets you watch rainbow and brown trout as they peacefully swim through

One Tough Horse

Tipperary was a bucking bronc who achieved fame along the rodeo circuit, and his name still remains a common and revered word for most Dakota rodeo folk. Born more than seventy years ago, no one knows what set Tipperary off on his one-horse campaign to rid the world of rodeo riders. Tales of Tipperary's vicious bucking and lightning speed spread through the West like wildfire. The legend grew to the point that cowboys refused to ride him, even though a handsome purse awaited the brave cowboy who could master this wild beast. Few managed the feat, and once he had passed his prime, Tipperary spent his golden years in the pastures near Buffalo. Today, what could be the only monument erected in honor of a bucking bronc reads: tipperary . . . WORLD'S GREATEST BUCKING HORSE.

the water. Hatchery tours run daily from 9 a.m. to 5 p.m. mid-May through mid-Sept. The museum and grounds, including the historic Booth House where the superintendent lived, are open year-round. It's a must-see place for families, especially with the free admission (605-642-7730; www.fws.gov/dcbooth).

Sanford's Grub & Pub (545 West Jackson Blvd.; 605-642-3204) is modeled after the junkyard theme of the popular 1970s TV sitcom, *Sanford and Son*. No matter how many times you eat here, you'll notice something else hanging on the wall—or from the ceiling. Sheet music and a military uniform are tacked to the ceiling, an interesting collage but totally unrelated to the car theme on the back wall. When Sanford's first opened, word spread quickly of its amazing sandwiches and pasta dishes. Folks rave about the Freddies: thickly sliced potatoes dipped in buttermilk and seasonings, then fried. Served with a side of sour cream, these potatoes are a match for the venerable french fry. The beer list is one of the most extensive in the state. They have a location in Rapid City, too.

A 1.7-mile detour southwest of Spearfish is worth it to see the exciting talent of Spearfish artist Dick Termes, who paints artwork on spheres and will graciously explain to visitors the amazing mathematical process he uses. The *Termesphere Gallery* is at 1920 Christensen Dr. (605-642-4805; www.terme spheres.com). If you take US 14A, you'll cruise through Spearfish Canyon, along the 19-mile designated National Scenic Byway. It's not only one of the prettiest, but one of the least crowded ones in the Hills. Peak time to go is fall when the vibrant gold of birch and aspen look most striking against the dark green of pine and spruce and the earth tones of the steep canyon walls. Colors usually peak around mid-Oct.

Thirteen miles south of Spearfish on US 14A, *Spearfish Canyon Lodge* provides top-of-the-line accommodations in the heart of the canyon. Rates start at $109 in winter and $139 in summer. Suites start at $199. The lodge's Latch-string Inn Restaurant & Lounge serves meals on the veranda, where the fresh scent of pine trees can be intoxicating (800-975-6343; www.spfcanyon.com).

Crow Peak Trails are designed to allow access to the top of Crow Peak and the north end of Beaver Ridge. The Spearfish Ranger District has a bro-chure and a map that outlines the different trails. Call (605) 642-4622 for infor-mation, or pick up a brochure at the information center. Crow Peak is a key landmark in the Northern Hills. The name Crow Peak is the English translation of the Sioux name for the peak, *Paha Karitukateyapi,* which means "the hill where the Crows were killed." It is located 7 miles southwest of Spearfish on Forest Developed Road (FDR) 214, also known as Higgins Gulch Road.

About 14 miles southeast of Spearfish on US 85, ***Deadwood*** buzzes with the colors and energy of a mini Las Vegas with 26 casinos and gaming halls and constant sound of slot machines ringing over and over. Gambling goes back more than 100 years when it helped the town flourish during the Gold Rush. Deadwood's residents (currently 1,282 of them) have seen their share of ups and downs. The town was wiped out three times in the 1880s, twice by fire and once by flood. It appeared that Deadwood's destiny was forever tied to sad times and a sad economy, until gambling came back when the state voted to allow $5 bets in 1989. They've since increased those bets to $100. It was an appropriate decision for Deadwood, because the economic rejuvena-tion helped restore many of Deadwood's Victorian buildings to their historic grandeur and several of the main thoroughfares have been repaved with brick. New buildings and businesses cropped up and continue to do so as business-people capitalize on the stream of people—and money—that gambling and its support industries bring to Deadwood. Fortunately, the bordellos didn't make a comeback. Prostitution was commonly practiced and acknowledged in Dead-wood until the industry was shut down in the 1970s.

Take a Trolley

One of the best ways to get around in Deadwood is to take the trolley that runs at regular intervals between the hotels, motels, and key points throughout Deadwood. The cost is $1 per person. The schedule is posted on the back of the Main Street Trolley signs. During the summer, from Memorial Day to mid-Sept, the hours of operation are 7 a.m. to 1:30 a.m. Sun through Thurs and from 7 a.m. to 3 a.m. Fri and Sat. Winter hours are from 8 a.m. to midnight Sun through Thurs, and 7 a.m. to 3 a.m. Fri and Sat.

Kevin Costner fans will love the **Midnight Star,** a casino owned by him and his brother, Dan. It's decorated with many costumes and props from his film career—from his never-seen role as the dead friend in *The Big Chill* to the epic filmed-in-South-Dakota *Dances with Wolves*. An elevator sweeps you to the top of the Midnight Star and opens into **Jakes** (800-999-6482), one of the most impressive restaurants in the Black Hills. The atmosphere is refined, and if you didn't know otherwise, you'd swear you were in New York City rather than Deadwood's Main Street. Both the food and service merit the same high accolades. Jake's has consistently received the prestigious AAA Four Diamond Award and *Wine Spectator* "Award of Excellence." It is one of the most romantic settings for dinner in the Black Hills.

More moderate prices are on the menu at **Diamond Lil's Bar and Grill** (605-578-3550). Here the Costners have given their favorite sandwiches and appetizers unique names—those of their family, friends, and favorite movie characters. The main level houses the casino (www.themidnightstar.com). Other casinos have matched the Costners' atmosphere with style and many perks for the gambler. You might get free drinks here or hors d'oeuvres there. It's all fun in the name of the game.

The majestic **Silverado Franklin Historic Hotel & Gaming Complex,** at 709 Main St., has a lot of history to bet on. The 1903, eighty-one-room Franklin hotel has been the choice of stars, including luminaries such as President William Taft, President Theodore Roosevelt, John Wayne, Buffalo Bill, Babe Ruth, Pearl Buck, Robert Kennedy Jr., and Mary Hart (a South Dakota girl, too). Call (605) 578-3670 or (800) 584-7005; www.silveradofranklin.com.

You can learn all about Deadwood's legendary past with gambling and brothels and larger-than-life characters such as Wild Bill Hickok and Calamity Jane at the fascinating **Adams Memorial Museum,** 54 Sherman St. There's something here to interest everyone with three levels of artifacts, including a rare plesiosaur dinosaur, folk art, vintage photographs and the museum's famous Potato Creek Johnny's gold nugget. At 7¾ troy ounces, the nugget ranks as one of the largest ever found in the Black Hills. It was recovered from a sluice on Potato Creek in western Lawrence County in May 1929. The massive chunk of gold was tucked away from public view until 1995, when it was on public display for two days to celebrate the museum's 65th anniversary. It now is safely back in the bank, and a replica of the nugget is on display. The museum is open year-round. Admission is free, but donations are suggested ($5 for adults; $2 per child 10 and under). It's open from 9 a.m. to 5 p.m. daily May 1 to Sept. 30, 10 a.m. to 4 p.m. Tues through Sat the rest of the year. Call (605) 578-1714 or visit www.adamsmuseumandhouse.org for hours.

The home of the museum's founder, W. E. Adams, also has been restored and opened as a museum. The city of Deadwood invested $1.5 million into returning the Victorian Queen-Anne-style home at 22 Van Buren St. to its earlier grandeur. It sits in the so-called presidential neighborhood of Deadwood.

Admission to the **Historic Adams House** tour is $5 for adults, $2 for children 12 and under, and free to members. Adams House hours are 9 a.m. to 5 p.m. May 1 to Sept. 30, and 10 a.m. to 4 p.m. Tues through Sat the rest of the year. The Deadwood Historic Preservation Commission also has opened the **Homestake Adams Research and Cultural Center** at 150 Sherman St. (605-920-8444).

When you're in this residential area, you can see how Deadwood feels like a sliver of San Francisco with its steep streets and historic homes. If you follow Lincoln Street uphill, you'll arrive at **Mount Moriah Cemetery,** the final resting spot for some of the Old West's biggest legends, including Wild Bill Hickok, Calamity Jane, and Potato Creek Johnny. Also buried at Mount Moriah, with her parrot and her husband, is madam Dora DuFran, Calamity Jane's gal pal. Dora ran brothels in the Black Hills in the 1920s and 1930s but was known for her humanitarian work as well. Melanie Griffith portrayed Dora in the 1995 made-for-TV movie *Buffalo Girls*.

One mile north of Deadwood on US 85 is **Tatanka: Story of the Bison.** Its centerpiece is the stunning, larger-than-life bronze sculpture by local artist Peggy Detmers, featuring fourteen bison being pursued by three Native American horseback riders. The Educational Center depicts the relationship between the bison and the Plains Indians through interactive exhibits and traditional Native American displays. Tepees, cultural demonstrations, storytelling, and music offer a snapshot of Indian life during the height of the Buffalo Culture—around 1840. Kevin Costner, who starred in and directed *Dances with Wolves,* founded the attraction, noting that the Black Hills gave him the feeling that he was part of history. Admission is $7.50 for adults, $6.50 for seniors, and $5.50 for kids age 6 to 11. For more information, call (605) 584-5678 or visit www .storyofthebison.com.

Just a few miles from Deadwood is **Lead,** Deadwood's sister city. After seeing the glitzy Deadwood, Lead might look much more bare bones, but you can find eateries, galleries, antique stores, and the Homestake Opera House. Mining was once the mighty force in this town until operations ceased in 2001. You can imagine the glory days, though, with a trip to the **Homestake Gold Mine Visitor Center** to see the largest, deepest, and oldest underground gold mine in the Western Hemisphere. Founded in 1876 by three California investors, including George Hearst, the Homestake mine extends 8,000 feet below the surface of the Black Hills. In addition to the underground mine, Homestake

Deadwood: The HBO Version

If you want to see a TV version of Deadwood that is far grittier than most fictional accounts of the town, then be sure to check out the HBO series *Deadwood*. The set looks like Deadwood, but it is actually a $5 million replica on the Gene Autry ranch in California.

The series captures life in Deadwood in 1876, just two weeks after Custer's Last Stand. The settlers, ranging from an ex-lawman to a scheming saloon owner to the legendary Wild Bill Hickok and Calamity Jane, share a restless spirit as they struggle to survive in this frontier town. The Emmy Award–winning show is not for the faint-hearted. There is an ample amount of profanity, nudity, and violence, and yet the show is mesmerizing. You can rent the show by season on DVD and easily watch four episodes in one night. Kudos to creator David Milch and an exemplary cast, including Timothy Olyphant, Ian McShane, Powers Boothe, and Keith Carradine.

operated the Open Cut surface mine, which was the original site of the Homestake claim. You can tour the Homestake May through Sept. The one-hour guided bus tour goes through the town of Lead before heading underground, taking a peek at surface operations and viewing the 1876 open-cut mine. Guides explain new and old mining technology, and you can learn more about the hoisting, crushing, and milling of gold-bearing ore. After the tour is finished, you will receive a sample of ore that was drilled from the ***Homestake Gold Mine.*** Tours are $6 for adults, $5.25 for seniors, $5 for students, and free for children 5 and under. There's also a $20 family rate (605-584-3110; www .homestakevisitorcenter.com).

For more on the history of mining, the ***Black Hills Mining Museum*** (605-584-1605) takes a detailed look at mining activity in the Hills during the past 120 years. The nonprofit educational corporation is dedicated to the preservation of the rich mining heritage of the Black Hills. In fact, you can take a fascinating tour of a simulated underground level of the Homestake Gold Mine. Count on realism—the simulation was created by more than 140 miners and former mine employees.

Open seven days a week during the summer, the museum is at 323 West Main St. For more information, visit the Web site at www.mining-museum .blackhills.com.

Mystic Miner Ski Resort at Deer Mountain and ***Terry Peak Ski Resort*** on Lead's southwestern edge take advantage of the 7,000-foot-plus elevation for thrills and maximum snowfall. You'll find 1,200-foot vertical drops, moguls, and snowboarding terrain with jumps, bumps, rails, and half-pipes. There also are plenty of runs gentle enough for beginning and intermediate skiers. For more information on ski packages, sleigh rides, and tubing, call Mystic Miner at (605) 645-6747 or go to www.skimystic.com. Terry Peak can be reached at (605) 584-2165 or www.terrypeak.com.

Twenty-one miles south of Lead and Deadwood on US 85 you'll find **Trailshead Lodge,** the most popular pit stop for the snowmobilers. They whoosh through powdery snow, wind through deep canyons, and weave through pines on roughly 350 miles of trails throughout the 1.3-acre Black Hills National Forest. It's little wonder *Snow Goer* magazine ranks the Black Hills among the top places to sled in the United States. Trailshead Lodge offers a convenient stopping point for gas, food, lodging, and a chance to thaw out as needed (605-584-3464; www.trailsheadlodge.com). You can rent snowmobiles here and at other resorts, including **Spearfish Canyon Lodge** (877-975-6343; www.spfcanyon.com), **Deadwood Gulch Resort** (800-695-1876; www.dead woodgulch.com) and **Recreational Springs Resort** (877-584-1228; www .recsprings.com). Deadwood, Lead, and Spearfish tend to be the winter hub for snowmobiling because the higher elevations often accumulate a four-foot snow pack. Snow and trail conditions are continually updated through the Sno-Wats phone line; (800) 445-3474.

If you prefer quieter winter sports, cross-country skiers and snowshoe enthusiasts will find close to 60 miles of trails to explore, along with national forest lakes for ice-fishing and several open-water where fly-fishing is practiced year-round by anyone willing to tolerate the cold for a few good trout.

Points Northwest

The northwestern corner of South Dakota is not as familiar as the Black Hills (even to South Dakotans), but this is a perfect place to get away from it all. Tiny towns occasionally crop up on the plains landscape here, with winsome names such as Promise, Bison, Prairie City, Meadow, Buffalo, and Faith, which gained notoriety when a Tyrannosaurs rex named Sue was found there. Names reflect the ranching spirit and determination of early settlers. This is a place where people tip their hats to fellow drivers, give a friendly finger wave from the steering wheel, or offer a full-blown wave out the window as you pass on the rural roads. These are gestures of warmth you'll never see in a big city. Folks assume they know you, or your kids, parents, employer—you get the idea. The degrees of separation are mighty thin in these big open spaces. It's a fine welcome, no matter how it's delivered.

If you take US 85 north 9 miles from Spearfish, you'll find the Western panorama of **Belle Fourche.** It means "pretty fork," honoring the confluence of the Belle Fourche and Redwater rivers. Dakotans, by the way, say *Bell Foosh*. The town of 4,900 people has two claims to fame. First, there's an official marker and a sheepherder's monument called a "Stone Johnnie" that mark the town's distinction as the geographical center of the United States (according to a U.S. Coast and Geodetic Survey). Second, is its ranching and cowboy culture. During its profitable era of big cattle drives from the late 1800s through the last roundup in 1902, the region attracted such notables as Butch Cassidy and the Sundance Kid. At the turn of the century, Belle Fourche became known as the largest cattle-shipping point in the world. Today the town claims the largest concentration of sheep in the United States and ships more wool from its warehouses than any other city.

You can join in on the community's rough-and-tumble spirit July 3–5 each summer for the annual **Black Hills Roundup Rodeo,** with fireworks, a carnival, and a historic parade. First held in 1918, this rodeo still attracts top Professional Rodeo Cowboy Association (PRCA) bull riders, bareback bronc riders, steer wrestlers, and other cowboys. Indeed, many Pro Rodeo athletes call Belle Fourche their home, including four-time World Bareback Riding Champion Marvin Garrett.

A handsome addition to the town's tourism offerings is the 4,000-square-foot **Tri-State Museum** (415 Fifth Ave.), which focuses on the early pioneer, rodeo, and Old West history of Western South Dakota, Eastern Wyoming, and Southeast Montana. The museum houses more than 5,000 artifacts, rodeo memorabilia, historical records, antiques, collectibles, fossils, and an 1876 cabin. For more information, visit the Web site at www.thetristatemuseum.com.

Just 9 miles east of Belle Fourche, **Orman Dam** makes a fabulous playground for the water-skiing, boating, camping, fishing, or swimming enthusiast. The yearly Fourth of July fireworks display, too, is legendary, and the surrounding prairies make for the perfect patriotic backdrop.

The world's largest earthen dam, Orman Dam was constructed with the use of horses around the turn of the 20th century to provide irrigation for a huge tract of sugar-beet farms downstream. Although corn, small grains, and alfalfa now dominate the agricultural scene, Orman Dam remains the area's primary dry-season water source. And there is plenty of water to go around: Orman has 185,000 acre-feet of water and 52 miles of shoreline with 13 square miles of water surface.

Continue on US 85 north, and you'll drive through cattle country, where one-pony towns like Redig and Ludlow can be missed with the blink of an eye. The sanctity of space keeps travelers mindful.

Historical landmarks like **Crow Buttes** crop up occasionally and offer interesting tidbits on the fascinating saga of the frontier. Located in Harding

County, Crow Buttes was the scene of a battle between Crow and Sioux Indians during the summer of 1822. Sioux men ravaged the Crow camp, destroying it and raping the women. Warfare ensued. The Crow warriors left the women, children, and older people at Sand Creek, north of the buttes, fleeing for a better vantage point on top of the Crow Buttes. The Sioux chased them. The Crow had no water with them, and no rain fell to soothe the sultry weather. The Sioux circled Crow Buttes and waited patiently for the trapped Crow to die from thirst. Subsequently, the nearby Canyon of Skulls to the northwest was filled with skeletons of the Sioux, who died en masse after contracting a fever from the Crow Indians.

Just before the town of Buffalo, take SD 20 east to find one of the best-kept secrets in South Dakota. Long before he became president, Theodore Roosevelt hunted bear in the region now known as *Custer National Forest.* (He later established forest reserves in the Cave Hills and Slim Buttes areas.) Custer National Forest is probably the most forgotten forest in the state. Even natives have a puzzled look on their faces when it's mentioned, which is understandable; there's Custer State Park to the southeast, so another Custer moniker seems at first repetitious, but that does not detract from the beauty of this rustic area.

The 73,000 timbered acres in the northwestern part of the state are anomalous to the barren, outlying landscape. Ride and hike, but don't expect a guide or user-friendly visitor center to take you by the hand. You're in the deep forest now, and there are no designated hiking trails.

The Cave Hills section of the forest was once a popular hiding place for outlaws. Ludlow Cave, the largest of the caves, sheltered many bandits during the stormy days of the Dakota Territory. Accordingly, ranchers have called this rugged, rough land the "jumping-off spot."

East of the Cave Hills lies the Slim Buttes section of forest, where lofty cliffs of limestone are split by dramatic canyons. The Slim Buttes battlefield is nearby, where Sioux veterans of the Custer battle were overtaken by the U.S. Cavalry. The Sioux were taken by surprise in the fall of 1876, but they took shelter high in the hills behind the limestone outcroppings and escaped during the night.

Stay east on SD 20 and you'll eventually run into SD 73. Take SD 73 north, and you'll inch your way toward literature and legend.

The first suggested stop on this stretch of highway is *Shadehill Recreation Area* (605-374-5114), one of South Dakota's largest reservoirs with 5,000 surface acre. In addition to the customary sporting opportunities one expects, the reservoir also boasts an intriguing historical marker on the southern shore. The marker describes the legend of Hugh Glass, who survived incredible odds and inspired the book *Lord Grizzly* by Frederick Manfred. In 1823, at the fork of the Grand River, Glass was hunting with the Ashley fur party when he was attacked by a grizzly bear. Horribly maimed, he could not be moved. Two members of the Ashley party were instructed to stay with him, but instead they took Glass's weapons and left him for dead. Amazingly, Glass survived on berries and buffalo meat acquired after driving away two wolves from a downed calf. Glass eventually crawled about 190 miles to Fort Kiowa on the Missouri River. Also in the area, the marking left by Custer's 7th Cavalry can be seen on a butte at Shadehill Reservoir.

Lemmon, just 12 miles north on the South Dakota–North Dakota border, is the home of Kathleen Norris, another fine contemporary writer from the state. She captured the essence of small-town life in *Dakota: A Spiritual Geography.* Her collection of poetry, *Little Girls in Church,* also speaks from the heart. Other excellent writers of western South Dakota include Linda Hasselstrom, Virginia Driving Hawk Sneve, and Dan O'Brien.

Also writing his way into the annals of history—and by different means—was Ed Lemmon, for whom the town was named. He was one of the first South Dakotans inducted into the prestigious National Cowboy Hall of Fame.

The Lemmon **Petrified Wood Park and Museum,** located at 500 Main Ave., five blocks north of US 12, has been around since the early 1930s when Lemmon men under the command of Ole S. Quammen put together this bizarre, yet intriguing blend of petrified wood and fossil sculptures across a city block. It was a labor of love for some and a necessity for others who were unemployed and depended on the project for sustenance during its construction. You can explore the 300-ton castle, a wishing well, a waterfall, and petrified wood cones up to 20 feet. You can envision trolls, or at least gnomes, feeling quite at home in this otherworldly place. The Lemmon Pioneer Museum also was built with petrified wood. It's open Memorial Day through Labor Day 9 a.m. to 5 p.m. Mon through Sat, and 10 a.m. to 6 p.m. Sun (605-374-3964). The **Grand River Museum** at 114 Tenth St. W features displays on ranching, Native Americans, and homesteaders, along with dinosaur fossils. The fossils, in particular, are fitting with the famous Hell's Creek formation in northwestern South Dakota. A Tyrannosaurus rex named Sue, who was found in Faith, straight south of Lemmon, is the area's most famous discovery and has a permanent home at Chicago's Field Museum. The museum is open 10 a.m. to 5 p.m. daily. For more information call (605) 374-3911 or go to www .grandrivermuseum.org.

Where to Stay in Western South Dakota

BELLE FOURCHE

Candlelight Bed & Breakfast
819 Fifth Ave. (US 85)
(800) 469-4568
Moderate

CUSTER

Best Western Buffalo Ridge Inn
224 Mount Rushmore Rd.
(605) 673-2275
www.bestwestern.com
/buffaloridgeinn
Moderate

DEADWOOD

Bullock Hotel
633 Main St.
(605) 578-1745
Moderate

Deadwood Gulch Resort
304 Cliff St. (US 85 South)
(605) 578-1294
www.deadwoodgulch.com
Moderate

First Gold Hotel
270 Main St.
(800) 274-1876
Moderate

The Lodge at Deadwood
100 Pine Crest Lane
(877) 393-5634
www.deadwoodlodge.com

Mineral Palace Hotel & Gaming
601 Main St.
(605) 578-2036
(800) 847-2522
www.mineralpalace.com
Moderate

HILL CITY

Best Western Golden Spike Inn
106 Main St.
(SD 15 and SD 85)
(605) 574-2577
www.bestwesterngolden
spike.com
Moderate

HOT SPRINGS

Sojourner Inn
1729 Minnekahta Ave.
(605) 745-3361
www.sojournerinn.net
Moderate

KEYSTONE

K Bar S Lodge
434 Old Hill City Rd.
(866) 522-7724
www.kbarslodge.com
Moderate

LEAD

Barefoot Resort
Across from Terry Peak
(605) 584-1577
www.barefootresort.com
Moderate

Golden Hills Inn
900 Miners Ave.
(888) 465-3080
www.goldenhillsonline.com
Moderate

RAPID CITY

Comfort Inn & Suites
915 Fairmont Blvd.
(800) 801-2671
www.choicehotels.com
Moderate

Flying B Ranch Bed & Breakfast
6539 Haines Ave.
(605) 342-5324
www.flyb.com
Moderate

Grand Gateway
1721 N. LaCrosse St.
(877) 742-1300
www.grandgatewayhotel
.com
Moderate

GrandStay Residential Suites
660 Disk Dr.
(605) 341-5100
www.grandstay.net
Moderate

Holiday Inn Rushmore Plaza
take exit 58 off I-90, then
travel 1 mile south
(800) 465-4329
www.rushmoreplaza.com
Moderate

Sleep Inn & Suites
4031 Cheyenne Rd.
(605) 791-5678
www.sleepinn.com
Inexpensive

SPEARFISH

Fairfield Inn
2720 First Ave. E
(605) 642-3500
Inexpensive

STURGIS

Holiday Inn Express & Suites
exit 30 off I-90
(605) 347-4140
www.hiesturgis.com
Moderate

Super 8 Motel
located off I-90 at exit 30
(605) 347-4447
Inexpensive

Where to Eat in Western South Dakota

CUSTER

Sage Creek Grille
607 Mount Rushmore Rd.
(605) 673-2424
Moderate

Sylvan Lake Lodge
junction of SD 87 and
SD 89 in Custer State Park
(605) 574-2561
www.custerresorts.com
Moderate

DEADWOOD

Jakes Atop the Midnight Star
677 Lower Main St.
(605) 578-3656
www.themidnightstar.com
Expensive

SELECTED CHAMBERS OF COMMERCE

Belle Fourche Chamber of Commerce
415 Fifth Ave.
Belle Fourche 57717
(605) 892-2676
www.bellefourchechamber.org

Custer Area Chamber of Commerce
615 Washington St.
Custer 57730
(605) 673-2244
www.custersd.com

Deadwood Chamber of Commerce
735 Main St.
Deadwood 57732
(800) 999-1876
www.deadwood.org

Hill City Chamber of Commerce
23935 Hwy. 385
Hill City 57745
(800) 888-1798
www.hillcitysd.com

Hot Springs Area Chamber of Commerce
801 South Sixth St.
Hot Springs 57747
(605) 745-4140
www.hotsprings-sd.com

Lead Chamber of Commerce
106 W. Main St.
Lead 57754
(605) 584-1100
www.leadmethere.org

Rapid City Convention & Visitors Bureau
444 Mt. Rushmore Rd. North
Rapid City 57709
(800) 487-3223
www.visitrapidcity.com

Spearfish Area Chamber of Commerce
106 West Kansas St.
Spearfish 57783
(800) 626-8013
www.spearfish.sd.us

Silverado Grand Buffet
709 Main St.
(800) 584-7005
www.silveradofranklin.com
Moderate

Tin Lizzie
555 Main St.
(605) 578-1715
Moderate

HILL CITY

Alpine Inn
(American/German)
225 Main St.
(605) 574-2749
Moderate

**Bumpin Buffalo
Bar & Grill**
245 Main St.
(605) 574-4100
www.bumpinbuffalollc.com
Moderate

**Slate Creek Grille and
Dry Creek Coffee**
198 Main St.
(605) 574-9422
www.slatecreekgrille.com
Moderate

KEYSTONE

**Powder House
Restaurant**
(American)
(605) 666-4646
www.powderhouselodge
.com
Moderate

RAPID CITY

**Arnold's Classic
1950s Diner**
1940 N. LaCrosse St.
(605) 721-9452
Inexpensive

**Botticelli's Ristorante
Italiano**
523 Main St.
(605) 348-0089
Moderate

Casa Real
2315 Mt. Rushmore Rd.
(605) 791-2272
Moderate

**Colonial House
Restaurant & Pub**
2501 Mount Rushmore Rd.
(605) 342-4640
Moderate

Curry Masala
510 St. Joseph St.
(605) 716-7788
www.currymasalainc.com
Inexpensive to moderate

The Fireside
(American/steak)
10 miles west of Rapid
City on SD 44
(605) 342-3900
Moderate to expensive

Pirates Table
(seafood/steak)
3550 Sturgis Rd.
(605) 341-4842
Moderate

ROCKERVILLE

The Gaslight
13490 Main St.
(605) 343-9276
Moderate

SPEARFISH

Roma's Italian Ristorante
701 Fifth St.
(605) 722-0715
Moderate

Sanford's Grub and Pub
545 West Jackson Blvd.
(605) 642-3204
Moderate

**Shoot the Bull
Steakhouse**
539 W. Jackson Blvd.
(605) 642-2848

STURGIS

**Phil Town Steakhouse &
Lounge**
(American)
2431 South Junction
(605) 347-3604
Moderate

WALL

Elkton House
(American)
exit 110 off I-90 and
SD 240
(605) 279-2152
Moderate

WESTERN NORTH DAKOTA →

Wallace Stegner once said that the West is America, only more so. In North Dakota you're privileged to experience an inconceivably huge chunk of the real West. There is no drugstore-cowboy posturing here. The ranchmen and women work tirelessly, and their careworn faces reflect the daily rigors of ranch life—from falling cattle prices and the unpredictable turns the weather can make to the inner knowledge that their children will likely graduate from college and leave the state.

The traveler will find long, lonely stretches of land—just like those that the settlers and Plains Indians of the past encountered—west of the Missouri River and few things of beauty to break up the monotony. At the same time, there's a timelessness here. It lacks the cookie-cutter feel of cities with homogenous big-box stores and look-alike commercial districts. This is an area where the ranches are large; the towns unfailingly small. Winds and shifting plains slowly bring prehistoric bones to the surface. Lightning strikes in the jagged peaks of the Badlands can ignite coal veins that smolder for years.

It serves the soul well to roam over the plains of North Dakota. To feel small. To feel vulnerable. To find strength.

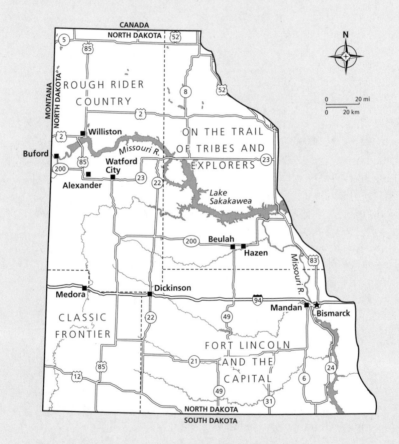

To breathe deeply and embrace the wide-open landscape as it ripples to the horizon. The self-reliance espoused by Ralph Waldo Emerson years ago is infectious in North Dakota. As Teddy Roosevelt once said, "My experience when I lived and worked in North Dakota with my fellow ranchmen, on what was then the frontier, was the most important educational asset of my life."

Classic Frontier

South Dakota may have Mount Rushmore and Badlands that look like a galactic moonscape, but when North Dakota pulls out its big guns for tourism promotion, you can be sure that ***Medora*** will hover at the top of the list. Small and compact, it's the commercial hub for exploring North Dakota's kinder, gentler Badlands. Still rugged and awe-inspiring, the Badlands are also rounder, greener, and filled with more wildlife than what you see in South Dakota.

The frontier town of Medora was founded in 1883 and named for the wife of the ambitious Marquis de Mores, a French nobleman whose thirst for adventure was matched only by his intense desire to be the richest financier in the world. When he and his beautiful wife arrived in the tiny, tough, railroad town of Little Missouri, he envisioned a unique meat-processing scheme that would process and ship meat—rather than cattle—in refrigerated train cars to the East Coast. Local residents called de Mores "the crazy Frenchman," yet it was Little Missouri that became a deserted pile of splinters when de Mores built his town of Medora and had a population of 251 only a year later. In addition to the meat-packing plant, it boasted a newspaper, a brickyard, several stores and saloons, a hotel, and St. Mary's Catholic Church.

What's in a Name?

On March 2, 1861, President James Buchanan signed the bill creating the Dakota Territory. It originally included the area covered today by both Dakotas as well as Montana and Wyoming. The word Dakota means *"friend"* in the Dakota and Sioux Indian language.

Beginning about 1887, efforts were made to bring Dakota into the Union as both a single state and as two states. The latter was successful, and on November 2, 1889, both North Dakota and South Dakota were admitted.

Since President Benjamin Harrison went to great lengths to obscure the order in which the statehood proclamations were signed, the exact order in which the states entered is unknown. However, because of the alphabetical position, North Dakota is often considered the thirty-ninth state.

The marquis often entertained neighbor Theodore Roosevelt at his twenty-six-room chateau that overlooked Medora. De Mores and the man who would be president did not always see eye to eye on everything, but they did agree on socializing over iced champagne. De Mores's dreams proved to be far-fetched, however, and he shut down the meat-packing operation in 1886, and he and his wife returned to France the following year. Medora became another pale Western ghost town when the wicked winter of 1887–88 wiped out most of the ranchers' herds. The De Mores's home, with its sweeping views of the valley, along with historical exhibits and the towering brick chimney from the slaughtering plant remind today's visitors of Medora's big dreams and ill-fated beginning.

The elegantly appointed, two-story de Mores chateau is now the ***Chateau de Mores State Historic Site.*** Lavish furnishings, Oriental carpets, and fine details in this frame house greeted the family when it arrived in 1884. For three years the family occupied the home seasonally, returning to New York during the winter months. The marquis and his wife loved hunting, music, and art. The chateau was given to the state in 1936. The interpretive center and chateau building are open 8:30 a.m. to 6:15 p.m. daily (last tour at 5:30) from May 16 through Sept 15. The interpretive center is open 9 a.m. to 5 p.m. Wed through Sun year-round. Call (701) 623-4355 or visit www.nd.gov/hist.

Medora's revival began in 1958, when the Burning Hills Amphitheatre was built and the drama *Old Four Eyes* was presented to mark Roosevelt's 100th birthday. Four years later, history buff Harold Schafer reignited de Mores's dream and brought the town back to life, this time as a premier vacation destination. In 1986 the Schafer family donated its holding in Medora to the Theodore Roosevelt Medora Foundation, a public, nonprofit organization that operates the public attractions.

In the summer of 1995, the ***Harold Schafer Heritage Center,*** 335 Fourth St., opened to tell the story of Schafer's engaging life at his Gold Seal

TOP HITS IN WESTERN NORTH DAKOTA

Dakota Dinosaur Museum	Maltese Cross Cabin
Fort Union Trading Post National Historic Site	Medora Musical
	Theodore Roosevelt National Park
Lake Sakakawea	
	Tobacco Gardens

Company, as governor, and as the promoter of Medora, the state's leading tourist attraction. The center's **Sheila Schafer Gallery** shows art exhibits each year. Harold's wife Sheila still spends summers in the couple's log cabin. She can be spotted around town, greeting longtime friends, welcoming visitors, and making sure Medora keeps its squeaky-clean image.

For families, Medora's a classic nostalgia trip, a throwback to tourism a generation or two ago (800-633-6721; www.medora.com).

surf**the**web

North Dakota Travel & Tourism has an eye-catching, well formatted, and easy to navigate Web site. Check it out at www.ndtourism.com.

The biggest ticket around is still the **Medora Musical,** which hit its 40th anniversary in 2009 and still serves up a rollicking song-and-dance variety show peppered with patriotism, a few special effects, cowboys on real horses, aw-shucks humor, history, and North Dakota pride. It might look a little schmaltzy at first glance, but the spirit of it pulls you in, especially in its jaw-dropping setting carefully nestled into the Badlands.

Showtime is 8:30 p.m. nightly in the **Burning Hills Amphitheatre,** with performances running mid-June through Labor Day weekend. Call for current ticket rates. Preschoolers are free.

It's easy to make a full evening of a musical outing. You can start by watching chefs plunge steaks speared by pitchforks into vats of boiling oil before dining on Tjaden Terrace with some of the most scenic views anywhere. Behind-the-scenes tours of the Medora Musical start at 7:15 p.m. nightly, but it's best for older children and adults. Leave time to browse new displays, costumes, and historical stories about the musical that were added to its welcome center.

To see the softer side of this land, stroll through the **Medora Doll House** (485 Broadway), which features exhibits of antique dolls and toys, all displayed in the historic Von Hoffman house. (The Von Hoffmans were the marquis' in-laws, and he built this home for them in 1884.) The Old Woman in the Shoe sits on a bench outside her shoe house, watching her children play outside. Small, all-bisque dolls—which cost anywhere from 5 to 25 cents in 1905—are displayed, along with many other types. Adults may enjoy this museum more than children. Medora Doll House Museum is open only during the summer from 10 a.m. to 6 p.m.

There are many other quaint shops—all within easy walking distance—in Medora, including the Joe Ferris General Store. Ferris, a hunting guide and friend to Theodore Roosevelt, was the original owner of the general store.

In 1884 Joe expanded his business by building a new glass-fronted building with a large porch. Business was good and the store flourished as a drugstore, hardware store, and saloon. Theodore Roosevelt stayed in the upstairs living quarters of the Ferris store upon his arrival in Medora before he departed for his ranch.

Rough Riders Gift Shop features jewelry, including Landstroms original Black Hills gold and sterling silver. And you must certainly visit the good folks at Corner Corral to dress up right in Medora. The store is filled with outerwear and sharp-looking western wear for men, women, and children.

Other shops worth a look-see include Teddy the Sharp Shirter (yes, the teddy bear is ubiquitous throughout this charming business district), Stage Barn Gift Shop, Touch of Dakota, and Butte Antiques.

While Medora used to close shop in the winter, that's changed thanks to a two-year expansion and renovation at the ***Rough Riders Hotel,*** 301 Third Ave., (701) 623-4444. The once cozy nine-room hotel now stays open year-round with a conference center and 68 rooms that artfully keep their Victorian Western look (oak armoires, shower tiles with Teddy Roosevelt's ranch brand) while adding the modern comforts of pillow-top beds and flat-screen TVs. It breathes much-needed fresh air into a fairly stale lodging scene. Look for a large new lobby, classic saloon with pressed-tin ceiling, and an expanded dining room with a new chef and entrees such as walleye, duck, and buffalo rib eye.

Riding Tall in the Saddle

When in Theodore Roosevelt National Park, do as Teddy did—go on horseback. The South Unit of the park features more than 80 miles of marked horse trails, and endless unmarked trails carved by the park's buffalo herd. Riders are permitted in all areas of the park except for the camping and picnicking areas and nature trails. A group horse campground is available in the South Unit by reservation, and back-country horse camping is allowed. The *Peaceful Valley Ranch* offers horse rentals and guided trail rides. Popular riding areas include Petrified Forest, Peaceful Valley Ranch, Halliday Wells, and Painted Canyon. Be on the lookout for bison, wild horses, long-horned cattle, elk, and deer.

Call the Peaceful Valley Ranch (701-623-4568) for trail rides May 1 to Oct 1. A variety of rides and trails are available: You can ride across the high plateaus to the largest outcropping of petrified stumps in the forest or see trails used by the pioneers to cross the Badlands. Medora Riding Stables also offers rides, but they fill fast so reservations are recommended (800-633-6721; www.medora.com).

TOP ANNUAL EVENTS

Cowboy Poetry Gathering
Medora
(701) 623-4910

Old-Fashioned Cowboy Christmas
Medora
(701) 623-4910

**The Fort Union Trading Post
Rendezvous**
held annually in June
(701) 572-9083

The Roughrider Days Rodeo
held over the Fourth of July weekend
Dickinson
(800) HELLO-ND

Frontier Army Days
every summer in Fort Abraham Lincoln
Park, Mandan
(701) 667-6340

If you want the best room, ask for No. 501, a king corner suite with seven windows facing the Badlands. Or try No. 503 with a balcony and you can pretend you're Theodore Roosevelt giving his presidential pitch in 1900.

The biggest winter event is the ***Old-Fashioned Cowboy Christmas*** the first weekend in Dec, with most of the events taking place in the community center. The highlight is sleigh or hay rides, but the event also includes an antiques and crafts show, as well as a Christmas quilt show, a family Christmas dance, a cowboy poker game, cowboy poetry, and a Best of the West doll show. The kids are entertained with a children's story hour and a chalk-art drawing session. To round off the activities, the chamber hosts a traditional Christmas supper, Western Parade of Lights, and a cowboy Christmas jamboree. In conjunction with all the holiday wonderment, the chamber honors a veteran each year.

Rough Rider Country

"It was still the Wild West in those days . . . and ours was the glory of work and the joy of living," Theodore Roosevelt said of North Dakota. The former president knew the Badlands intimately, and his passion for these endless buttes and clay-streaked bluffs inexplicably pulses throughout the region. You'll start to understand it with that first sweeping glance across Painted Canyon overlook just off I-94. To truly appreciate the landscape, you need to enter the park, hike its buttes, watch bison take a dirt bath in a wallow, photograph majestic wild horses as they trot alongside a curve in the Little Missouri River.

Earn Your Badge

If you're taking kids to any national park, check out the Junior Ranger Program, which is usually free. Our three children, ages 5 to 10, love the workbooks and the incentive to pay keen attention to a park's geology, history, and wildlife. When kids complete their work, a local Ranger gives a short ceremony, including a pledge to protect nature, before awarding plastic junior ranger pins or a commemorative patch. Our trio earned bragging rights for both Theodore Roosevelt National Park (explored in a freak June snowstorm) and Mount Rushmore National Monument. Teddy easily wins as their favorite president. For more information, go to www.nps.gov.

The park is divided into three distinctly different units: the South Unit (accessible from Medora via I-94), the Elkhorn Ranch site, and the North Unit, which can be reached via US 85 near *Watford City.* Although the park is open year-round, some portions of the road system may be closed during winter. The park includes 110 square miles of Badlands and is considered one of the nation's least crowded gems. Since the withdrawal of an ancient salt sea 130 million years ago, rain, wind, and the Little Missouri River have shaped a curious, mystical landscape in the Badlands. Exposed seams of lignite coal create a band of black below one ridge. On another butte, clay is baked into red scoria, the result of smoldering lignite, ignited by lightning strikes or prairie fires. The burning of lignite beds through the ages has helped lend color as well as shape to the Badlands, as the baked rocks become more resistant to erosion than the neighboring layers. Painted canyons, ash coulees, and broad cottonwood river bends are breathtaking.

North Dakotans like to call the park Rough Rider Country, and no doubt it was the rough-and-tumble lifestyle of the West and the starkness of the North Dakota Badlands that primed the young Roosevelt for a much larger role later in his life, that of a Rough Rider leading his men to battle in Cuba. The *Medora South Unit Visitor Center* (701-623-4466) will formally introduce you to Teddy, and if you haven't already fallen madly in love with the former president, you certainly will here.

Just a few steps away from the visitor center is the *Maltese Cross Cabin,* a small, efficiently organized three-room cabin. The cabin was originally located about 7 miles south of Medora in the wooded bottomlands of Roosevelt's Maltese Cross Ranch near the Little Missouri River. At Roosevelt's request, ranch managers built a 1½-story cabin complete with shingle roof and cellar. In its day the cabin was considered a mansion, for it had wooden floors and three separate rooms. The steeply pitched roof, an anomaly on the

Dakota plains, provided an upstairs sleeping loft for ranch hands. You can see the desk at which Teddy wrote his book, *Hunting Trips of the Ranchman,* which he completed between 1884 and 1885. The rocking chair in the living room was his favorite piece of furniture. During the Roosevelt presidency the Maltese Cross Cabin was exhibited in Portland, Oregon, and St. Louis, Missouri. It was then moved to the Capitol grounds in Bismarck and finally relocated to its present site and renovated in 1959.

While the cabin helps you visualize what life was like for Roosevelt in the 1800s, the highlight for most visitors is the awe-inspiring 36-mile scenic loop drive through the wide expanse of the park's South Unit.

Along this paved road you will see panoramic views of the Badlands with plenty of opportunities to get out and hike through this 46,158-acre section. A word to the wise: Drive carefully and make sure you're not in a hurry. On my first visit to the park, a herd of bison took its sweet time crossing the road. A few shaggy males rumbled so close to our vehicle and seemed so huge, it was like we were in a sardine tin. Don't even think about getting out to shoot a photo unless it's from the car or a good distance away with a telephoto lens. They look tame (and even slow) until you see a national park service clip of ignorant tourists getting swiftly head-butted like a game-winning field goal.

You'll likely see elk and deer in the park, as well, especially during early morning or late afternoon drives when wildlife are most active. Park rangers can clue you in on where the wild horses were recently spotted and show you where to watch for prairie dog towns. The prairie dogs are especially entertaining as they interact and pop up and down their intricate towns. They may seem cute and timid, but do keep your distance to avoid painful bites or disease. Also be on the watch for prairie rattlesnakes, which might strike if surprised on the trails.

The North Dakota Game and Fish Department urges people not to touch wildlife, especially baby animals that appear to be abandoned. It is illegal to

Vibrant Souvenirs

Pottery lovers head 25 miles west of the national park on I-94 to visit the studio of Tama Smith at 127 East Main St. in the tiny border town of Beach. A self-proclaimed "fire potter," Smith's most distinctive palette of colors is prairie fire. The mix of brilliant red, rich ochre, and earthy browns grace her pots, vase, mugs, and other practical works of art. Her studio is open 8 a.m. to 6 p.m. MST daily through the summer and 9 a.m. to 5 p.m. Mon through Sat Oct to Dec. Call (888) 229-9496 for winter hours (www.prairiefirepottery.com).

The Great Survivor

As many as sixty million bison once roamed over one-third of the entire land mass of North America. It was not unusual for a herd to contain four million animals and cover an area 50 miles long and 20 miles wide.

On the Dakota prairies, bison provided food, clothing, shelter, arrow points, ropes, and ornaments for the Plains Indians. As late as 1866 a huge herd of bison estimated at 100,000 was sighted 18 miles north of Fargo. Often mistakenly called buffalo, bison are not related to the true buffalo of Africa and Asia. Their ancestors, wild cattle that found their way across the now-vanished land bridge from Siberia to Alaska, came to North America during the Pleistocene era.

Prized for their meat and hides and as trophies, bison were hunted almost to extinction; by 1891 the United States bison population had been reduced to a mere 541 animals. The species was saved from annihilation by concerned conservationists, ranchers, and lovers of the outdoors who protected the remaining bison, gradually replenishing their number and building today's herds.

take wild animals home, and captive animals returned to the wild will lack the necessary survival skills. Motorists also should watch for deer along roadways throughout the entire region—not just the park. June and Nov are the peak months for deer-vehicle accidents when deer are more on the move.

When Roosevelt first came to the Badlands, he was an asthmatic young man who scoured the wild ravines—in bad weather for two weeks—until he finally found and shot a bison. The adventure thrilled Roosevelt so much that before he left he bought a cattle ranch about 7 miles south of Medora and renamed it the Maltese Cross Ranch. Unfortunately, when Roosevelt returned to North Dakota the next year it was for far grimmer reasons. His wife and mother had died within hours of each other, and Roosevelt was inconsolably grief-stricken. In a move to further isolate himself from civilization and his own pain, he bought another cattle operation, the **Elkhorn Ranch,** 35 miles north of Medora. The ranch buildings no longer exist but interpretive signs tell where the house and outbuildings were. You can visit the ranch, but be forewarned that it can be reached only on rough dirt roads. Call the visitor center at (701) 623-4466 for conditions before attempting the trip.

Teddy's cattle ranches during the late 1800s let him practice and nurture his philosophy of practical conservation. He also was aware of the problems of the West and possessed the rugged spirit of its settlers, an enviable asset when he became president in 1901. His time in North Dakota greatly shaped his ground-breaking conservation efforts that helped national parks and the nation's wildlife thrive in the 20th century.

If you take US 85 north from Belfield, you're well on your way to the North Unit of **Theodore Roosevelt National Park.** The highway first will take you through Grassy Butte, where you can find the **Old Sod Post Office.** Construction materials were scarce in 1912, so the Grassy Butte Post Office was built of logs and sod. The building was used until 1964. Now listed on the National Register of Historic Places as a historic site, the building serves as a museum that is filled with sundry antiques and relics from the 1800s and early 1900s. The museum is open 9 a.m. to 4 p.m. Memorial Day to Labor Day, weekends in May and June then daily through Labor Day. Admission is free. Call (701) 863-6604.

anybodygot thetime?

In the less-visited **North Unit of Theodore Roosevelt National Park,** the buttes are taller and certain areas are heavily forested. Squaw Creek (1.1 miles) and Caprock Coulee (1.5 miles) nature trails are self-guided and interpret the Badlands, coulees, and breaks. Upper Caprock Coulee, Achenbach, and Buckhorn trails will take you into the backcountry. A 14-mile scenic drive has turnouts with spectacular views and interpretive sites.

Like South Dakota, North Dakota has two standard time zones. The southwest corner uses mountain time and the rest of the state uses central time. North Dakota observes daylight saving time.

Watford City, which bills itself as a slice of the New Old West, celebrates the beginning of summer each year with the three-day **Homefest.** Street dances, golf and bowling tournaments, and free swimming in the community pool are just a few ways the town welcomes visitors. Likewise, the annual **Art-in-the-Park** festival brings together the best of art, entertainment, and food

Glorious Golf Courses

North Dakota has three of the nation's top golf courses, which frame up some of the state's most stunning scenery. It costs $140 to play all of them with the Triple Golf Challenge. The Links of North Dakota (866-733-6453; www.thelinksofnorthdakota .com) boasts a pure links style, taking advantage of gently rolling bluff-tops overlooking Lake Sakakawea west of Williston on ND 1804. Bismarck's Hawktree (800-620-6141; www.hawktree.com) also takes a links-style approach with greens tucked into the Burnt Creek Valley and framed in native grasses. Bully Pulpit, three miles south of Medora, looks the most dramatic with vibrant greens tucked into the Badlands (800-633-6721; www.medora.com).

Hit the Trail

My first taste of mountain biking was on a section of the 126-mile Maah Daah Hey Trail near Medora. It took almost 30 minutes to ease the death grip I had on the brakes. When I finally relaxed and let myself speed down the hills and let momentum carry me up new ones, it was an exhilarating breakthrough. I've been hooked ever since. Dakotah Cyclery (888-321-1218; www.dakotacyclery.com) offers great introductory experiences for beginners and families, along with bike rentals, shuttles, and anything an expert will need, from repair parts to having your gear waiting at your campsite when you're ready for an epic ride. They're open from 9 a.m. to 6 p.m. MST daily May through Oct. People come from across the nation to tackle this trail, following the iconic posts marked with the simple outline of a turtle. In the Mandan language, Maah Daah Hey means a place that will be around for a long time. We can only hope so. While the scenery isn't as colorfully intense as the red rock in the Moab, Utah, mountain biking mecca, North Dakota makes up for it with solitude and only slightly more muted colors in this gorgeous and challenging terrain. The newest section, "The Deuce," climbs buttes and zig-zags through switchbacks in the 30-mile extension south from Sully's Creek State Park to the U.S. Forest Service's Burning Coal Vein Campground. The trail also is popular with horseback riders. The trail extends north to the USDA Forest Service CCC Campground in McKenzie County 20 miles south of Watford City. For maps or more information, contact the U.S. Forest Service at (701) 250-4443 or www.fs.fed.us. The Another great source is the Maah Daah Hey Trail Association at www.mdhta.com.

from western North Dakota and eastern Montana for one sunny day at Watford City's Tourist Park each June.

For family fun, head for the **Wild West Water Park** (315 Third St.; 701-570-3677), which offers two tower water slides, a children's water play area, a large hot tub, and concessions. Swimming lessons and a senior program are also available.

You can see North Dakota's largest fossil at **Long X Visitor Center and Museum** in Watford City (100 Second St. SW; 701-444-5804). The petrified bald cypress tree stump is estimated at 17,000 pounds and measures about 6 feet in diameter and 8 feet tall. The 60-million-year-old fossil was discovered in the Badlands south of Watford City during an archaeological dig in 2001. You'll also find tourist information and a pioneer museum on-site. Hours are 9 a.m. to 9 p.m. Mon through Sat year-round and 1 to 5 p.m. Sun from Memorial Day through Labor Day.

Follow US 85 back south to I-94 and some of the state's best hunting and fishing grounds. Mourning dove, sharp-tailed grouse, Hungarian partridge, and ring-necked pheasant are just some of the upland bird-hunting opportunities. Wing-shooters take to the fields and prairie water holes on the first of Sept, as mourning dove hunting traditionally kicks off North Dakota's shotgun season. Drive almost anywhere among the rolling green grasslands, and you'll be sure to see and hear the honk of pheasants.

Belfield, some 18 miles east of Medora and the Badlands south unit, is a magnet for weary travelers and hunters with **Trapper's Kettle** (701-575-8585) restaurant and gift shop. It incorporates the hunting/trapping theme through-out its decor and menu. Authentic traps serve as door pulls in the restaurant, and the cedar dining tables have inlaid traps. Examples of taxidermy of almost every animal imaginable seem to stare vacantly in the dining areas. The hearty and well-prepared food is stick-to-your-ribs good here; the thick and beefy chili is served in a crock with grated cheese—perfect winter fare. Pan-fry dishes and mini-kettle soups also hit the spot. Prices are moderate.

Bright orange is the fall fashion color of choice in these parts as hunters remind their buddies to reset watches to mountain standard time and team up to land the biggest bucks. White-tailed deer are found almost everywhere, but the mule deer tend to cluster in the jagged country of the Badlands and other broken terrain. Lightning-swift antelope inhabit the western borders of the region, and the regal white elk and bighorn sheep confine themselves primar-ily to the Badlands and the Killdeer Mountains.

If you climb out of your car in **Dickinson** (19 miles west of Belfield off I-94), you'll see honest-to-goodness cowboys and cowgirls there. Even coun-try-western music blares through the loudspeakers over the gas pumps at the service stations. This is the way Dickin-son, the Queen City of the Prairies, likes it. Put on your Stetson and your cowboy boots, because this is the most natural-feeling way to experience Dickinson.

This sprightly community of 16,010 people is the rodeo capital of North Dakota, with two world champions and every level of rodeo, from the young-

hunting101

For more information on resident and nonresident hunting require-ments and licenses, call the North Dakota Game and Fish Department at (701) 328-6300 or check out the Web site at www.gf.nd.gov.

sters' "showdeo" to the Professional Rodeo Association. The **Roughrider Days Rodeo** and festivities are held during the Fourth of July weekend every year.

Dickinson is just part of a statewide passion for rodeo: About fifty rodeos throughout the state attract hundreds of cowboys each year.

In case you didn't know, the word *rodeo* is actually derived from a Span-ish word meaning "roundup." The history of the rodeo traces back to the 1800s when most ranches had untamed horses (or broncos). Cattle outfits often challenged one another to bronc-riding contests in which cowboys could prove their mettle. Eventually someone reckoned there would be good money to be made if there was an admission charge to see the battle between the bronc and the cowboy.

Rodeos remain a popular, breathtaking event in both North Dakota and South Dakota. Basically there are four types of rodeo: high school, college, amateur, and professional. For a listing of rodeos in North Dakota, call (800) HELLO-ND.

Dickinson's other claim to fame is its *Dakota Dinosaur Museum* (701-225-3466; www.dakotadino.com), a fantastic earth science museum that features dinosaur bones found in North Dakota, including a complete triceratops, which lived in the Badlands when they were a swampy and warm area, and a duck-billed edmontosaurus. Ten other full-scale dinosaurs, a complete fossil rhino, and rocks and minerals are impressive displays as well. Located right on I-94 at 200 E. Museum Dr., it's attached to the Joachim Regional Museum

Famous North Dakotans

Theodore Roosevelt isn't the only famous person to have kicked up his boots in North Dakota. Some famous North Dakotans include:

- **Warren Christopher,** who served as deputy secretary of state in the Carter administration and was awarded the Medal of Freedom on January 16, 1981. In 1993, Christopher was sworn in as the sixty-third U.S. secretary of state.

- **Angie Dickinson,** who has appeared in more than fifty major movies and television productions, but is best known for her roles in the movie *Dressed to Kill* and the TV series *Police Woman.*

- **Phil Jackson,** who will go down in National Basketball Association history not only for his dynamic leadership, but also as the only person to both play for and coach teams (New York Knicks, Chicago Bulls, and Los Angeles Lakers) to titles for the NBA and the Continental Basketball Association.

- **Louis L'Amour,** the award-winning western author and screenwriter, who published more than 400 short stories and more than 100 novels. He wrote sixty-five TV scripts and sold more than thirty stories to the motion-picture industry, including *Hondo,* starring John Wayne.

- **Roger Maris,** baseball's former single-season home-run king, who hit sixty-one home runs during the 1961 season while he was a member of the New York Yankees.

- **Lawrence Welk,** who became one of the greatest entertainers in the world through his weekly TV show featuring his distinctive "champagne music."

complex. It is open 9 a.m. to 5 p.m. daily May 1 through Labor Day. Admission is $7 for adults, $6 for seniors, and $4 for children.

The dinosaur museum is adjacent to the *Joachim Regional Museum and Prairie Outpost Park* (www.dickinsonmuseumcenter.org), where through a self-guided tour you get an idea of how rugged pioneers settled southwestern North Dakota. The museum offers tours of a Norwegian *stabbur* (storage house), a Germans-from-Russia homestead house, a one-room schoolhouse, a railroad depot, a church, and other buildings that reflect the area's ethnic and immigrant past. For more information call (701) 456-6225.

If you travel 3 miles west on I-94, then 1 mile south, you'll be at *Patterson Reservoir* (701-225-2074), ideal for swimming, fishing, boating, camping, and picnicking during the summer. The reservoir is part of the Missouri River Valley reclamation project. The park is open daily June through Aug.

About 20 miles east of Dickinson at exit 72, a 110-foot-tall sculpture of Canada geese looms over the Interstate, dwarfing the cars that pull over the admire it. It's just a hint of what's to come along one of North Dakota's most quirky, surprising drives: the Enchanted Highway. This 32-mile ribbon of road stretches from the freeway to tiny *Regent.* North-Dakota-inspired sculptures pull you forward as they rise from the wide-open rolling landscape about every 10 to 15 miles. Former teacher and school principal Gary Greff—with no welding or art training—was worried his hometown of Regent (pop. 200) would disappear like so many other farm-dependent towns. One day he saw drivers pulling over to snap pictures of a giant figure of a man created out of hay bales. He then dreamed up the idea of metal sculptures. In 1991, he finished the first sculpture of a tin family made from used farm equipment and erected it a few miles out of Regent. He has built and put up seven more in the years since with each getting more complex, more artsy, and less folksy. Look for Teddy Roosevelt, pheasants, deer, Canada geese, and the delightful "Fisherman's Dream," featuring a lively group of fish made from recycled scrap metal, oil well pipes, drums, and tanks. We also enjoyed the 40-foot-tall grasshoppers, where we had our B-movie moment, looking miniature and posing with looks of terror beneath the insects that plagued pioneers.

Regent is a tiny town, but you can find a Metal Magic gift shop, the Enchanted Highway gift shop with ice cream and a restroom (most welcome after the drive), plus two bed-and-breakfasts: the 1900s *Crocus Inn* (www .crocusinn.com, 701-563-4562) and Prairie Vista (701-563-4542).

Back on the Interstate, two exits east of the Enchanted Highway is *Richardton,* population 625. The twin spires of its historic *St. Mary's Catholic Church* on 418 Third Ave. W are quiet testaments to the faith that has steadfastly guided Dakotans through lean and prosperous times. Benedictine monks built this stunning structure a century ago. The original building and its immovable central altar are the focal point amid the vaulted ceilings, original medallion paintings, ornate altars, and more than fifty stained-glass windows. St. Mary's is a wonderful example of Bavarian–Romanesque–style architecture. Today the church is lovingly tended by about 35 resident monks living in the Assumption Abbey, which is connected to the church. They warmly welcome visitors. Be sure to see their gift shop, printing facility, wine cellar, church, and library. Nuns of the Benedictine order at nearby Sacred Heart Monastery also welcome visitors. Call (701) 974-3315 for an appointment or visit www .assumptionabbey.com.

On the Trail of Tribes and Explorers

Whether you head north of Theodore Roosevelt National Park or follow the Missouri River from the east, you'll find many of North Dakota's most historic and storied places by following the *Lewis and Clark Trail* (www.lewisand clarktrail.com).

The explorers and their crew bravely headed across uncharted territory to seek a route west across the continent from St. Louis to the Pacific Ocean, meticulously recording their discoveries and adventures along the way. The Lewis and Clark Trail comprises two developed highways along the Missouri River. The highway numbers—1804 and 1806—appropriately match the years that the explorers entered and returned to North Dakota. ND 1804 follows the eastern side of the Missouri River, while ND 1806 follows the western side. Historical sites and recreation can be discovered along both banks of the river.

On the far western border of the state, astounding history unfolds at the *Fort Union Trading Post National Historic Site* (701-572-9083 or www.nps .gov/fous), which stands near the confluence of the Yellowstone and Missouri Rivers in the town of *Buford.* Open daily year-round, the site is accessible from ND 1804, a 24-mile drive southwest from Williston. From 1829 to 1867, the Fort Union Trading Post was the "vastest and finest" of a string of trading posts along the northern rivers. Twenty-foot-high whitewashed palisades, anchored by two-story stone bastions, surrounded Fort Union. Capitalist John Jacob Astor reasoned that the imposing structure would impress the local Native Americans. Here, Scots, Germans, French, and Spanish bargained with the Assiniboin, Crow, Cree, Blackfoot, and Sitting Bull's Hunkpapa band of Sioux. Furs and hides were traded for iron tools, guns, blankets, and other manufactured goods.

Much of what we have learned about the cultures of the Northern Plains Indians comes from Fort Union's adventurous staff and often rich-and-famous guests. John James Audubon, Germany's Prince Maximilian, and renowned artists George Catlin and Karl Bodmer left lasting legacies in their paintings, sketches, and words about this incredible mosaic. You can enjoy the rich tapestry of culture and feel like a part of the past by timing a visit with the annual Rendezvous festival. The site is free and includes tours of Bourgeois House and visitor center and the Trade House with living history actors throughout the summer.

Trade flourished here until smallpox ravaged most of the trading tribes. The friendly trade ultimately ended when Fort Union was occupied by the Thirtieth Wisconsin Infantry in 1864. It dismantled the private-enterprise fort to help construct the military's *Fort Buford,* now a state historic site about a mile upstream. The fort is probably best known as the place where Hunkpapa leader Sitting Bull surrendered in 1881. Chief Joseph also surrendered here after defeat in the Nez Perce War. Buildings here date from the 1870s. The site is open mid-May to mid-Sept. Admission is $5 for adults and $2.50 for children and includes admission to the *Missouri–Yellowstone Confluence Interpretive Center* half a mile away. The center is open year-round and includes exhibits on geology, prehistoric times, geography, and the impact of people, the river, and roads through the area. The best attraction, though, is the chance to see the same magnificent views that Lewis and Clark saw as they reached the confluence (701-572-9034; www.history.nd.gov).

Twenty-two miles northeast of Fort Buford on ND 1804 is *Williston,* an energy town proud of its history. *Buffalo Trails Day* each summer features a parade, a chuck wagon breakfast, old-time music, and lots of games. You can glimpse the town's past throughout the summer at the *Frontier Museum,* northwest of Spring Lake Park on Main Street. The complex comprises a 1910 rural church, complete with furnishings, two modern buildings filled with artifacts, a 1903 two-story house filled with antique furniture, an 1887 grocery store, a restored Great Northern depot, and a complete country school. The Williston Tourist Information Center is housed in the Great Northern depot. Contact the Williston Convention and Visitors Bureau for more information, (800) 615-9041.

A detour 26 miles south of Williston leads to the tiny town of *Alexander* with its charming *Lewis and Clark Trail Museum* on US 85. Housed in a 1914 brick schoolhouse, it features Lewis and Clark memorabilia (including a scale model of Fort Mandan), plus extensive displays with a country store, a hall of fame, and unusual exhibits such as one on the last lynching in North Dakota. Outside, antique farm machinery is displayed. A playground and picnic facilities are available just a few blocks away in *Alexander Park.* The museum is open from Memorial Day. Plan a couple of hours to fully appreciate the museum, which is one of the largest and most interesting museums in western North

Dakota. Call (701) 828-3595 for hours or get a sneak preview at www.alexander museum.com.

If all the Lewis and Clark sites inspire you to try your own adventure, the folks at *Lund's Landing Lodge* 23 miles east of Williston on SD 1804 will take guests canoeing or kayaking on the same routes Lewis and Clark followed along Lake Sakakawea. Packages include lodging in their cedar cabins, plus breakfast and evening meals that are likely topped off with their beloved Juneberry pie a la mode (701-568-3474; www.lundslanding.com).

On the south shore of the lake, *Tobacco Garden Bay* was once a fuel stop for steamboats It now includes a restaurant, 70 campsites, and three log cabins. Nearby, the 2.5-mile Birnt Hills Trail offers lovely scenic views of Lake Sakakawea. The name Tobacco Garden Bay is derived from the Sioux and Assiniboin Indian name for the reed that grew in the area. Call (701) 842-4199 for reservations.

Fort Berthold Reservation is home of the Three Affiliated tribes (Hidatsa, Arikara, and Mandan Indians) on Lake Sakakawea. The boundaries for the reservation have changed many times since its inception in 1880, and today the reservation encompasses 980,000 acres of tribally and individually owned lands. Historically the Mandan and Hidatsa Indians were a peaceful and agricultural group, stable and not as nomadic as the other Plains Indians. The Arikara, previously part of the Pawnee, separated from their relatives on the Loup River in Nebraska, worked their way north, and eventually joined the Hidatsa and Mandan Indians. At present about 3,696 of the tribes' members live on the reservation.

Lake Sakakawea is named for the young Shoshone woman who guided the intrepid explorers Lewis and Clark from North Dakota to the Yellowstone River in 1805. The nation's "Sixth Great Lake" is artificially made, formed by the mighty barrier of the Garrison Dam. This massive body of water draws thousands of visitors each year because of its superb sailing, camping, hunting, and fishing. At 200 miles long and covering 909 square miles, it is the largest body of water in the state.

The *Three Affiliated Tribes Museum* (www.mhanation.com) is located on the Fort Berthold Reservation about 4 miles west of New Town on ND 23. One of the newest exhibits at the museum honors Fort Berthold World War I veterans. At that time Native Americans were not allowed to vote, yet they valiantly volunteered to serve their country. Memorabilia, photographs, and a forty-eight-star United States flag are highlights in the display. The museum is open Apr through Nov. Call (701) 627-4477 for more information. It's possible for visitors to feel even more a part of the tribes' history by touring and staying overnight in an Earth Lodge Village, which is in being developed.

You can get a feel for the vastness and beauty of the tribes' historic communities with a visit to the **Knife River Indian Villages** (www.nps.gov/knri), a national park that commemorates Native Americans. The remains of the villages arc along the banks of the Knife and Missouri Rivers, approximately 60 miles north of Bismarck. This is one of the oldest inhabited sites in North America, dating back 9,000 years. The Hidatsa and Mandan Indians, two of the oldest tribes on the continent, lived here in earth lodges, planting and harvesting gardens of corn, squash, beans, and sunflowers, which they exchanged in an ever-growing trading network between tribes. The locally produced Knife River flint has been traced to villages in the far southeastern part of the United States. In the winter of 1804–05, they were gracious hosts to Lewis and Clark and the Corps of Discovery. President Thomas Jefferson had appointed Lewis and Clark to explore and document America's new Louisiana Purchase territory. The Corps, which departed from near St. Louis, comprised forty-five men operating a 55-foot keelboat and five other boats. After arriving in North Dakota for the winter, the explorers met the teenage girl Sakakawea (the Dakotas' alternate spelling of Sacagawea). She helped guide them through her native Shoshone lands as they searched for a water route to the Pacific Ocean. In April 1805 the group left Fort Mandan to continue the westward expedition. Lewis and Clark returned to North Dakota in August 1806 on their way back to St. Louis.

Knife River Indian Villages can be reached via US 83 and ND 200A near Stanton. The site is part of North Dakota's American Legacy Tour. This world-class archaeological park boasts an earthen lodge at the modern visitor center. Trails lead to three village sites, where remnants of earth lodges and scattered bones and tools are easily seen. Ten miles of hiking and Nordic ski trails offer opportunities to view wildlife. The center is open 7:30 a.m. to 6 p.m. Memorial Day through Labor Day; excluding federal holidays, the center is open 8 a.m. to 4:30 p.m. the remainder of the year. For more information call (701) 745-3300.

Ready for another detour? Take ND 49 North to **Beulah,** which prides itself on being the Energy Capital of the Midwest. And for good reason. The Freedom Mine delivers 6 million tons of coal a year, mostly to the East Coast. The **Great Plains Synfuel Plant** is the nation's only commercial-scale coal gasification plant, which turns coal into natural gas. Tours are available by appointment Mon through Fri. For more information call (701) 873-6667 or visit www.dakotagas.com.

Fort Mandan in Washburn ranks among the best Lewis and Clark sites, recreating the Corps of Discovery's winter camp with interpreters explaining their daily life and how they prepared to keep heading west in the spring.

Admission is $7.50 for adults and $5 for children and is also good for admission into the nearby North Dakota Lewis and Clark Interpretive Center. Among its treasures are a canoe hand-carved from a cottonwood trunk, exhibits on steamboats and frontier trade, and the Berquist Gallery with rare watercolors from Swiss artist Karl Bodmer and written observations from German Prince Maximilan who both traveled through the area in 1833 and lived among the Native Americans. Hours are 9 a.m. to 5 p.m. daily in the summer and Mon through Sat in the winter. Also open noon to 5 p.m. Sun in the off-season (701-462-8535; www.fortmandan.com).

Another jumping-off point for the adventurous is the *Cross Ranch Nature Preserve,* managed by the Nature Conservancy. The ranch is located 30 miles north of Mandan via ND 1806 (a gravel road). This 6,000-acre nature preserve has mixed grass prairies, Missouri River floodplain forest, upland woody draws, and a bison herd. You can hike along self-guided nature trails. The preserve is open year-round to the public. Activities include bird-watching, canoeing, wildlife viewing, and cross-country skiing. The adjacent Cross Ranch State Park has a visitor center, cabins, primitive camping, picnicking, and fishing. Call (701) 794-8741 for more information.

Fort Lincoln and the Capital

Most people think of South Dakota and Montana when they hear the name George Armstrong Custer, and for good reason. He led the army expedition into the Black Hills of South Dakota, where he had been sent to quell rumors of gold on parts of Sioux land. Instead he found that the prospectors' tales of extractable quantities of gold throughout the area were bona fide. Later he and his troops were killed at the famous Battle of the Little Big Horn in Montana. Prior to these illustrious times in history, however, Custer was a young Civil War hero stationed at Fort Lincoln in what was then the Dakota Territory.

You can visit Custer's home at the *Fort Abraham Lincoln State Park* (701-667-6340; www.parkrec.nd.gov/Parks/FLSP.htm). The only thing dry about these tours might be a sample of hard tack or spicy jerky. The park in

a worldly capitol

The North Dakota Capitol was built in the early 1930s for $2 million. A Judicial Wing was completed in 1981. Although it ranks as one of the nation's most practical and economically built state capitols, this art deco structure is enhanced by a unique blend of raw materials, including Indiana limestone, Montana yellowstone, Belgian marble, Tennessee marble, Honduras mahogany, East Indian rosewood, English brown oak, Burma teak, and laurel wood.

Mandan has some of the best living history actors around, adding a sense of fun with plenty of audience interaction doled out with stories on food, manners, day-to-day operations, and old-fashioned gossip from 1875 before the battle. If you're there on a summer weekend, you can catch a melodrama Fri and Sat evenings for $2 or $1 for the Sun matinee. You also can see the central barracks, the commissary store, the blockhouses standing guard over the old fort, and the cemetery where the marked graves of soldiers tell stories never found in history books.

Guided living-history tours run May through mid-Oct. For more information, call (701) 663-4758 or visit www.fortlincoln.com.

Each summer, *Frontier Army Days* brings reenactment cavalry and infantry groups—the Frontier Army of Dakota—to Fort Abraham Lincoln for cannon firing, cavalry charges, drills, and the living history of Custer's pivotal presence in the development of the West.

The story of ill-fated Custer isn't the only legend at Fort Abraham Lincoln State Park. Mandan Indians settled *On-a-Slant Village.* With a population once as high as 15,000 people. They farmed miles of Missouri River bottomland from ten or twelve fortified cities here on the Slant River. The villages were empty and wiped out by disease by the time Lewis and Clark visited. At the pinnacle of their wealth and power, the Mandans built remarkably cozy, round, earth lodges, like those seen at Knife River. On-a-Slant Village shows traces of seventy-five lodges, including the large ceremonial lodge that is 84 feet in diameter. Visitors also can capture the spirit of the time through trail rides.

In downtown Mandan at 401 Main St., the *Five Nations Arts Museum* (701-663-4663; www.fortlincoln.com) brings the talent of local tribes into the present tense. Inside, the soothing sounds of Native American music can be heard and an amazing selection of native arts and crafts admired. Located in an old train depot, the colonial revival redbrick building affords a unique sense of the architecture in 1929, the year in which it was built. The original interior is still gracefully intact, with stone floors, oak woodwork and trim, and a beautifully meticulous wainscoting of tan tiles. The gallery carries the work of more than 200 artists from the Mandan, Hidatsa, Arikara, Chippewa, and Sioux tribes who manage this portion of Fort Abraham Lincoln State Park. The gallery is open 9 a.m. to 6 p.m. Mon through Sat and noon to 5 p.m. Sun with extended hours during the summer and holidays. Just across the Missouri River from Mandan, you'll find *Bismarck,* the state capital and, with 55,532 people, the second-largest city in North Dakota. Located on a natural ford of the Missouri River, Bismarck served as an early-day steamboat port. It was named for German chancellor Otto von Bismarck in hopes of encouraging German investment in the railroad.

SHOPPING SAMPLER

Junk Yard Chic
201 West Main, Bismarck
Specializes in finding new uses for old items, giving this place a creative, fun vibe.
(701) 223-3784
www.junkyardchic.com

Wildhorse Western Furnishings
2600 East Rosser Ave., Bismarck
It's the place to go if you love home decor and gifts with cowboy flair.
(701) 258-4692

Urban Girl Beads & Gifts
208 E. Broadway, Bismarck
Encourages do-it-yourself jewelry but also sells ready-made items from local artists.
(Classes are available)
(701) 323-9222
www.urbangirlnd.com

Latitudes Gallery & Gifts
107 North Fifth St., Bismarck
Sells a variety of unique artwork, gifts, and jewelry.
(701) 224-9034

Among Bismarck's most lauded eateries is ***Peacock Alley*** (701-255-7917) at 422 East Main Ave., at the corner of Fifth Street. Proprietor Bill Hixson has retained the aura of the former Patterson Hotel, which in its heyday was the off-hours headquarters for state and national politicos. Theodore Roosevelt, Calvin Coolidge, John F. Kennedy, and Lyndon Johnson swept through the hotel on presidential campaign stops, and legislators still meet in the bar and grill. Like the proud peacock, the restaurant's blue-and-green decor handsomely fans a posh yet down-to-earth attitude. This is the perfect place for drinks after the theater, but then again, it's also the perfect place to take the family for Sunday brunch. There's nothing snooty about the restaurant—or anything in North Dakota, for that matter. Like at most places in North Dakota, you can dine here formidably on a modest budget. You can load up with fresh fruits, muffins, sticky homemade caramel rolls, French toast, pancakes, hash browns, two kinds of sausage, bacon, ham, and more at the Sun buffet. Equally mouthwatering is the dinner menu. Temptations abound in dishes like sliced tenderloin with brandy peppercorn sauce, roast duckling, and cannelloni bolognese. The restaurant is open 11 a.m. to 2 p.m. and 5:30 to 10 p.m. (9 p.m. on Mon). Sun brunch is served from 9 a.m. to 1 p.m. The bar is open until 1 a.m. except Sun.

Across from Peacock Alley on Main Avenue is a Mission-style depot that sets the festive atmosphere for Mexican cuisine. ***Fiesta Villa*** (701-222-8075) is famous for its fajitas and chimichangas, and the margaritas are highly recommended to quench your thirst after a fiery meal. In the summertime diners can enjoy their meals on the outdoor patio. The restaurant is open 11 a.m. to 10:30 p.m. Mon through Thurs and 11 a.m. to 11 p.m. Fri and Sat.

No trip to Bismarck would be complete without at least a walk or drive past the **State Capitol** (600 East Blvd. Ave.). If you take Sixth Street north 10 blocks, you'll run into Boulevard Avenue and be at the foot of the grand nineteen-story Capitol, which is topped with an observation tower. It's hard to miss The Skyscraper of the Prairies—it's the tallest building in North Dakota. Built in the 1930s, the Capitol boasts an art deco interior as fashion-forward now as it was then, with exotic wood paneling, stone, and metal. It's open year-round, and free tours are available hourly Mon through Fri with weekend hours in the summer. Large groups can tour by appointment with one week's notice. Call (701) 328-2480.

The **North Dakota Heritage Center** (701-328-2666; www.nd.gov/hist) is on the Capitol grounds, and its permanent and changing exhibits reflect the history and settlement of the northern Great Plains. The artifacts cover the gamut of time periods, from a sinew-sewn buffalo-hide tepee to a mastodon skeleton. Admission is free, and the center is open daily, with limited hours on Sun. For outdoor sculpture, the statue of Sakakawea—her baby on her back—is a lovely memorial to the woman who guided Lewis and Clark through the territory.

Just a few blocks south is the **Former Governor's Mansion State Historic Site** (701-328-2666; 320 East Ave. B), the restored Victorian mansion that was occupied by the state's first families from 1893 to 1960. Interpretive exhibits and governors' portraits now occupy this elegant three-story structure. Tour the mansion (corner of Fourth Street and B Avenue) for free; it's open mid-May through mid-Sept Wed through Sun afternoons.

To see the great state of North Dakota in a similar fashion to Lewis and Clark over 200 years ago, hop aboard the **Lewis and Clark Riverboat,** a 150-passenger boat. Charters are available from Apr through Oct for weddings, family reunions, and office parties, and the riverboat offers daily excursion cruises, dinner cruises, sunset cruises, and special events for the entire family. The riverboat is located at the Port of Bismarck on North River Road, exit 157 off I-94. Call (701) 255-4233 for more information or visit the Web site at www .lewisandclarkriverboat.com.

North Dakota is again timelessly joined to South Dakota through the **Standing Rock Reservation,** which extends into both states. The people of the Standing Rock Sioux tribe are part of the Yanktonai and Teton Sioux Nation, which formerly controlled a vast domain that extended from the James River in North Dakota and South Dakota west to the Big Horn Mountains of Wyoming. In 1868 the Treaty of Fort Laramie reduced this area to the Great Sioux Reservation, setting the boundaries of a 25-million-acre tract that covered all of South Dakota west of the Missouri. When gold was discovered in the

BEST BISMARCK-MANDAN FAMILY ATTRACTIONS

**North Dakota Heritage Center
and the Capitol Grounds**
612 East Boulevard Ave.
Bismarck, ND 58501
(701) 328-2666

Dakota Zoo
602 Riverside Park Rd.
Bismarck, ND 58504
(701) 223-7543
www.dakotazoo.org

**Fort Abraham Lincoln
State Park**
4480 Fort Lincoln Rd.
Mandan, ND 58554
Park Information:
(701) 667-6340
Interpretive Programming:
(701) 663-4758
www.fortlincoln.com

Fort Lincoln Trolley
Departs from Third Street
Station in Mandan summer
afternoons, early June
through Labor Day
(701) 663-9018

Raging Rivers Waterpark
2600 Forty-eighth Ave. SE
Mandan, ND 58554
(701) 663-3393
www.ragingriverswaterpark.com

Papa's Pumpkin Patch
5001 Fernwood Dr.
Bismarck, ND 58503
(701) 222-1521
www.papaspumpkins.com
(Select weekends in the winter
it becomes Papa's Polar Patch.)
www.papaspolarpatch.com

Black Hills, Congress ratified an invalid agreement and took the Black Hills shortly thereafter. The Great Sioux Reservation was broken into six small reservations in 1889, one of which is Standing Rock (formerly called the Grand River Agency), situated on the North Dakota–South Dakota border between the Badlands and the Missouri River. On the western edge of Fort Yates, located on the Missouri River on the North Dakota portion of the Standing Rock Indian Reservation, is the original grave site of renowned Hunkpapa Sioux spiritual leader Sitting Bull.

On the Standing Rock Reservation, the powwow is a vital element of Lakota life today. Originally powwows were held in springtime to celebrate the beginning of life. In the Sioux tradition the celebration also was a prayer to *Wakan-Tanka,* the Great Spirit or Grandfather. Call (701) 854-7201 or visit www.standingrock.org for more information on powwows, which are highly educational and entertaining for all ages. The costumes are breathtaking.

Where to Stay in Western North Dakota

ALEXANDER

Ragged Butte Inn
US 85
(701) 828-3164
Inexpensive

BELFIELD

Cowboy Inn
2 blocks west of US 85
on US 10
(701) 575-4245
Inexpensive

BEULAH

Dakota Farms Inn
1200 Hwy. 49 North
(701) 873-2242
Inexpensive

BISMARCK

AmericInn of Bismarck
3235 State St.
(800) 634-3444
Moderate

Comfort Inn
1030 Interstate Ave.
(701) 223-1911
(800) 228-5150
Moderate

Expressway Inn
200 East Bismarck
Expressway
(800) 456-6388
Inexpensive

Kelly Inn
1800 North Twelfth St.
(701) 223-8001
Moderate

Radisson Hotel
605 East Broadway
(800) 333-3333
Moderate

BOWMAN

North Winds Lodge
US 85 South
(888) 684-9463
Inexpensive

MANDAN

**Best Western Seven
Seas Inn**
2611 Old Red Trail
(800) 597-7327
Moderate

**Colonial Motel and
RV Park**
4631 Memorial Hwy.
(701) 663-9824
Inexpensive

MEDORA

AmericInn Motel
75 East River Rd. S
(701) 623-4800
Moderate

Badlands Motel
located on the east side of
Medora
(701) 623-4422
Moderate

Rough Riders Hotel
301 Third Ave.
(800) 633-6721
Moderate

WILLISTON

Airport International Inn
3601 Second Ave. W
(701) 774-0241
Moderate

El Rancho Motor Hotel
1623 Second Ave. W
(800) 433-8529
Inexpensive

Where to Eat in Western North Dakota

BELFIELD

Trapper's Kettle
US 85
(701) 575-8585
Inexpensive to Moderate

BISMARCK

Bistro: An American Café
1103 East Front Ave.
(701) 224-8800
Moderate

83 Diner
(American)
1307 Interchange Ave.
(701) 258-3470
Moderate

Fiesta Villa
411 East Main Ave.
(701) 222-8075
Inexpensive

**Golden Dragon
Restaurant and Lounge**
410 East Main
(701) 258-0282
Moderate

Kroll's Kitchen
(German)
1915 East Main
(701) 255-3850
Moderate

Little Cottage Cafe
(American/German)
2513 East Main
(701) 223-4949
Moderate

**North American Steak
Buffet**
2000 North Twelfth St.
(701) 223-1107
Moderate

Paradiso
(Mexican)
2620 State St.
(701) 224-1111
Moderate

Peacock Alley
corner of Fifth Street
and Main Avenue
(701) 255-7917
Moderate to Expensive

Red Lobster
1130 East Century
(701) 222-2363
Moderate

Rock'n 50's Cafe
(American)
Gateway Mall
(701) 222-4612
Moderate

Space Aliens Grill & Bar
(American)
1304 East Century Ave.
(701) 223-6220
Moderate

The Walrus Restaurant
(Italian)
Arrowhead Plaza
North Third Street
(701) 250-0020
Moderate

DICKINSON

China Doll Restaurant
583 Twelfth St. W
(701) 227-1616
Inexpensive

German Hungarian Club
20 East Broadway
(701) 225-3311
Inexpensive

SELECTED CHAMBERS OF COMMERCE

Beulah Convention & Visitors Bureau
120 Central Ave. N
Beulah, 58523
(701) 873-4585

**Bismarck–Mandan Convention and
Visitors Bureau**
1600 Burnt Boat Dr.
Bismarck, 58503
(800) 767-3555
www.bismarckmandancvb.com

**Bottineau Convention and Visitors
Bureau**
519 Main St.
Bottineau, 58318
(701) 228-3849
www.bottineau.com

**Dickinson Convention and Visitors
Bureau**
72 East Museum Dr.
Dickinson, 58601
(800) 279-7391
www.dickinsoncvb.com

McKenzie County Tourism Bureau
201 Fifth St. NW
Watford City, 58854
(800) 701-2804
www.4eyes.net

**Williston Convention and Visitors
Bureau**
10 Main St.
Williston, 58801
(800) 615-9041
www.willistonndtourism.com

**Rattlesnake Creek
Brewery and Grill**
(American)
2 West Villard
(701) 225-9518
Inexpensive to Moderate

MEDORA

Cowboy Café
half-block north of historic
St. Mary's Catholic Church
(701) 623-4343
Moderate

**Little Missouri
Dining Room**
corner of Pacific and
Third Streets
(701) 623-4404
Moderate

WILLISTON

**Gramma Sharon's
Cafe Inc.**
US 2 and 885 North
(701) 572-1412
Inexpensive to moderate

Kalley's Kitchen
US 2 and 86 North
(701) 774-1103
Moderate

Trapper's Kettle
3901 Second Ave. W
(701) 774-2831
Inexpensive

CENTRAL NORTH DAKOTA →

With woods to explore, lush lakes, prairie potholes, and an international garden of incredible magnitude, Central North Dakota lures its share of visitors. They come for the world-class birding and outdoor activities, the chance to immerse themselves into the German–Russian or Nordic character of early pioneers, to walk the childhood paths of celebrities, and to experience Native American culture and rare opportunities such as seeing the albino bison the Dakota consider sacred. No matter which direction you point your vehicle, look for the vast patchwork of wheat and brilliant sunflowers that thrive in North Dakota's glacial soils, and listen for the songbirds and waterfowl that gather along rivers, potholes, and lakes, and also thrive across this region of prairie.

Germans-from-Russia Pocket

Start in the southern corner of Central North Dakota, an easy jaunt from Fort Yates to the home communities of North Dakota's German–Russians: Strasburg, Wishek, Linton and other area towns. Their European homelands are no longer in Germany. They left Alsace (then a German province, now part

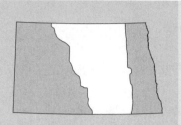

of France) around 1804 and resettled in Ukraine to farm and escape the Napoleonic Wars. In 1808–09 another wave of immigration created Roman Catholic communities along the Kutschurgan River in Russia, with names brought from Germany: Strassburg, Baden, and Selz. Those names arrived in North Dakota with yet another wave of immigration, fueled by overpopulation and Russian desires to turn the Germans into Russians. The name **Strasburg** underwent its second spelling change (Strasbourg, Strassburg, Strasburg), and Selz was bestowed upon two towns, the first of which, near Hague, disappeared. The second, in Pierce County, is still a thriving community. Black Sea Germans, or *Russlanddeutsch,* as they are called, are so far removed from Germany that the customs and language they preserve are ancient history in present-day Germany. Whereas French and Scottish immigrants quickly assimilated into North Dakota society, the Black Sea Germans maintained their cultural identity longer and were generally aloof to community involvement.

Nowadays the residents are eager to share their food and festivities. Oktoberfest, a traditional event in Germany, is replicated in many communities in south-central North Dakota, as well as in the western part of the state. The town of **Wishek,** for instance, has paid homage to fermented cabbage every Oct for seventy years with its **Sauerkraut Days.** Schoolchildren get out of school early for the free wiener-and-kraut lunch. If kraut's not your style, try *knoephla* soup (spelled many ways, but the soup is always buttery with potatoes and dumplings) and *fleischkuekle,* a beef-filled pasty, or pierogi. The festival is replete with food and drink, and you can hear the oompah-pahs of polka throughout the community.

The family histories of the people who live here are strikingly similar to that of "wunnerful, wunnerful" **Lawrence Welk,** the famous Champagne

TOP HITS IN CENTRAL NORTH DAKOTA

Devils Lake

International Peace Garden
on the U.S. border
(888) 432-6733

National Buffalo Museum
Jamestown
(701) 252-8648

Norsk Hostfest
Oct, Minot
(701) 852-2368

North Dakota Birding Trail

North Dakota State Fair
July, Minot
(701) 857-7620

Turtle Mountains

Music Maker. Welk's father had grown increasingly unhappy with life in Russia, and in 1892 he and his wife came to America. Their voyage was financed by an uncle who ran a store in Strasburg. Lawrence Welk was born in 1903, and he spoke only German until he was twenty-one years old. This was not uncommon for children of German–Russian descent, as parents were reluctant to send their children to school, only allowing them to attend when their work was finished on the farm.

Welk was the sixth of nine children, and on his twenty-first birthday he left for Bismarck. He played his accordion at weddings and dances until his great break came in 1955 with a chance to appear on national TV.

Welk's birthplace, officially known as the ***Ludwig & Christina Welk Farmstead,*** is nestled among wheat fields north of Strasburg. Although the home is made of sod, with 3-foot-thick walls, it has white siding on the exterior and wallpaper inside. It is open Fri through Mon from 10 a.m. to 5 p.m. Memorial Day through Labor Day and by appointment. Welk died in sunny southern California in 1992, the year the homestead restoration was completed. It's no wonder that Welk's greatest aficionados come from North Dakota and neighboring Minnesota and Iowa. More than 7,000 Welk fans visit the site each year. Admission is $5 for adults; $3 for children age 6 to 12. For more information call (701) 336-7103.

North Dakota is a paradise for birds, with 63 National Wildlife Refuges. That's more than any other state. More than 320 species and an estimated 53 million songbirds, shorebirds, birds of prey, wading birds, upland birds, and nesting waterfowl make their home here in the summer. What makes this area unique is its convergence of eastern and western species and the thriving prairie potholes that polka-dot the landscape east of the Missouri River. Several lie between the German–Russian communities and just north of I-94 as it stretches west to east across the state. Look for Long Lake National Wildlife Refuge, Blade National Wildlife Refuge, and Chase Lake National Wildlife Refuge, which is known for harboring white masses of pelicans. You can get complete details on the best birding hot spots in the region of Steele, Carrington, and Jamestown, by calling (888) 921-2473 or checking out www.birdingdrives .com. Most towns throughout Central North Dakota also have birding festivals or birding drives. Ask for birding brochures at visitor centers or check out the birding section in the State of North Dakota's annual Travel Guide (800-435-5663; www.ndtourism.com).

East of Wishek on ND 13 is the tiny town of ***Kulm,*** hometown of actress Angie Dickinson and near one of the more haunting sites in the state. ***Whitestone Hill Battlefield Site*** was the site of North Dakota's most deadly clash of Native Americans and U.S. Calvary. It's truly off the beaten path, a 23-mile

Prairie Birding Checklist

Birds unique to the pristine prairies include the western grebe, ferruginous hawk, Hungarian partridge, sharp-tailed grouse, piping plover, upland sandpiper, marbled godwit, clay-colored sparrow, and the chestnut-collared longspur. Several endangered or threatened birds have been documented in North Dakota by the U.S. Fish and Wildlife Service, including the interior least tern, bald eagle, whooping crane, peregrine falcon, and piping plover. For details on the refuges, including maps and trails, go to www.fws.gov/mountain-prairie/refuges/nd.

detour that heads 15 miles south of Kulm on ND 56, then east on an unimproved road.

The battle lasted about two hours as General Alfred Sully's troops attacked a tepee camp of Yanktonai, some Dakota, Hunkpapa Lakota, and Blackfeet (Sihasapa Lakota) on September 3, 1863. It was part of a military mission to punish participants of the Dakota Conflict of 1862. Tribes were being forced west by European settlers in Minnesota, and the bison herds on the Dakota plains were being decimated. By sunset an estimated 150 to 300 Sioux had lost their lives and 156 were taken prisoner. The cavalry's death toll was considerably less: Only twenty cavalrymen died, and fifty to sixty were wounded. There are memorials to both sides of the battle on-site, alone with a self-guided tour and a small museum, picnic area, and playground. The North Dakota Historical Society (701-328-2666; http://history.nd.gov/historicsites/whitestone) operates the museum mid-May to mid-Sept Thurs through Mon. The local Whitestone Historical Society hosts an annual summer event at the site to commemorate the battle.

Land of Louis L'Amour

Jamestown, nestled in the valley where the James and Pipestem Rivers meet, is appropriately known as Buffalo City. You should be able to see the herd of about 30 bison from either side of the Interstate, but it absolutely deserves a closer look. Native Americans have long revered the rare albino bison as sacred, and Jamestown's **National Buffalo Museum** now has three: White Cloud, who has been here since 1997; Dakota Miracle, whom she gave birth to in 2007; and Dakota Legend, an albino calf born to another member of the herd in 2008.

The **Frontier Village** (701-252-6307) details the way humans came to live and learn on the land. A post office, trading post, 1881 church, fire department, and barbershop are some of the structures that re-create small-town life in the

1800s. If you have children, be sure to take the stagecoach ride so they appreciate the modern wonders of paved roads and shock absorbers. The village is open 9 a.m. to 9 p.m. Memorial Day through Labor Day. Admission is free.

One of the favorite stops at the village is the writing shack of famed western novelist and Jamestown native **Louis L'Amour,** the highest-selling western author of all time. He wrote 117 books and is best known for his frontier books, such as *Mustang Man, The Sackett Brand, Ride the Dark Trail,* and *The Daybreakers.* More than thirty of his books became movies, including *Hondo,* with John Wayne; *Shalako,* starring Sean Connery; and *The Burning Hills,* which featured Tab Hunter and Natalie Wood.

If you want to learn more about the man who lassoed the American West spirit with words, walk the **Louis L'Amour Trail** in Jamestown. The first stop is the Dakota Territory Courthouse, where L'Amour's father worked as the county and the state veterinarian. He also doubled as a deputy sheriff for several years. The courthouse is located at Fifth Street and Third Avenue Southeast in Jamestown.

The Stutsman County Memorial Museum (located in the Lutz Mansion) and the Jamestown City Hall are next along the trail, then the L'Amour Family Home Site. This is where L'Amour's boyhood home was originally located, at 113 Third Ave. SE. The home was later moved to another part of Jamestown and structurally changed.

Legend of the White Buffalo

The white buffalo is sacred to the Lakota people. Legend says the White Buffalo Calf Woman brought them their most sacred pipe. This beautiful woman in a white buckskin dress spent four days and four nights showing the Lakota how to smoke the pipe, on which a bison calf was carved on one side. As the White Buffalo Calf Woman left, she walked in the direction of the setting sun, stopped, and rolled over four times. The first time, she got up and became a black buffalo; the second time, a brown buffalo; the third time, a red buffalo; and the fourth time she rolled over, she became a white buffalo. This buffalo walked on farther, stopped, and after bowing to each of the four directions of the universe, disappeared over the hill. Head into the rustic log building on the *Frontier Village* campus, 500 Seventeenth St. SE, to learn about the significance of buffalo from prehistoric times to the present, from legends and artifacts, to artwork and interpretive panels that also explain how buffalo helped Lewis and Clark survive. There is a viewing deck at the museum to truly study the herd as it roams across 200 acres. Hours are 8 a.m. to 8 p.m. daily Memorial Day through Labor Day; 9 a.m. to 5 p.m. Mon through Fri and 10 a.m. to 5 p.m. Sat the rest of the year, plus noon to 5 p.m. Sun in May, Sept and Oct (701-252-8648; www.buffalomuseum.com).

The First United Methodist Church, the Alfred Dickey Library (one of the young boy's favorite places), Franklin Grade School, and Walz Pharmacy, once owned by L'Amour's friend Reese Hawkins and stocked with all of the writer's books, also are highlighted along the trail.

L'Amour's writing reflects his Dakota roots. "The sort of men and women it took to open the West were the kind of whom stories were told. Strongly individual, willing to risk all they possessed as well as their lives, they were also prepared to fight for what they believed was theirs," he wrote in *The Sackett Companion.*

L'Amour is the only writer to receive the Presidential Medal of Freedom and the Congressional Gold Medal. An elephant handler, a professional boxer, a seaman, and a journalist, L'Amour, who died in 1988, is warmly remembered in his hometown.

An attractive brochure charting the Louis L'Amour Trail is available at the Jamestown Visitor Center, 404 Louis L'Amour Lane, at Frontier Village or call (800) 222-4766 or (701) 251-9145. They also have information on the area's 30 miles of hiking and biking.

Louis L'Amour wasn't Jamestown's only world-famous firstborn. Norma Deloris Egstrom, better known as the singer Peggy Lee, was also born in Jamestown, on May 26, 1920.

At the north end of town on US 281, the ***Fort Seward Historic Site and Interpretive Center*** (701-252-8421), which overlooks Pipestem Lake, sheds light on the early military history of the region. The center is open daily 10 a.m. to 6 p.m. Memorial Day through Labor Day, although the grounds and picnic area are open year-round. Homesteading by covered wagon is commemorated each year in the ***Fort Seward Wagon Train*** (www.covered-wagon-train.com). Participants don mandatory pioneer costumes during a one-week wagon train reenactment. The wagon train was first organized in 1969

Nicknames for North Dakota

- **Peace Garden State,** the official license-plate nickname inspired by the International Peace Garden since 1957.

- **Flickertail State,** referring to the Richardson ground squirrel that flicks or jerks its tail while running or just before entering its burrow.

- **Roughrider State,** referring to the first U.S. Volunteer Cavalry that Theodore Roosevelt organized to fight in the Spanish–American War. In fact, the Roughriders included several North Dakota cowboys.

as a one-time experience, but promoters found it so worthwhile they made it a yearly event. The wagon train starts rolling at the crack of dawn, and it averages 3 to 4 miles per hour. At the end of the day, singing and storytelling around the campfire foster camaraderie, pioneer style—a memorable family affair. Just north on US 281 the 840-acre **Pipestem Dam and Lake** offers year-round recreational opportunities, and the lovely lake fascinates bird-watchers, boaters, anglers, and others. Conservation of wildlife and the natural environment is a major objective of the U.S. Army Corps of Engineers, and 4,200 acres of creek valley and rolling upland at Pipestem are home to a wide variety of wildlife and waterfowl. The natural setting has been enhanced by selective planting of more than 250,000 trees around the lake.

Jamestown's **Arts Center** (115 Second St. SW; 701-251-2496) features monthly visual-art exhibitions. The **1914 Basilica of St. James** (701-252-0119), at 622 First Ave. S, is the only basilica in North Dakota and one of less than fifty in the entire United States. The **North Dakota Sports Hall of Fame** (located in the civic center at 212 Third Ave.) pays tribute to those who have shaped the growth and development of sports in North Dakota. Hall of Famers include basketball's Phil Jackson, baseball's Roger Maris, and football's Dave Osborn. For more information call (701) 252-8089.

The **Stutsman County Memorial Museum,** at 321 Third Ave. SE, is housed in the George Lutz mansion, a monument to the early-day history of the area. Four floors in the stately brick museum are devoted to the culture and life of the early pioneers. The first floor, with a complete dining room, kitchen, and butler's pantry, highlights items that a pioneer homemaker might have used. Military life and the railroad's strength in the state are featured on the second floor, and pioneer medicine, wildlife, and church relics round out this eclectic collection on the third floor. A room in the basement has been turned into a claim shanty. Many visitors love the home's art nouveau-style stained glass and Tiffany lamps the best. The museum is open Mon through Fri from 10 a.m. to 5 p.m. and Sat and Sun from 1 to 5 p.m. Memorial Day through Sept 30 Free admission. For more information call (701) 252-6741.

For swimming, camping, fishing, and boating, the **Lakeside Marina and Recreational Area** (701-252-9200) is just 3 miles north on ND 20 at the Jamestown Dam. Camping and tent and trailer sites are available. There is a fee for some activities. Open early May through late Sept.

If you go 25 miles northwest of Jamestown on US 281, which joins US 52, you'll drive into the 16,000-acre **Arrowwood National Wildlife Refuge** (701-285-3341), where the Jamestown River meanders among marshes and lakes. A self-guided automobile tour affords breathtaking views of duck broods in summer and migrating snow geese in fall.

All Creatures Great and Small

As you are traveling along the highways and byways of North Dakota, be on the lookout for small, brown-and-white roadside signs featuring binoculars, which indicate one of the state's eighty-plus roadside viewing areas.

Watch the birds and beasts from a distance with good-quality binoculars, a spotting scope, or a telephoto lens. If the animals you are watching are watching you—with their heads up and ears facing your direction—or are nervous, you are probably too close or moving too quickly.

Obviously, be kind to these bashful critters. Patience will reward you. Keep quiet and wait for animals to return to or enter an area. The early and late hours of daylight are generally the best times to watch and photograph most wildlife.

North on US 281 and 52 is *Carrington,* which, like most of the communities in North Dakota, can trace its development to the arrival of the railroad. By 1882 the Northern Pacific line ran through the yet unnamed prairie settlement. Agriculture formed the base for Carrington's early- and present-day economy. It's home to the state-of-the-art Dakota Growers Pasta Co., which markets pasta made from the durum wheat grown in the region.

History and art buffs, be sure to check out the *Putnam House* (533 Main St.), an American Foursquare home built in 1907 by Thomas Nichols Putnam, the area's pioneer lumberman, and his wife Clara Belle Putnam. The 4,300-square-foot home is testament to the precise craftsmanship and architecture of the turn of the 20th century. The grand staircase is a breathtaking focal point, and the dining room features a built-in oak buffet with leaded-glass doors. It's more than a majestic, though. It's also a rural cultural and community center, providing an inspiring setting for summer concerts on the wraparound porch, art exhibits, and hands-on classes in stained glass, jewelry, ethnic cooking, and more. For details and upcoming events, call (701) 652-1213 or go to www.putnamhouse.org.

Just 6 miles southwest of Carrington on US 52 is *Hawk's Nest,* a butte standing 300 feet above the surrounding plains on 100 acres of unfenced land. The area has one of the few remaining stands of buffalo grass and pine oaks. Visitors to Hawk's Nest, which is maintained by the local Kiwanis Club, can hike, camp, and ski there.

Detour straight east of Carrington to Cooperstown for a look at the Cold War era and one of the newest attractions: *Ronald Reagan Minuteman Missile State Historic Sites,* opened in 2009. Here visitors can go 50 feet into a concrete capsule to the control center for 10 Minuteman Missiles. The site is one of 15 command centers and 150 missile sites manned by the **Grand Forks Air Force Base** and set up to defend the country at the peak of the Cold War that began in the mid-1960s. The sites were decommissioned starting in 1991. It's open 10 a.m. to 6 p.m. daily mid-May through mid-Sept and Thurs through Sat and Mon Mar through May and Sept through Oct. 31. Off-season, it's open by appointment only. Call (701) 797-3691 or go to http://history.nd.gov/historic sites/minutemanmissile. Admission is $10 for adults; $3 for children. The facility is four miles north of Cooperstown at 555 113-1/2 Ave. NE along ND 45.

Devils Lake and the Rendezvous Region

Head an hour north of Carrington on US 281 to reach the emerald waters of **Devils Lake** at the crossroads of ND 19 and ND 20. Don't let the name fool you. This spring-fed lake was once dubbed "Enchanted Waters." Some speculate the nickname was mistranslated. Others point to its legend as "Bad Spirit Lake," after a group of Sioux drowned in 4-foot waves while returning from battle. Either way, the name Devils Lake stuck. The state's largest body of water covers more than 70,000 prairie acres and nurtures forests of hardwood oak, ash, and elm that provide year-round recreation. Walleye and white bass are the top draws, and yellow perch are found in winter. Migrating geese, ducks, and sandhill cranes take over the skies each spring and fall. Devils Lake State Parks comprises three parks and recreation areas. Call (800) 233-8043 or visit www.devilslakend.com for more information.

On the south shore of Devils Lake, **Sullys Hill National Game Preserve** shelters swans, bison, elk, deer, prairie dogs, and other wildlife with its native habitat. Don't miss the beautiful lake overlook, and bring binoculars for the four-mile auto tour open May through Oct. In the winter, you can ski the trails. Stop in the visitor center for maps, exhibits, and a look at native species in the 180-gallon aquarium. The preserve is 12 miles southwest of the town of Devils Lake on ND 57. Admission is free. Call (701) 766-4272 or visit www.fws.gov/sullyshill for information.

Thirteen miles southwest of Devils Lake on ND 57, one of the best-preserved military outposts west of the Mississippi West is found at the **Fort Totten State Historic Site** (701-328-2666; www.nd.gov/hist). Fort Totten was built in 1867 to protect the overland route to Montana and was the last outpost before 300 miles of wilderness. It later became an Indian boarding school, health care facility, and then a reservation school. Self-guided tours of the 17 original buildings can be enjoyed year-round. In the summer months, check out performances at the Fort Totten Little Theatre.

To get a firsthand frontier experience, stay at the ***Totten Trail Historic Inn.*** The bed-and-breakfast inn right on the historic site is furnished in period style (1870–1910). Rooms are available year-round, with prices ranging from $80 to $110. Some rooms have a private bath, and others share a bath with one other room. A stay includes breakfast and a Victorian-style afternoon tea. Proceeds fund continuing renovations at the fort. For more information, call (701) 766-4874 or go to www.tottentrailinn.com.

Norsemen and the Turtle Mountains

Norwegians accounted for a large number of the immigrants who came to North Dakota. Seventy-five percent of the soil in their homeland was not suitable for agriculture, so it was natural these Norwegians sought the fertile farmland of North Dakota. Only Ireland lost a greater percentage of its people to America.

Norwegian culture thrives at the renowned ***Norsk Hostfest*** at the state fairgrounds in ***Minot,*** which is located at the crossroads of US 2 and US 83 and is home to 36,567 people. An estimated 60,000 people attend North America's largest Scandinavian festival, where you can catch a heady whiff of cardamom-spiced sweet breads, tap your feet to fiddles, and enjoy the kaleidoscope whirl of dancers in ethnic costumes. Held each fall for more than 30 years, the Host-fest brings in big-name entertainers on seven stages and more than 200 artisans and craftsmen with everything from delicate silver jewelry to sturdy tine boxes. Bite into favorite desserts such as lefse, rommegrot, rosettes, and krumkake or bravely sample the infamous lutefisk. For multicourse fine dining, reserve a seat at En to Tre. Chefs prepare a buffet with traditional dishes such as smoked salmon, shrimp, herring, lingonberry preserves, roasted meats, cold plates, flat-breads, and cheeses to be savored by Norwegians and non-Norwegians alike. Call (701) 852-2368 or check out www.hostfest.com.

The ***Scandinavian Heritage Center,*** at South Broadway and Eleventh Avenue, is the world's only outdoor living museum that is dedicated to preserving the ethnic heritage of all five Scandinavian countries. Buildings on the premises include a visitor center; a stabbur (storage house) from Telemark, Norway; a Finnish sauna; Danish windmill; Dala horse; Stave church museum; an eternal flame brought to North Dakota from Norway; and a 230-year-old house from Sigdal, Norway. Hours vary by season. Call (701) 852-9161 or check www.scandinavianheritage.org for details.

The ***Minot Holiday Inn*** (located directly across from the State Fairgrounds and All Seasons Arena) combines modern architecture with contemporary, finely appointed interiors. The poolside restaurant, Ground Round Bar & Grill (a favorite in North Dakota), lounge, and casino complete a memorable stay. Rates start at $84. For reservations call (800) 468-9968. If you're in the bed-and-breakfast mood, try the **Dakotah Rose Bed & Breakfast** at 510 Fourth Ave. NW (701-838-3548). Call for rates.

The must-go summer event is the **North Dakota State Fair** in Minot. How big is it? Think of it by the numbers: 300,000 visitors; 46,000 competitive exhibits; 600 vendors; 24 buildings; 10 free stages; nine days of fun; and three nights each of rodeo contests and rumbling car and truck competitions. The new grandstand opens in 2010 and will be able to hold 15,000 spectators.

Call (701) 857-7620 or visit the Web site at www.ndstatefair.com. Also on the fairgrounds is the Ward County Historical Society Pioneer Village and Museum, open May through Sept.

The nineteen-acre **Roosevelt Park Zoo** (701-857-4166; www.rpzoo.com) is the home of a black-footed penguin collection. No doubt these flightless seabirds enjoy the chilly temperatures during North Dakota winters. Warmer-blooded residents include spider monkeys, kangaroos, a white Bengal tiger, giraffes, and llamas. Concessions, a children's zoo, a gift shop, and an educational center also are part of the zoo, which is located on the east side of town off the Burdick Expressway. The zoo is open daily 10 a.m. to 8 p.m. in the summer and 10 a.m. to 6 p.m. in May and Sept. Admission is $6 for adults, $3 for children ages 4 to 12, and free for children 3 and younger.

The Roosevelt Park and Zoo is the fifth point along the 2.5-mile **River-walk,** a walking and biking trail. Riverwalk starts at the **Railroad Museum** (701-852-7091) at 19 First St. NE. The museum presents the history and progression of the railroad through photographs and other memorabilia. A two-fifths-scale train, located at the north end of Roosevelt Park, travels down a milelong track.

The second point of interest is the **Lillian and Coleman Taube Museum of Art** (701-838-4445) at 2 North Main St. The Minot Arts Association renovated the former Union National Bank building as a center for the visual arts, educational programs, and cultural and social events. Hours are 10:30 a.m. to 5:30 p.m. Tues through Fri and 11 a.m. to 4 p.m. on Sat.

As you traverse the Riverwalk, you will also discover **Val's Cyclery** (701-839-4817) at 222 East Central, where Rocky and Rory Schell continue the cycling and fitness tradition started by their father, Valentine, more than forty years ago. **Eastwood Park** is the next stop. This is a splendid place to check out the architectural styles of homes from Minot's early days: Princess Anne, English Tudor, and arts and crafts. In 1986 the neighborhood was designated a National Historic District.

Other sites along the Riverwalk are Lowe's Garden Center (701-839-2000), which is housed in a replica of an early North Dakota train depot; North

Dakota State Fair and All Seasons Arena; MotorMania, which takes place every Labor Day weekend at the fairgrounds; and the **Ward County Historical Society Pioneer Village and Museum** (701-839-0785). Pioneer Village and Museum, located at the west entrance to the fairgrounds, is a collection of preserved and restored historic buildings, housing vintage automobiles and thousands of artifacts that illuminate Minot's past. Starting in May and ending in Oct, the museum is open from 10 a.m. to 6 p.m. Tues through Sun.

For more information about Riverwalk, call the Minot Convention and Visitors Bureau at (800) 264-2626.

And before leaving Minot, by air or by land, be sure to check out the **Dakota Territory Air Museum** (701-852-8500; www.dakotaterritoryair museum.com), which is adjacent to the northwest corner of the Minot International Airport. It features civilian and military aircraft from 1928 to the present. If you love things that fly, this is the place to be. You'll find civilian aircraft, from a 1928 Waco to a 1946 Piper J-3 Cub, as well as a Lockheed T-33 jet trainer, a Douglas C-47 World War II transport, and a Curtis P-40 Hawk. Also prominently displayed—and still operational—is the Minot Airport beacon, which guided pilots in the area from 1949 to 1993. And the price can't be beat: $2 for adults and $1 for children ages 6 to 17. The museum is open from 10 a.m. to 5 p.m. Mon through Sat and from 1 to 5 p.m. Sun. The museum is mid-May through mid-Oct.

One of the prettiest places to take a fall drive is along the 28-mile Des Lac River Valley, which kisses the Canadian border and stretches southeast along US 52 to Kenmare, about 50 miles northwest of Minot.

Hop onto the 12-mile scenic drive along Des Lac Lake from near the Baden overpass to a picnic area five miles northwest of Kenmare. There are several scenic pull-outs and 13 interpretive panels about the area, famous for vast fields of wheat and cheery sunflowers. In the town of Kenmare, look for the 1902 **Old Danish Mill,** a restored flour mill with millstones that weigh 1,800 pounds.

For a truly stunning sight, head to the **Des Lacs National Wildlife Refuge** one mile west of Kenmare. While it's great for picnics, hikes, and birding year-round, it's best known as a staging area for up to 500,000 snow geese as they gather and prepare for migration (701-835-4046; www.fws.gov/ jclarksalyer/desclacs).

East of Kenmare and northeast of Minot, the bustling community of **Bottineau** is the gateway to the Turtle Mountain area. Travel 37 miles north of Minot on US 83, then 43 miles east on ND 5. Up north there's something to do every season at **Lake Metigoshe State Park,** a wooded natural area with numerous lakes. Lake Metigoshe is one of the most popular year-round vacation spots in the state.

Crossing the Border

If you plan to travel between Canada and North Dakota at any of the 18 border crossings, heightened security measures means you'll need a passport or a U.S. passport card. The card, a slimmed down version of a passport, is good for travel in Canada, Mexico, and the Caribbean. Apply for one and find out more about customs procedures at www.travel.state.gov.

The best way to avoid delays and hassles when crossing the international border is to be prepared.

In either direction, customs officials will ask you where you live, your citizenship, the purpose of your trip, how long you intend to stay, and if you have any goods to declare. There may be questions about alcohol, tobacco, and firearms. If you made a duty-free purchase, state how much you bought. When returning home, you may be asked what you have purchased, so it's a good idea to save your sales slips and pack your items so they can be easily inspected at the border. Oral declarations are the general rule.

Imagine this: It's July 14, 1932, and you're one of the 50,000 people who have traveled 13 miles north of Dunseith, North Dakota, for the dedication of the *International Peace Garden*—a lavish garden on the border that commemorates peace between Canada and the United States. Dr. Henry J. Moore, a horticulturist from Islington, Ontario, Canada, conceived the idea for the garden when he was on his way home from the 1928 annual meeting of the National Association of Gardeners, a U.S. organization. He thought it was a fitting tribute to the peaceful existence between the two countries.

The proposal was approved at the association's 1929 meeting, and the search began for an appropriate site. Moore liked what he saw when visiting the Turtle Mountains. After a plane ride over the area, he remarked: "What a sight greeted the eye. Those undulating hills rising out of the limitless prairies are filled with lakes and streams. On the south of the unrecognizable boundary, wheat fields everywhere; and on the north, the Manitoba Forest Preserve. What a place for a garden!"

The tablet on a cairn of native stone reads: TO GOD IN HIS GLORY . . . WE TWO NATIONS DEDICATE THIS GARDEN AND PLEDGE OURSELVES THAT AS LONG AS MAN SHALL LIVE WE WILL NOT TAKE ARMS AGAINST ONE ANOTHER. The two countries chose a place situated on ND 3, the longest north-south road in the world, and about centrally located on the continent of North America (Turtle Mountains).

The border walk through the Formal Gardens is a one-of-a-kind chance to see an enormous carpet of flowers in bloom across two nations. The 1.5-mile walk takes you past fountains, pools, cascades, the Perennial Garden, Arbor Garden, arboretum, bell tower, and the recently renovated Sunken Garden, Conservatory and Visitor Center.

If you visit between July 15 and Aug 15, you'll be dazzled by hundreds of orange and yellow Asiatic lilies. Most gardens hit their peak color in Aug. Self-guided driving tours will allow you to see Lake Udall on the United States side and Lake Stormon on the Canadian side.

One of the most touching displays at the garden is the 9/11 Memorial Site, which pays tribute to the more than 2,800 lives lost in the September 11, 2001, terrorist attack. On June 3, 2002, the International Peace Garden received ten 10-foot girders from the World Trade Center wreckage. The girders lie at rest at the 9/11 Memorial Site as an everlasting reminder of the human tragedy that occurred one quiet Sept morning in New York City, Pennsylvania, and Washington, D.C.

The park isn't only for the green thumbs in the family; it's also the perfect spot for the culturally inclined. The International Music Camp is held annually during early summer at the park, featuring Sat concerts with guest conductors and an old-time fiddlers' contest.

The International Peace Garden is one of the prettiest spots in the nation for picnicking, camping, or just sitting back and absorbing the scents and beauty of nature. The grounds are open daily, with camping available May through mid-Oct. For detailed information call (888) 432-6733 or, in Canada, (204) 534-2510. You can also visit the Web site at www.peacegarden.com. To get to the garden from Bottineau, travel 13 miles east on ND 5 until you

24-hour Ports of Entry

Pembina, North Dakota, and Emerson, Manitoba
I-29
(701) 825-6551

Dunseith, North Dakota
(International Peace Garden),
and Boissevain, Manitoba
US 281
(701) 263-4460

Portal, North Dakota, and North Portal, Saskatchewan
US 52
(701) 926-4241

All other ports of entry are open daily with varied hours.

reach Dunseith; then take US 281 north for 13 miles.

If you drive US 281 south back to Dunseith, check out the quirky Wee'l Turtle statue, made from more than 2,000 tire rims. Then take US 281 east approximately 18 miles, which will take you right through Belcourt, near the lovely town of **Rolla** and the heart of the magnificent Turtle Mountains.

Peace among nations is nothing new in this territory. Ancient tribes became nations of Mandan, Hidatsa, Arikara, as well as Yanktonai, Sisseton, Wahpeton, Pembina Chippewa, Cree,

asprawling tributetopeace

The International Peace Garden has:

- 2,339 acres of gardens
- 150,000 annuals
- 50,000 perennials and hardy bulbs
- 5,000 flower shrubs
- 300 shade and flowering trees

and Metis. Each had its own culture, yet many worked together during years of peace and years of turmoil and change. Their traditions, philosophies, and spirituality have made an unparalleled contribution to the sumptuous cultural landscape of North Dakota.

The Turtle Mountain Band of Pembina Chippewa live in the wooded, rolling hills of north-central North Dakota. Their ancestors came from the Great Lakes region in the late 1700s, essentially drawn west by the fur-trade business. As trappers, voyagers, entrepreneurs, and caretakers of the land, the Pembina Chippewa formed enduring relations with other indigenous and European peoples, most significantly the Cree and the French. The Chippewa and Metis people built and developed North Dakota's oldest still-existing community: **Pembina,** located east of the Turtle Mountains and tucked into the far northeast corner of the state. The Red River Valley and northern North Dakota were the choice hunting territories of the Pembina Chippewas after the 1800s. As part of the continuing westward migration and following a stir of treaty making, Chief Little Shell III brought his band across the Dakota prairie to the Turtle Mountains, an area much like the woodlands of Minnesota. On December 21, 1882, the **Turtle Mountain Indian Reservation** was established. It is now located on 33,100 acres in Rolette County, where the community of Belcourt is situated.

The reservation is surrounded by the beautiful **Turtle Mountains,** which offer endless recreational opportunities that include cultural centers, gaming facilities, powwows, fishing, swimming, skiing, golfing, and sundry community-sponsored events. Named the Turtle Mountains 200 years ago by explorers, these hills, flecked with lovely lakes, have long been home to native tribes.

One of the safest bets for accommodations and entertainment is the *Sky Dancer Hotel & Casino,* located 5 miles west of Belcourt on US 281. The hotel, which is operated by the Turtle Mountain Band of Chippewa, features ninety-seven guest rooms, the Chippewa Trails Restaurant, and a 37,000-square-foot casino with poker and blackjack tables, bingo, and 525 slot machines. For more information, call (866) 244-9467 or visit the Web site at www.skydancercasino.com.

Two miles from Belcourt on ND 5, the *Anishinaubag Intercultural Center* (701-477-5519) offers a hands-on living-history experience in a reconstructed Plains Indian village. In a natural wooded 100-acre setting, visitors can see Native American architecture, villages, a trading post, log cabins, and a log round house, used for dances and meetings. Canoe rental also is available at this exquisite lake setting.

enchantedforests

The oak and aspen forests of the Turtle Mountain State Forest provide refuge to a variety of birds, including rugged grouse, magpies, and vireos. Also commonly seen are deer, moose, and small mammals such as squirrels, woodchucks, raccoons, and snowshoe hares.

Six miles east of Belcourt on US 281 is Rolla, which hosts the annual *International Ragtop Festival* each July. The three-day salute to America's automotive gem—the convertible—rolls out a parade, rock 'n' roll concerts, and other activities. For more information call (701) 477-3610.

Twenty-three miles south of Rolla on Highway 30 is the *Dale and Martha Hawk Foundation Museum,* with North Dakota's largest collection of antique farm machinery and the only known working Hackney Auto Plow. The collection is housed in five historic buildings, including a church, a store, and a schoolhouse. It's open 9 a.m. to 6 p.m. seven days a week May through Sept. Camping also is available. Call (701) 583-2381 or visit www.hawkmuseum.org.

SELECTED CHAMBERS OF COMMERCE

Jamestown Tourism Center
404 Louis L'Amour Lane
Jamestown 58401
(800) 222-4766
www.tourjamestown.com

Minot Convention and Visitors Bureau
1020 South Broadway
Minot 58702
(800) 264-2626
www.visitminot.org

Where to Stay in Central North Dakota

BOTTINEAU
Norway House
1255 Hwy. 5 SE
(701) 228-3737
Inexpensive

DEVILS LAKE
Comfort Inn
215 US 2 East
(701) 662-6760
Inexpensive

Davis Motel
702 US 2 West
(701) 662-4927
Inexpensive

Super 8
1001 US 2 East
(701) 662-8656
Inexpensive

Totten Trail Historic Inn
14 miles south of Devils
Lake
(701) 766-4874
www.tottentrailinn.com
Moderate

MINOT
Dakotah Rose Bed & Breakfast
510 Fourth Ave. NW
(701) 838-3548
Moderate

Days Inn
2100 Fourth St. SW
(701) 852-3646
Inexpensive

Grand International Inn
1505 North Broadway
(701) 852-3161
Inexpensive to Moderate

Where to Eat in Central North Dakota

DEVILS LAKE
Cedar Inn Family Restaurant
US 2 West
(701) 662-8893
Inexpensive

Dakotah Buffet
ND 57 South
Fort Totten
(701) 766-4747
Moderate

Mr. & Mrs. J's Restaurant
US 2 East
(701) 662-8815
Inexpensive to Moderate

MINOT
Homesteaders Restaurant
2501 Elk Dr.
(701) 838-2274
Moderate

Michael's Restaurant
515 Twentieth Ave. SE
(701) 837-6133
Moderate

EASTERN NORTH DAKOTA

→

As you travel toward the North Dakota–Minnesota border, the alluvial Red River Valley defines the history and economy of the far eastern third of North Dakota. It is one of the greatest agricultural regions in the world and is often compared with the Valley of the Nile.

The Red River Valley is the remnant of the lakebed of the huge, ancient glacial Lake Agassiz, and its waters flow into the Hudson Bay and eventually into the Arctic Ocean. The valley varies from 10 to 40 miles in width from north to south along the border of North Dakota and Minnesota and is relatively flat, with an average elevation of 900 feet. Rich chernozem (black) soils are found in the Red River Valley; promoters in the 1800s hailed the valley as the Garden of Eden, conveniently omitting the fact, however, that early spring flooding or a lack of water coupled with a short growing season could be less than idyllic.

North Dakota's livelihood, nonetheless, has always depended upon its soil, and that soil has made the state the land of plenty, whether in agriculture, crude oil, or lignite (a brown variety of very soft coal). North Dakotans simply call this long eastern corridor of woodlands in the north and agricultural bounty in the south *The Valley.*

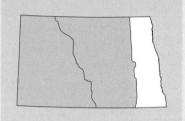

CANADA
NORTH DAKOTA

Grafton

NORTH
DAKOTA
HERITAGE

Grand
Forks

NORTH DAKOTA · MINNESOTA

EDEN

Valley
City

Fargo

Wahpeton

NORTH DAKOTA
SOUTH DAKOTA

N

0   50 mi

0   50 km

TOP HITS IN EASTERN NORTH DAKOTA

Bagg Bonanza Farm
45 miles south of Fargo
(701) 274-8989

Fargo Theatre
314 Broadway
(701) 289-8385

Fort Abercrombie State Historic Site
Abercrombie
(701) 553-8513

Pembina State Museum
(701) 825-6840

In the very northeast corner of the state, the four communities of Walhalla, Pembina, Langdon, and Cavalier successfully meld various traditions and nationalities. The largest Icelandic settlement in America is located within the region—providing a fascinating chapter in the rich history of the frontier West. The towns of Mountain, Gardar, Hallson, Svold, and Akra were settled in 1873–79 by Icelanders coming from a sister colony in Gimli, Manitoba. After traversing the fertile Red River Valley, the immigrants reached the Pembina Escarpment, a hilly wooded region that overlooks the valley. They put down roots and thrived here. Quality education for their children was paramount to the settlers, and the vision was not only to assimilate into this new world but also to become its leaders. Icelandic pioneers and other ethnic groups are remembered in the Pioneer Heritage Museum, Akra Hall, Cranley School, and the Gunlogson Homestead at Icelandic State Park near *Cavalier.* In Mountain you'll find the oldest Icelandic church in America.

One and one-half miles northeast of Walhalla on ND 32, the *Gingras Trading Post State Historic Site* (701-825-6840, www.history.nd.gov) preserves the home and trading post established by prominent Metis trader Antoine B. Gingras in the 1840s. (Gingras was one of the signers of the charter of Winnipeg.) His hand-hewn oak-log home and store are among the few tangible remains of the fur trade in the Valley of the Red River of the North. The site is open from May 16 through Sept 15 from 10 a.m. to 5 p.m. daily. Admission is free.

Today Walhalla is more of a vacation outpost. *Frost Fire Ski and Snowboard Area* is a fully developed ski area, with chairlifts, a lodge, and spectacular views. Summer musicals in an outdoor amphitheater draw audiences from near and far. The covered amphitheater, on the slopes of the heavily wooded Pembina Gorge, sees sellout crowds that like to come early, shop in the crafts barn, and grab lunch before the curtain rises. For information call (701) 549-3600 or visit the Web site at www.frostfireskiarea.com.

Located 2 blocks southwest of the intersection of ND 32 and County Road 55 in Walhalla, the **Walhalla State Historic Site** (701-328-2666) marks the birthplace of **Walhalla.** The town first was called St. Joseph, after a mission was established near Pembina in 1848 by Father George Belcourt. An original trading post founded by trader Norman Kittson in 1851 was later moved to the site, where a marker is now located.

If you travel 11 miles south of Walhalla on ND 32, you'll discover a reminder of frontier Protestantism at the **Oak Lawn Church State Historic Site.** This site marks the location of a Presbyterian church built by the Reverend Ransom Waite and his congregation in 1885. The church was a prominent landmark until it burned in 1954. A sign and stone marker today represent the faith and fortitude of the church. Call (701) 328-2666 for more information.

Four miles east of Walhalla on ND 5 is Lake Renwick and **Icelandic State Park,** one of the jewels of the park system. Its newest addition is the historic Akra Hall community center, joining the old homestead, a one-room schoolhouse, and nature trails of the Gunlogson Arboretum, which in winter are groomed for cross-country skiing. The **Gunlogson Homestead and Nature Preserve,** located within the park and the focal point of the Pioneer Heritage Center, elucidates the homesteading days of American history, when immigrants bravely settled land at the edge of the wilderness. The two-story frame homestead was built by Icelandic immigrants between 1882 and 1890. The formidable Pioneer Heritage Center is open mid-May through Labor Day (call 701-265-4561 for information). The six time periods that are featured include the early fur-trapping days, as well as the era of pioneers such as the Gunlogsons.

If you truly want to savor Dakota hospitality, check into the **221 Melsted Place Bed & Breakfast** (701-993-8257; www.melstedplace.com) one mile east of nearby Mountain on ND 3. This elegant bed-and-breakfast has hosted Olafur Grimsson, the president of Iceland, who stayed in its Matriarchal Suite, an original bedroom for the maternal grandparents. It's appointed with an ornate, gold-leaf headboard and a king-size bed. There are three other rooms at this historic farmstead built in 1910 by Sigurdur Magnusson Melsted, an engineer, businessman, farmer, and active citizen. He built the impressive estate for his wife, Rosa, her parents, and their ten children. The home has remained in its original form except for removing the upstairs veranda in the 1950s.

Savor sweets at the inn's Chocolate Festival in Feb, enjoy the site of swans at the Spring Celebration in Apr, tour the haunted granary in Oct or enjoy sleigh rides, Victorian teas, and candlelight dinners during the Christmas season. Room rates range from $80 to $120. Amenities include a spa, evening bonfires, and a host of nature activities, including bird-watching, stargazing, and berry picking.

The town of **Mountain** holds its own treasures: the 1884 Historic Vikur Church, an Icelandic Festival in Aug, and the Borg Pioneer Memorial Home.

Two pleasant diversions await travelers heading east on ND 5 at Cavalier and the wooded hills of the Pembina Escarpment. The **Pembina County Historical Museum** (701-265-4941), located at Division and Main Streets, features pioneer replica rooms, rotating theme displays, and a research library. Three buildings contain antique pioneer machinery. The museum is open from 9 a.m. to 6 p.m. daily Memorial Day through Labor Day; closing time is 5 p.m. during the winter. Four miles west of town is Lake Renwick, a lovely nine-hole golf course.

A second museum in Pembina is the **Pembina State Museum** (exit 215 off I-29; 701-825-6840). Here, visitors can see 100 million years of history, dating from the Cretaceous period to modern times, in the permanent exhibit gallery. Or they can view the Red River Valley from the seven-story-high observation deck. Open daily.

North Dakota Heritage

Grab I-29 south from Pembina, and you'll follow the Red River Valley to the heart of Grand Forks, the state's oldest community. The junction of the Red River of the North and the Red Lake River, has been a meeting place for centuries—first for Native Americans who camped and traded there, then for French, British, and American fur traders who ambitiously peddled their wares around "la Grande Fourches." The regional population of about 100,000 encompasses North Dakota's Grand Forks and Minnesota's East Grand Forks, established on the opposite river bank in 1870 by steamboat captain Alexander Griggs.

thestateflower

The wild prairie rose (Rosa blanda or Rosa arkansana) has bright pink petals with a tight cluster of yellow stamens in the center. This rose grows wild along roadsides, in pastures, and in native meadows.

The population grew dramatically after the Great Northern Railroad came to town in 1880. From the 1880s to 1910, pine logs were floated down the Red Lake River or brought in by rail to sawmills in the city. Many homes in Grand Forks were built of regal white pine from the immense forests of northern Minnesota.

Grand Forks remains the center of trade and processing for an agricultural area where wheat, potatoes, sugar beets, and livestock are produced. Cream of Wheat is synonymous with childhood—and Grand Forks; here, in 1893, miller Frank Amidon invented the

Crunch into Chippers

Enjoy Red River Valley potatoes in an addictive new way at Widman's Candy Shop. They drench salty, crispy potato chips in smooth, sweet milk or dark chocolate made from a family recipe. The candy shop founded in 1949 sells Chippers at 106 South Third St. in Grand Forks (701-775-3480) or 4325 13th Ave. South in Fargo (701-281-8664). They put a North Dakota twist on other chocolates, too, pouring almond bark across nutty sunflower seeds and coating roasted flax seed in dark chocolate. Enjoy the sweet goodness.

creamy white porridge. Together, Fargo and Grand Forks are considered North Dakota's most cosmopolitan cities. A thriving state university, Air Force base, and world-class sports facilities distinguish Grand Forks. Locals are mighty proud of the **Alerus Center** (1200 Forty-second St. S), which hosts conventions, concerts, sports events, exhibitions, meetings, and banquets. It's also home of UND Football. The Alerus Center is the culmination of many years of hard work by area leaders. Although many public facilities face an uphill battle in getting funding approval, the Alerus Center had to overcome a second public vote of confidence, a disastrous flood in 1997 that virtually shut down the town, a redesign, and a roof collapse before becoming the jewel of the Grand Forks crown in 2001. The center has hosted such acts as Black Eyed Peas, KISS, Aerosmith, Keith Urban, and Cher. Free walking tours are offered at 2 p.m. Mon through Fri. Call (701) 792-1200 for more information or visit www.aleruscenter.com.

The Wheat King of America, as Thomas Campbell was known in the early 1900s, was born here, and he earned his nickname because of the enormous farm acreage he owned. Campbell's home, the **Campbell House,** is a white, clapboard structure on 2405 Belmont Rd. The house shares space on the old family ranch with an original 1870s post office, a 1920s one-room schoolhouse, a carriage house, the original log Grand Forks post office, and the **Myra Museum.** The house and property were deeded to the historical society in 1971. The house has been restored and the Centennial Corner has exhibits devoted to local personalities. The Myra Museum, similar in architecture to the Campbell House, was named in honor of John Myra, a Grand Forks County farmer. Dedicated in 1977, the museum houses a wide variety of artifacts from local history. Exhibits are rotated on a regular basis. All buildings are open daily mid-May through mid-Sept, from 1 to 5 p.m. The museum also can be toured during the off-season by appointment. Call (701) 775-2216 for more information.

Although Grand Forks lost several downtown buildings to the flood and fire of 1997, many remaining structures reflect the innate style and grace of the architects who shaped the city at the turn of the 20th century. For instance, art deco style is seen in the 1931 Grand Forks Herald Building at 120 North Fourth St. The building, designed by architect Theo B. Wells, housed the *Herald* newspaper's editorial offices. In Grand Forks, art deco, a signature style of the 1920s and '30s, was not common since there was little construction of commercial buildings during the Great Depression. Other architectural styles found in Grand Forks include classical revival, colonial revival, Romanesque, Greek revival, and Dutch colonial.

If you need more than history and architecture to lure you downtown, tempt your tastebuds with a taste of the Red River Valley. Paul Holje and George Kelley use local honey, eggs, butter, fruits and vegetables, as well as flour from nearby North Dakota State Mill for artisan breads, savory soups and sweet desserts at **Dakota Harvest Bakers,** 17 Third St. N, (701) 772-2100. They opened in 2004, baking bread in stone-deck ovens, with menu items changing daily and often including vegetarian or vegan options. Try their oatmeal whole wheat or Cream of Wheat bread, buffalo beer chili, red velvet cake with cream cheese frosting, or bittersweet chocolate cookies with sea salt.

In an 1893 building at the other end of the block, **The Toasted Frog,** 124 N. Third St., relies on the creativity and experience of Shawn Clapp and Jon Holth for its regional, trendy dinners. They each worked at Grand Forks most famous fine dining destination, Sanders 1907, before working at Fargo's Hotel Donaldson and returning to Grand Forks. They specialize in wood-fired cooking, serving Moroccan-spiced lamb burgers, seafood lavosh, spiced pears tarts, and even wood-fired s'mores with raspberry sauce. Appetizers include fried cheese-wrapped pickles and, of course, frog legs (701-772-3764; www .toastedfrog.com).

Beyond downtown and at the west end of University Avenue, the **University of North Dakota** (UND), reigns as the state's largest school and its oldest after being started in 1883. It feeds the minds of just under 13,000 students. Many of them are drawn to its highly respected medical and law schools and its internationally known John D. Odegaard School of Aerospace Sciences.

The **North Dakota Museum of Art** (701-777-4195; www.ndmoa.com), located on the UND campus in a renovated gymnasium, is renowned for its cutting-edge contemporary art and human-rights exhibitions. Its collection spans art in all media starting with the early 1970s, including the visual history of the region. Leave time to browse the eclectic gift shop with ethnic gifts, children's books, jewelry, and art work. The museum is open 9 a.m. to 5 p.m. Mon through Fri, and 1 to 5 p.m. Sat and Sun; admission is free.

Also on the UND campus, the **Chester Fritz Auditorium** is a 2,300-seat venue for a wide array of performances, from country acts and classical music to Russian ballet and Broadway shows. There's a permanent photo gallery of past performers at "The Fritz," world-renowned for acoustic brilliance. Call (701) 777-4090 or visit www.cfa.und.edu.

You don't have to be a sports fan to be bowled over by UND's $100 million Ralph Engelstad Arena (www.theralph.com). The luxurious 400,000-square-foot, five-story arena, with seating for 11,700, is truly the envy of the NCAA. Chalk it up to an Italian marble lobby, cherrywood leather-padded seats, and 300 televisions sets that can even be found in the bathroom so fans won't miss a bit of the action. The arena hosts family shows, ice events, concerts, and games featuring the Division I National Champion men's hockey team and the up-and-coming women's team. Also onsite is a pro shop and a Fighting Sioux Museum. The Betty Engelstad Sioux Center, a 50,000-square-foot expansion to the arena, houses four regulation-size practice volleyball and basketball courts, all of which can be converted into one main game court. Tours are available at 1:30 p.m. Mon through Fri. Call the Sioux Shop at (701) 777-6636 for reservations.

Aerospace progress is carefully chronicled at UND's **John Odegard School for Aerospace Sciences,** located at the intersection of University Avenue and Tulane Drive. Tours of its facilities are available on Tues and Thurs at 3:15 p.m. For information or reservations, call (701) 777-2791. For a tucked-away UND gem, follow the dinosaur tracks to the free Geology Museum in Leonard Hall, open weekdays year-round, with fossil and geological displays and a 70-million-year-old Triceratops skull. Families can continue the prehistoric theme at **Canad Inns Destination Center** at 1000 S. Forty-second St. by the Alerus Center. There are 14 kid-themed rooms with bunks and murals with cavemen, tropical scenes, or Arctic animals plus a few themed Jacuzzi rooms with Egyptian, Japanese, and Mayan decor. The hotel's 40,000-square-foot water park is the North Dakota's largest. Non-guests also are welcome to use the water park. Call (701) 772-8404 or go to www.canadinns.com for current prices and details.

For a more historic lodging, try the **511 Reeves Bed & Breakfast.** Hosts Bill and Wanda Graveline have three rooms in this historical residence, each with a distinct personality: the Audubon Room, appointed with masculine tastes in mind; the Americana Room, quaint, right down to the red chenille loveseats; and the Cottage Room, which wistfully recalls the more carefree days of childhood. Call (701) 775-3585 for rates and reservations.

For an easy weekend getaway and perfect place to introduce children to fishing, check out **Turtle River State Park** (701-594-4445; www.parkrec.nd

.gov), 22 miles west of Grand Forks on US 2 in the breathtaking Turtle River Valley. You can borrow fishing gear at the park office and try catching rainbow trout in the river. Not your thing? Hike, mountain bike, or return in the winter for cross-country skiing and sledding. Camping spots and rustic cabins are available May through Sept.

Eden

Hit I-29 and head south to *Fargo,* North Dakota's largest city with 90,700 residents. Its visitor center, a replica of North Dakota's iconic grain silos, appropriately welcomes visitors to an area that profits immensely from the Red River Valley rich soil. More than a century ago, this land was called *Eden,* and that still works today. Fargo has been a vital trade and distribution center for sugar beets, wheat, and livestock produced in the surrounding region. Settlers, enticed by the promise of prosperity in the Great West, forded the river in carts. Farm products and by-products keep many factories bustling, and legalized casino gambling has made Fargo a regional tourism center. (Fargo's counterpart, Moorhead, is located just across the state line in Minnesota.) Not surprisingly, Fargo was named one of the top 100 places to live in 2006 by *Money* magazine. And *SELF* magazine added to the city's accolades by naming the area the "Happiest City in the Nation." Low crime, great schools, and short commutes add to the praise, as does a stable economy bolstered by Microsoft and the health care industry.

Fargo was established in 1871 at the point where the Northern Pacific Railway crossed the Red River. Its first name was Centralia, but the town later was renamed to honor William George Fargo, who was founder of Wells, Fargo and Co. and one of the railroad's directors. Low railroad freight rates and the land's incredible wheat-producing potential attracted settlers.

Fargo wears its heritage like a badge of honor. The city has all the accoutrements of culture and higher education in an ambience of small-town hospitality. It gives an earnest tip of the hat to the past with such events as the *Red River Valley Fair* and *Pioneer Days.* Parades, arts and crafts, and people in period costume set the tone for Pioneer Days, held during the third weekend in Aug. It brings to life *Bonanzaville,* a restored and extensive pioneer village of more than 45 buildings from the early 20th century. It proudly touts itself as "fifteen acres of valley heritage," including a Plains Indian Museum, train depot, machinery shed, church, general stores galore, log cabins, and even a hanger for historic planes. Plan to spend at least a few hours here or you'll miss the fun details like the telephone company offering local calls in exchange for "two eggs or five cents." Bonanzaville is named for the large and well-capitalized Bonanza farms (not to be confused with the ranch of 1960s TV fame) that were built by early railroad boosters as a way to attract settlers to this "slice of Eden in the West." Sure enough, settlers followed with their plows and dreams. Between 1879 and 1886 about 100,000 people, many of them Scandinavian and German, came to live in Dakota Territory. This period became known as the Dakota Boom. Several of the Bonanza farms endured to the early part of the 20th century—the last threads in the fabric of a powerful era in agriculture.

Bonanzaville's visitor center does a great job commemorating what was one of North Dakota's most colorful eras. The village (located 4.25 miles west of I-29 on Main Avenue or via I-94, exit 343), is open daily Memorial Day through Labor Day. Call (701) 282-2822 or go to www.bonanzaville.com for details and special events such as Christmas on the Prairie.

Children can have their own lesson on the merits of agriculture through the enchanted ***Children's Museum at Yunker Farm,*** at 1201 Twenty-eighth Ave. N in Fargo Here they can see a display of live bees, then crawl through a honeycomb section designed just for them. The exhibits were constructed to involve kids in demonstrations and hands-on experiments. Housed in a renovated, century-old redbrick farmhouse, the museum is naturally inviting. The fifty-five-acre grounds include a miniature train, a carousel, a playground, a pumpkin patch, nature trails, and a community garden.

TOP FAMILY ATTRACTIONS

Fargo–Moorhead RedHawks professional Northern League baseball games
(701) 235-6161
www.fmredhawks.com

Red River Zoo
4220 Twenty-first Ave. S
near I-94 and I-29,
(701) 277-9240,
www.redriverzoo.org

Rheault Farm
2902 Twenty-fifth St. S
a one-acre renovated
1918 farm site
(701) 241-1350
www.fargoparks.com

Scheels with its in-store Ferris wheel
(701) 298-2918
www.scheelssports.com

Thunder Road Family Fun Park
(701) 282-5151
www.thunderroadfargo.com

Waterparks at the Holiday Inn's Shipwreck Bay
(701) 282-2700 or at the
Best Western Kelly Inn
& Suites
(701) 282-2143

Admission is $4 for children and adults. Open daily except during the school year when it's closed on Mon. Call (701) 232-6102 or check www .childrensmuseum-yunker.org for details.

For hip, sophisticated fun, head to downtown Fargo. On balmy Thurs nights, it might be lined with the vibrant colors and throaty rumbles of classic cars. Pick any night, though, and you'll find Broadway hopping with restaurants, upscale stores, and the glowing neon of ultra-trendy Hotel Donaldson on one end and the vintage *Fargo Theater* marquee on the other.

The renovated *Art Deco theater* at 314 Broadway hums with the artsy, quirky spirit that helped independent films thrive in the last decade. It helps that one of the most famous independent flicks, the Academy Award-winning *Fargo,* carries the town's namesake. Sure, some might be annoyed at Joel and Ethan Coen's dark crime thriller filmed in Fargo; Brainerd, Minnesota; and Minneapolis. They took a great deal of poetic license with the North Dakota–Norwegian accent and expressions—lines like "You betcha," "You're darn tootin'!," and "Oh yawhhh!" At the same time, it embraced the character of the even-tempered, well-grounded pregnant police chief, Marge Gunderson, which won Frances McDormand a best actress Oscar. You can pose with her famous character on the theater's second floor with the larger-than-life chainsaw carving affectionately referred to as "Woodchip Marge." They added a second 99-seat theater in

AUTHOR'S FAVORITE SHOPS

Boucle Yarn Studio
311 Broadway
(701) 356-9276
Gorgeous, vibrant yarn along with guidance and classes for passionate knitters.

O'Day Cache
317 Broadway
(701) 293-2088
These Asian imports add up to beautiful decor, clothing, jewelry, housewares, furniture, and vibrant paper lanterns.

Shannalee
313 Broadway
(710) 232-3300
Funky clothing, cosmetics, and accessories.

Vlana Vlee and The Red Shoe
102 Broadway
(701) 297-8533
Home decor and furniture, hip women's clothing and high-end shoes and boots, baby clothes and gifts, and unexpected accessories.

Zandbroz Variety
420 Broadway
(701) 239-4729
Best bet for beautiful stationery and pens, kitchenwares and cookbooks, jewelry, off-beat and retro kids' toys, and a great read, whether it's a brand-new book or a rare vintage edition.

2009, giving patrons the choice of two movies each night when the theater isn't hosting dance groups, comedians, bands, and orchestras.

The theater opened in 1926 as a vaudeville and silent-film hall. There are still a handful of rare talents, local men who can improvise the sound effects and background music for silent films with the theater's rare, still-functioning Wurlitzer pipe organ. Your best bet for hearing it is attending the annual Fargo Film Festival in early Mar. Call (701) 239-8385 or visit www.fargotheatre.com.

Within a block of the theater, you'll find a wonderful cluster of stores.

For the best view of downtown, head up to Sky Prairie Lounge and watch the sunset from **Hotel Donaldson**'s rooftop gathering place. It's open to the public summer evenings, Mon through Fri. Guests in the 17-room boutique hotel each enjoy the work of a different artist and can use the hot tub on the rooftop. The centerpiece of its premiere room—No. 17—is a Japanese soak tub with water cascading from the ceiling. The hotel boasts some of the area's best dining with an emphasis on local ingredients creatively served. Splurge on bison tenderloin with bacon wilted spinach or go light with tiny tapas-style desserts for $2 a piece. Lunch in the HoDo lounge is popular with its afford-able gourmet burgers and salads. It really hops on Thurs nights with live music.

A short stroll from the hotel, a strikingly renovated, turn-of-the-century warehouse has been elegantly transformed into the **Plains Art Museum** (704 First Ave. N; 701-293-0903). It hosts regional, national, and international exhib-its, large permanent collections, special events, performances, and art classes. If you need a quick bite, the onsite cafe touts from-scratch salads, soups, and paninis.

Head south two blocks on Eighth Street to Nichole's Fine Pastries just south of Main Street, for tasty and artistic indulgence. The detail-oriented owner Nichole Hensen grew up on a North Dakota farm, fell in love with fine foods at Sanders in Grand Forks, went to pastry school in California, and found her way back home again. She and her staff craft fine chocolates and artful European fruit pastries so beautiful they sing a siren song. Just try to decide between lemon curd tarts, chocolate-caramel sea salt tarts, chocolate-pistachio strawberry mousse layer cake, twice-baked and lusciously filled almond crois-sants, and more. Even better: cool down a hot day with a creamy gelato or tart sorbet in unique flavors such as spicy ginger, tangy rhubarb, cherry-kiwi, or blood orange. You can get sandwiches, soups, and salads, too, along with breakfast with a cafe expansion that opened in spring 2010. It's also a great late-evening weekend destination, pairing wines with their sweet temptation (701-232-6430; www.nicholesfinepastry.com).

Just across the Red River from the hub of downtown Fargo is Moorhead, Minnesota. You can see the white peaks of its Historical and Cultural Society of Clay County from the North Dakota side. Beneath the unusual awning is its centerpiece—the **Hjemkomst Viking Ship,** a replica built by Robert Asp, a Moorhead school counselor whose dream was to sail it to Norway. Leukemia took him before he could, but his family completed the harrowing, adventurous, and historic Atlantic crossing, landing in Bergen, Norway, in the 1980s. You can get up close to the ship, watch a movie about it and also go outside to tour the impressive Hopperstad Stave Church. To get the best feel for these Nordic cultures—through sights, music, costumes and food—time a visit with the Scandinavian Festival the last weekend in June or the Viking Village in late July. Call 218-299-5511 or go to www.hjemkomst-center.com.

Adjacent to the museum you'll also find the **S.S. Ruby** with narrated tours of the Red River. The relaxing cruises will raise your appreciation for the Red River's history, geography, and wildlife. You also can rent a canoe or kayak and explore on your own Memorial Day through Labor Day (701-793-7829; www.riverkeepers.org).

Stop for lunch at the nearby **Usher's House,** a restaurant that looks almost fortresslike with its sturdy stone walls. Don't let that fool you, though. While the front tavern is cozy like an English pub with lots of dark woodwork, the back room is all glass with lovely views of the wooded park alongside the Red River. There also is plenty of patio or screened-in gazebo dining for those balmy summer days (218-287-0080; www.ushershouse.com).

You can find plenty of riverside trails especially in the downtown areas, but one of the nicest places to enjoy the peaceful river is 17 blocks south of Main Avenue. Here, tucked back behind residential streets, you'll find **Lindenwood Park** with spacious, wooded picnic grounds, playgrounds, bike rentals and trails, and places to pitch a tent along this scenic oxbow in the river (1712 Fifth St. S, 701-232-3987; www.fargoparks.com).

Like Grand Forks, Fargo hums with pride when it comes to aviation. Check out the local heritage at **Fargo Air Museum** (1609 Nineteenth Ave. N; 701-293-8043). Besides educating the public about aviation and North Dakotans' role in it, it celebrates the freedom, thrill, and exhilaration of flight and commemorates those who sacrificed their lives in times of war. Some of the planes on display include the F2G-1D, the world's only flying Super Corsair and one of the only three existing in the world; and a Beech Staggerwing, a classic airplane known as Queen of the Sky that was used during World War II on reconnaissance missions and to carry generals. For more information, go to www.fargoairmuseum.org.

Baseball, too, is revered with a patriotic fervor at the **Roger Maris Museum** (West Acres Shopping Center; 701-282-2222), which traces the career of the legendary Fargo athlete. As a New York Yankee, Maris gained fame when he hit sixty-one home runs during the 1961 season, breaking the longstanding record of the great Babe Ruth. At the exhibit you'll see actual film of Roger's last twelve homers of 1961, along with his uniforms, baseball equipment, and other memorabilia. Visit the Web site at www.rogermarismuseum.com.

Maple River Winery (628 Front St. in Casselton, just west of Fargo; 701-347-5900) is enjoying increasing popularity with wine from fruits native to North Dakota. They specialize in chokecherry, wild plum, and the unusual apple jalapeño pepper. The wine is available at many retailers across the state. Tours are available from 10 a.m. to 5 p.m. Mon through Fri. Weekend and evening tours are also available by appointment. The Web site is www .mapleriverwinery.com.

If you take I-29 south (actually old US 81, parallel to the Interstate), you'll find **Fort Abercrombie,** the site of a six-week siege in 1862. Located at the eastern edge of Abercrombie, this site preserves the military post that served from 1857 until 1878 as the gateway to the Dakota frontier. A museum here interprets the history of the fort and the area. Only one original building remains, but blockhouses and the palisade wall have been reconstructed. The museum is open Thurs through Mon from 8 a.m. to 5 p.m. For more information call (701) 553-8513.

Near Wahpeton, check out the **Bagg Bonanza Farm,** 45 miles south of Fargo on I-29, Mooreton exit. This twenty-one-building farm is the sole remnant of the boom for "king wheat" in the 1800s, when a 6,000-acre factory farm was not even one of the biggest in the area. This is the last restorable Bonanza farm in the United States. Guided tours are available from noon to 6 p.m. Fri through Sun or by appointment. The season opens Memorial Day weekend and ends Labor Day weekend. Special events are scheduled throughout the season, including the annual Old-Fashioned Fourth of July Celebration. Concessions and a gift shop are on-site. For more information call (701) 274-8989.

The Bridges of Sheyenne Valley

Head an hour west of Fargo to reach **Valley City,** gateway to the Sheyenne Valley. Two of the valley area's most prominent features are not always found in North Dakota: trees and winding roadways. It's no surprise then that it became the Sheyenne Valley National Scenic Byway and one of the Midwest's most beloved fall treks with the valley dappled in vibrant shades of gold, yellow, and red. Of course, it's lovely and relaxing any season of the year as the road curves 68 miles from Lake Ashtabula to Lisbon. The southern end of the byway heads through tiny Kathryn with its 1900s main street and Clausen Springs Park, which is popular for camping.

Valley City in the heart of the byway also is one of the state's most beloved small-town destinations with enough elegant and dramatic bridges—there are eight right in town—to make *The Bridges of Madison County* look a little ho-hum.

The impressive **Highline Bridge,** for instance, is a three-span, 255-foot bridge. At 3,860 feet long and 162 feet above the riverbed, the Highline Bridge is one of the longest and highest single-track railroad bridges in the nation. The first train officially crossed the trestle on May 12, 1908, and regular train service over the bridge began May 20. Because it was of vital importance in moving supplies and men, the bridge was closely guarded during both World War I and World War II to prevent sabotage. You can learn more about the local history at **Barnes County History Museum** (701-845-0966).

Pick up a beautifully photographed *Scenic Bridges and Hidden Treasures* brochure at the Rosebud Visitor Center, 250 West Main St., or contact the Valley City Area Chamber of Commerce at (701) 845-1891 or go to www.hello valley.com. Give yourself at least a few hours to stroll along the river and back and forth across the pretty bridges, many of which are on the campus of *Valley City State University.*

On the campus you find a planetarium (701-845-7452) in the **Rhoades Science Center,** where visitors are treated to an incredible view of the solar system. If you're inspired by the stars, check out the power of the sun at Medicine Wheel Park where strategically placed rocks create a Native American solar calendar. Interpretive signs explain how it works, and you can catch celebrations here during the equinox and seasonal solstices.

Northwest of Valley City, the **Baldhill Dam and Lake Ashtabula** boasts eight recreational areas where you can swim, fish, boat, picnic, and camp. The Valley City Federal Fish Hatchery (701-845-3464), one of two such facilities in the state, also is located at the park. Thirty miles south of Valley City on ND 1, you can steer toward **Fort Ransom** and **Fort Ransom State Park.** The community and park inherited the name of a frontier cavalry fort, which was situated to protect the settlers' path to the Missouri River. Nowadays, the small Norwegian town of Fort Ransom is regarded as a scenic arts community. The **Ransom County Museum** is open afternoons, May 1 through Oct. The Sheyenne Valley Arts and Crafts Festival is another popular attraction and takes place the last full weekend in Sept. Call (701) 973-4491 for more information.

Sodbuster Days takes place every summer. Here you can revisit the horse-powered days of threshing, haying, and plowing. Wagon rides and entertainment round out two weekends of living history. For more information call (701) 973-4331 or go to www.ransomcountynd.com.

While cross-country skiing and snowmobiling are the major winter activities at the Fort Ransom area, Bears Den Mountain Ski Area boasts a chairlift, a T-bar lift, and a beginner's tow rope. Call (701) 973-2711 or go to www .skibearsden.com for more information.

Where to Stay in Eastern North Dakota

FARGO

Best Western Doublewood Inn
3333 South Thirteenth Ave.
(701) 235-3333
Moderate

Comfort Inn East
1407 Thirty-fifth St. S
(701) 280-9666
(800) 228-5150
Moderate

Fairfield Inn
3902 Ninth Ave. S
(701) 281-0494
Moderate

Hilton Garden Inn
4351 Seventeenth Ave. S
(701) 499-6000
Moderate

Howard Johnson Inn Downtown Fargo
301 Third Ave. N
(701) 232-8850
Moderate

Kelly Inn
4207 Thirteenth Ave. S
(701) 277-8821
Moderate

Radisson
201 North Fifth St.
(701) 232-7363
Moderate to expensive

GRAND FORKS

AmericInn
1820 South Columbia Rd.
(701) 780-9925
Inexpensive to moderate

Canad Inns Destination Center
1000 South Forty-second St.
(701) 772-8404
Moderate

Clarion Inn
1210 North Forty-third St.
(701) 772-7131
Moderate

C'mon Inn
3051 Thirty-second Ave. S
(701) 775-3320
Inexpensive

Comfort Inn
3251 Thirtieth Ave. S
(701) 775-7503
(800) 228-5150
Moderate

Days Inn
3101 South Thirty-fourth St.
(701) 775-0060
(800) 329-7466
Inexpensive

Econo Lodge
900 North Forty-third St.
(701) 746-6666
(877) 424-6423
Inexpensive

511 Reeves Bed & Breakfast
511 Reeves Dr.
(701) 775-3585
Moderate

Guest House International
710 First Ave. N
(701) 746-5411
(800) 867-9797
Moderate

Lakeview Inn & Suites
3350 Thirty-second Ave. S
(701) 775-5000
(877) 355-3500
Moderate

Ramada Inn
1205 North Forty-third St.
(701) 775-3951
(800) 570-3951
Moderate

Where to Eat in Eastern North Dakota

FARGO

Café Aladdin
1609 Thirty-second Ave. S
(701) 232-4200
Inexpensive

HoDo Lounge
101 Broadway
(701) 478-1000
Moderate to expensive

Monte's Downtown
220 Broadway
(701) 526-0149
Moderate to expensive

SELECTED CHAMBERS OF COMMERCE

Carrington Area Chamber of Commerce
871 Main St.
Carrington, 58421
(701) 652-2524
www.cgtn-nd.com

Devils Lake Area Tourism Office
208 Hwy. 2 W
Devils Lake, 58301
(800) 233-8048
www.devilslakend.com

Fargo–Moorhead Convention & Visitor Bureau
2001 Forty-fourth St. SW
Fargo, 58103
(800) 235-7654
www.fargomoorhead.org

Grafton Area Chamber of Commerce
432 Hill Ave.
P.O. Box 632
Grafton, 58237
(701) 352-0781
www.graftonevents.com

Grand Forks Convention & Visitors Center
4251 Gateway Dr.
Grand Forks, 58203
(800) 866-4566
www.visitgrandforks.com

Valley City Area Chamber of Commerce
250 West Main St.
Valley City, 58072
(701) 845-1891
www.hellovalley.com

Wahpeton Visitor Center
118 Sixth St. North
Wahpeton, 58075
(800) 892-6673
www.wahpetonbreckenridgechamber.com

Nichole's Fine Pastry
13 S. Eighth St.
(701) 232-6430
Inexpensive

Saffron
3003 Thirty-second Ave. SW
(701) 241-4200
Inexpensive to moderate

GRAND FORKS

Amazing Grains
214 DeMers Ave.
(701) 775-4542
Inexpensive

Bella Vino
108 North Third St.
(701) 757-8466
Moderate

Big Sioux Café
4401 Thirty-second Ave. S
(701) 738-0441
Inexpensive

Happy Joe's Pizza & Ice Cream Parlor
2909 Washington St. S
(701) 772-6655
Inexpensive

The Kegs
(Open summer only)
901 Fifth St. N
(701) 775-4993
Inexpensive

Kon Nechi Wa's
3750 Thirty-second Ave. S
(701) 775-3421
Moderate

The Red Pepper
415 North Forty-second St.
(701) 772-8226
Moderate

Sanders 1907
22 South Third St.
(701) 746-8970
Expensive

Index